New Edition

first certificate
expert

RESOURCE BOOK

Drew Hyde • Jan Bell • Roger Gower • Nick Kenny

PEARSON
Longman

£17.20

Pearson Education Limited
Edinburgh Gate
Harlow
Essex CM20 2JE
England
and Associated Companies throughout the world.

www.pearsonlongman.com

First published 2003

Second edition published 2008
Second impression 2008

ISBN 978-1-4058-4847-3

Set in 10/12pt Times New Roman

Printed in Malaysia, PJB

Author's Acknowledgements

The author would like to thank Bernie Hayden, Fran
Banks and Jacqui Robinson for their help and guidance,
all his colleagues and students at Frances King School
of English for their suggestions and Annie, Louis and
Freya for their patience.

Publisher's Acknowledgements

We are grateful to the following for permission to
reproduce copyright material:

Consignia plc for an extract adapted from their
advertisement "Sorted ... Royal Mail delivers a solution
to the home delivery problem" published February
2000; Financial Times Limited for an extract adapted
from "Jobs on the line" published in *FT Weekend: How
to Spend It* February 2002; Focus Magazine for the
article "A quick chat with Ellen MacArthur" by Sally
Palmer published in *Focus Magazine* November 2002;
Media Generation Limited for an extract adapted from
"Best boot forward" by Kenric Hickson published in
Quicksilver Magazine Autumn 2000; New Crane
Publishing for an extract from "Roll up, roll up!
Change your life" by Richard Barber published in
Sainsbury's Magazine October 2002; Penguin Books
Limited for an extract adapted from "The little girl and
the wolf" by James Thurber published in *The Thurber
Carnival* © James Thurber 1953; Peter Shepherd for a
questionnaire adapted from www.trans4mind.com;
Telegraph Group Limited for an extract adapted from
"The man who was driven by jaguars" by Nigel
Blundell published in *The Telegraph* 5th August 2000 ©
Telegraph Group Limited 2000; and Times Newspapers
Limited for an extract from "Speechless? Now we're
talking" by Elizabeth Judge published in *The Times*
10th August 2002 © Times Newspapers Limited,
London 2002; the journalist Liz Gill for an extract
adapted from her article "Me and my wheels" published
in the *Financial Times Magazine* October 2000.

In some instances we have been unable to trace the
owners of copyright material and we would appreciate
any information that would enable us to do so.

Sample answer sheets are reproduced by kind
permission of Cambridge ESOL.

Illustrated by Francis Blake, John Coburn, Fran Jordan,
Sandy Nichols, Rachel Oxley, Chris Pavely, Nadine
Wickenden and Russ Wilms

Cover photo © Raven Design

Designed by Jennifer Coles

Second edition layout by 320 Design Ltd.

Second edition edited by Alison Ramsey and
Alice Kasasian

Contents

Introduction to the course

Components

FCE Expert New Edition consists of:

a Coursebook for classroom use with CD ROM

a Student's Resource Book for homework, private study or classroom use (with or without Answer key) with audio CD set

Teacher's audio CD pack

this Teacher's Resource Book

Interactive exam practice at www.iTests.com allows students to test themselves, monitor their progress and improve exam performance.

Five key features

1 *FCE Expert* is flexible. It is designed in a modular way so that teachers can either follow the order of the material in the book or choose their own route through the course to meet the needs of specific classes. Each page or double-page spread is freestanding, and almost always follows the same order in each module, making it easy to access and isolate separate elements of the course and integrate them in a different way.

So, a teacher might follow the linear route presented in the book:

(Modules 1A, 2A etc.)
Reading → Language development → Writing

(Modules 1B, 2B etc.)
Speaking → Listening → Use of English/Language development

Or a teacher might follow different, tailored routes, such as:
Language development → Reading → Writing

Writing → Reading → Speaking

Speaking → Language development → Use of English → Listening

2 While each section can be taught independently, there are links between the sections to provide a coherent progression when the more linear route is chosen. For example, the Language development in the first unit of each module provides language which will be useful for students in the following Writing section; the Speaking has a topic which relates to the Listening in the same unit; in the second unit of each module, the grammar and vocabulary in the Language development sections are tested in the Use of English sections on the opposite page.

3 Most of the Use of English/Language development spreads follow a test–teach approach in which the language is first tested by means of a Use of English task, then focused on in the Language development section using the examples from the Use of English task to clarify form and meaning.

4 The general skills required for Reading and Listening (e.g. for reading: skimming, scanning, predicting, etc.) are presented first in the early units, through tasks which simulate the exam but are graded in terms of their level of difficulty.

5 The Writing and Speaking sections focus more on approach than end-product. In other words, students are trained to build up good habits, develop the skill of self-monitoring and so become more independent learners.

Coursebook

The Coursebook consists of twelve modules, each divided into two units. Each module includes grammar consolidation and vocabulary development, and practises all the Papers of the exam.

Each module is designed around a theme. There is an Overview showing what is to be studied in the module, followed by a lead-in discussion. Then each of the two units is based around a topic linked to the overall theme of the module. For example, Module 5 (A and B) has the theme Discovery. Under that general heading 5A focuses on Technology whereas 5B focuses on The modern world.

This Teacher's Resource Book also contains photocopiable Exam practice for Paper 2 Writing and Paper 4 Listening.

Other elements of the Coursebook are:

- Top 20 Questions asked about FCE

- Exam overview, giving an at-a-glance outline of what is included in each paper

- Exam reference, giving more detailed information about what to expect in each part of each paper, and what skills or language are tested in each section

- Grammar reference, which gives detailed information about the main grammar points practised in the course

- Writing reference, which provides:
  - a checklist to help students monitor and edit their own writing
  - a sample question for each type of writing task in the exam, with model answer, specific guidance, and another question for further student practice

- a spelling and punctuation section, giving useful support in these areas as practised in the Writing sections

- Speaking material, with photographs and tasks for Parts 2 and 3 of the Speaking paper

- Functions reference, which brings together all the language functions introduced in the Speaking sections, so that they can be easily accessed for reference and revision

Module and unit structure

Each module contains the following sections. For ease of use and flexibility, the sections are nearly always in the same order.

Modules 1A, 2A, 3A etc.

Reading

The texts have been chosen for their interest value and their potential to provide a 'window on the world' and generate discussion.

Stage 1 A *Before you read* section to establish the topic and a purpose for reading. It also aims to motivate students and generate vocabulary. For example, in Module 4A (Personal challenges) students discuss a photo of the man featured in the article. Then they look at the title of the article and the introduction and write three questions they would like to find the answers to in the text.

Stage 2 An activity to encourage reading for gist, followed by a Paper 1 Reading exam task, with advice on the relevant task strategy. For example, in Module 4A there are three Task strategy points to follow. As the exam preparation is carefully graded and stepped throughout the course, these Task strategy sections are reduced as the course progresses.

Stage 3 A discussion and/or a vocabulary activity, both based on the text. In Module 4A the vocabulary is phrasal verbs.

This Teacher's Resource Book contains photocopiable lead-in or follow-up activities.

In the Student's Resource Book, there is more extensive vocabulary work related to the reading texts, and further practice of each Paper 1 Reading exam task.

Language development 1

Language development 1 can be used independently of any exam training. However, the section revises and extends general grammar areas which students will need for the exam, not only because they are tested in the Use of English papers but because they will be needed for the Writing and Speaking papers.

This section follows a three-stage approach.

Stage 1 Students find examples of the grammar in context, and match them to form and meaning.

Stage 2 Controlled practice, linked to the context.

Stage 3 A practice activity which links the language to the exam task in the following Writing section. So, in Module 4A the final Language development exercise involves students using narrative forms and time conjunctions to continue a story, then the Writing section consists of training in how to write a story for Paper 2.

At appropriate stages of the Language development sections, students are referred to the Grammar reference at the back of the book for a detailed grammatical summary of the language point being practised.

This Teacher's Resource Book contains photocopiable activities directly linked to these Language development sections, providing communicative language practice.

Writing

The Writing sections cover all the types of writing that students may be required to do in the exam, with particular emphasis on the compulsory transactional letter (Paper 2 Part 1). In terms of language, each Writing section has a link to the Language development section which precedes it, and a *Language spot* which practises an important area of language needed for writing.

The principle behind the Writing section is to establish 'good practice' through a clear set of procedures consistently applied and monitored, which can be used when completing any exam Writing task. Each spread is graded, and the aim is to give carefully guided preparation, so that students build up to complete the main task at the end of the section. In each section there is considerable language support; in particular a range of functional exponents is given and linked to the task.

In the units, the approach focuses on process more than end product. However, in the Writing reference there are exam tasks with model answers, notes for guidance, and more tasks for further practice.

The procedure in the Writing sections is as follows:

1 Lead-in → **2** Understanding the task → **3** Planning the task → **4** Thinking about the language and content needed → **5** Writing → **6** Checking and improving the writing

For example, in Module 4A (Writing a story):

Stage 1 *Vocabulary.* An opportunity to expand students' vocabulary topic by topic.

Stage 2 Analysing the exam task and discussing what will make a good story

Stage 3 Brainstorming ideas from pictures and making notes

Stage 4 Comparing opening/closing paragraphs and practising useful functional exponents and the use of adverbs

Stage 5 Writing the story

Stage 6 Editing the story using a checklist.

Students are then referred to the appropriate page in the Writing reference. The *Language spot* section gives practice in making language vivid. The *Language spot* sections are linked but not integrated with this procedure, and could be used at any point in the lesson, including the beginning.

Modules 1B, 2B, 3B etc.

Speaking

This section follows similar principles to the Writing section, in that it aims to build up 'good practice' through a clear set of procedures consistently applied. The sections are graded throughout the book. They cover the strategies needed in the exam and provide useful functional exponents. These functions are all in the Functions reference at the back of the book.

In the earlier units, there are recorded sample answers on the cassette/CD for students to listen to critically from the point of view of appropriate language and effective strategies.

Each section has the following structure:

Stage 1 *Vocabulary.* An opportunity to expand students' vocabulary topic by topic.

Stage 2 *Lead-in.* In this part, the students discuss the pictures and generate the vocabulary they will need to perform the task. For example, in Module 3B students are asked to identify the jobs of two people who work with animals.

Stage 3 Guided exam preparation for the task. In Unit 6 the task is the 'individual long turn' (Paper 5 Part 2). First students compare and contrast the pictures, then they listen to a sample answer, identify the examiner's instructions, and analyse the student's answer for both content and language.

Stage 4 Students perform the exam task, following the guidelines provided in the Task strategy section, and afterwards reflect on how they performed.

Listening

This section can be covered before or after the Speaking section, which has a linked topic.

The sections are graded through the book to develop the skills needed to perform the tasks in the four parts of Paper 4 Listening. Early units have Task strategy sections in the margin to guide students.

Each Listening section has three stages:

Stage 1 *Before you listen*: This aims to establish the context, to build up motivation, to predict the content and to generate the vocabulary needed for the task. For example, in Module 3B (*Our natural heritage*) the students are asked to talk about the photograph and guess the man's job and his likes/dislikes about being in the rainforest.

Stage 2 A task with relevant strategies. Module 3B practises the general skill of listening for specific information and introduces the exam task of completing sentences.

Stage 3 Discussion and/or vocabulary related to the text. In Module 3B there is a discussion about the way in which students completed the task.

Further practice of useful vocabulary linked to the topic can be found in the Student's Resource Book.

Use of English 1

This section usually focuses on the more 'grammatical' Use of English tasks and so it is nearly always either Paper 3 Part 2 (open cloze) or Paper 3 Part 4 (key word transformation). Its aim is to develop the exam strategies needed for each task and, in terms of language, follow a test–teach procedure, in that the Use of English task here tests the students' knowledge of the language, some of which is then practised in Language development 2.

Those sections which practise Paper 3 Part 2 include texts related to the topic of the unit and have the following structure:

Stage 1 *Lead-in.* This aims to build up motivation in relation to the topic of the text and generate some of the vocabulary needed.

Stage 2 Graded guidance for completing the exam task.

Stage 3 The students complete the exam task, supported by a Task strategy section and a Help section, which gives specific guidance for individual answers. This support is reduced throughout the book. This is followed either by discussion about the content of the text or analysis of the language tested in the task.

A similar procedure is followed for Paper 3 Part 4 (key word transformation) but since there is no specific text or topic, more attention is given to the exam strategies needed.

Language development 2

This section focuses on some of the language from the Use of English task.

Some of the areas practised are 'large' grammar points, such as comparatives, quantity or articles; others are relatively small, such as *as/like*, but all are frequently tested in the Use of English paper.

Stage 1 Analysis of examples of the target language from the preceding Use of English task where appropriate. Students are either guided to the grammar rules for themselves, or given input on the page. In some cases (e.g. comparatives) students are referred to the Grammar reference.

Stage 2 A range of controlled and semi-controlled practice activities.

Stage 3 A short personalised task.

Further communicative practice is provided in the photocopiable material in the Teacher's Resource Book.

Use of English 2

The task in this section focuses on vocabulary and is usually Paper 3 Part 1 (multiple-choice cloze) or Paper 3 Part 3 (word formation). Since vocabulary is also tested in Paper 3 Part 4, one unit has a key word transformation task.

The texts are related to the topic of the unit and the page has a similar structure to Use of English 1 (see above).

Language development 3

This section practises and extends the vocabulary tested in the Use of English task.

The page has a similar structure to Language development 2 (see above).

Student's Resource Book

The Student's Resource Book is an integral part of the *FCE Expert* course. It contains 12 modules that mirror the themes and contents of the Coursebook units. It aims to consolidate areas of grammar practised in the Coursebook, extend vocabulary and give extra practice of Reading, Listening and Use of English. A Colloquial English section adds useful English idioms to students' vocabulary.

There is an accompanying audio CD set. The Listening material is also available on the Teacher's cassette/CD pack.

Module and unit structure

Each module contains the following sections:

Modules 1A, 2A, 3A etc.

Vocabulary

Extension of topic vocabulary based on the Coursebook reading text; other vocabulary areas such as phrasal verbs; exam practice exercises for the vocabulary-based tasks in Paper 3 Use of English.

Language development 1

Consolidation and practice of language covered in Language development 1 in the Coursebook; extension of certain language areas; graded exam practice exercises.

Writing

Further practice of the exam task type covered in the Coursebook, focusing on structure and organisation based on analysis of a sample answer.

Listening

Paper 4 Listening text and task, practising strategies and task types that have already been covered in the Coursebook.

Modules 1B, 2B, 3B etc.

Vocabulary

Extension of topic and other vocabulary or functions based on the Coursebook listening and/or speaking tasks.

Language development 2

Consolidation and practice of language covered in Language development 2 in the Coursebook; extension of certain language areas; graded exam practice exercises.

Reading

Paper 2 Reading text and task, practising strategies and task types that have already been covered in the Coursebook.

Complete practice exam

A complete exam which you can use when you think your students are ready for it, or in separate parts at any stage in the course.

Teacher's Resource Book

As well as this Introduction, the Teacher's Resource Book contains:

Unit-by-unit teacher's notes

Guidance on how to use the Coursebook material, with further suggestions; 'books closed' activities to set the ball rolling at the beginning of modules and units; annotated answers for exercises and exam tasks.

OMR Answer sheets (photocopiable)

Replicas of the Answer sheets students have to use in the exam. They can be photocopied and given to students when they do the Exam practice sections in the Coursebook, and the complete Practice exams in the Student's Resource Book.

Photocopiable activities

A pre-course exam quiz; three photocopiable activities to supplement each coursebook module, providing further lead-in and follow-up material and communicative language practice; full teacher's notes and answer keys for each activity.

Module tests: How much do you remember? (photocopiable)

One photocopiable page per module, testing the grammar and vocabulary covered in the module. There are four exercises on each page. The items reflect the four Paper 3 tasks, but for ease of administration and checking, they use discrete sentences rather than full-length texts. Answer keys are at the appropriate points in the unit-by-unit teacher's notes.

Exam practice (photocopiable)

Six exam practice sections for use after Modules 2, 4, 6, 8, 10 and 12. This material provides practice in Paper 2 Writing and Paper 4 Listening. The recordings for the Paper 4 Listening tests can be found on the Coursebook CDs after Modules 2, 4, 6, 8, 10 and 12. Answer keys are at the appropriate points in the unit-by-unit teacher's notes.

Audio scripts

These are all at the back of the book for ease of reference.

Teacher's CD pack

The Teacher's CD pack (four CDs) contains all the listening material from the Coursebook, Teacher's Resource Book and Student's Resource Book. There are two CDs for the Coursebook, (which include the listening tests in the Teacher's Resource Book) and two CDs for the Student's Resource Book.

Abbreviations used in the Teacher's Resource Book
CB = Coursebook
TRB = Teacher's Resource Book
l./ll = line/lines
p./pp = page/pages
para. = paragraph

Module 1 Lifestyles

Module 1 includes topics such as family, homes, routines, festivals and celebrations.

> ### Photocopiable activity
>
> Photocopiable activity (pre-course) on page 125 provides an introduction to the FCE exam. After the quiz, it would be useful to show students other features of the book, by asking questions such as *Where can you find the Grammar reference?* (pp. 182–195) *What can you find on pages 196–208?* (Writing reference).

To set the ball rolling ...

Lead-in p.9

Get students to discuss the dictionary extract together, then ask them for the key points: *way someone lives; place they live; things they own; job they do; activities they enjoy.* Then they should discuss the other questions in pairs or small groups before feedback to the class to compare ideas.

Module 1A Family life

To set the ball rolling ...

With books closed get students to tell a partner about their family and childhood. If necessary provide prompts such as *Who did you live with? Were you happy? Were you ever bored? Were your parents strict?*.

Reading pp.10–11

1 Get students to look at the first strategy box before they do this. Ask them to give reasons and so encourage them to give fuller answers. Ask them to look at the photos and predict what type of families they are.

2 Use the strategy box to clarify what the term skimming means and why it is important. As well as giving a general understanding, skimming helps to establish the type and style of the text, the writer's intention (to inform, amuse, entertain) and the general organisation and layout of the text. Suggest a suitable time to skim this article. Suggestion: 1–2 minutes.

2b This would best be discussed as a whole class.

3 Before students scan the article, use the strategy box to clarify what scanning is and why it is useful. In the exam it is important to use time well and scanning will help students do this.

3c Students should do this in pairs or small groups.

4 This would be a good point to introduce the concept of phrasal verbs and ways in which students should record them in vocabulary books. Ask them to find the underlined words/phrases in the text and to guess what they mean. If they find it difficult, put the following words on the board and ask the students to match them to the phrases in the text; *sent, practise, relax.*

Follow with a discussion using questions such as: How do you chill out? Where were you packed off to as a child? What interests would you like to keep up if you had time?

5 These discussions would be best in small groups.

> ### Photocopiable activity
>
> Photocopiable activity 1A on p.126 could be done at this point. It is a board game about students' lifestyles, containing questions typical of those asked in Paper 5 Parts 1 and 4.

Language development 1 pp.12–13

1a First get students to describe the picture. What is the relationship of the people and what are they doing? Check/Clarify the difference between *grow* – to become physically bigger, used for people, plants, animals, towns, etc. – and *grow up* – to develop from a child to an adult, used only for people.

1b Check that students are familiar with the basic names of the verb forms before they do the exercise. When they have completed the exercise, you may want to show them the Grammar reference on page 187.

2a Students should work on their own to complete the dialogues before checking their answers with the Grammar reference and each other.

2b Before students practise the questions together point out how the answers in the book are more than simple responses; the answers are expanded to give further information. E.g. in question 2 the answer *My father* is expanded to say why. Encourage students to do the same.

3a You may need to clarify the difference between a state and an action, e.g. by saying: *I live in Madrid. It's not an action, I don't actually do anything, I just live. Every day I ride a bike to work. It's a physical action, something that I do.*

3b After students have completed the box give them time to read the Grammar reference on page 187.

4 Students can either refer to the Grammar reference as they do the exercise or try on their own before checking. Ask them to justify their answers and say whether each one is a state or an action.

5a First check that students know who Jamelia is.

Background

The British R&B singer Jamelia had her first hit, aged 18 in 1999. Her most famous songs include 'Money' and 'Superstar'. She was 'spotted' when her aunt persuaded her to perform at the Notting Hill Carnival in London.

5c After completing the box, students should read the Grammar reference on page 189.

6 Students should be able to justify their choices and be able to say why other answers are or aren't possible.

7a Students should write their answers, to give them time to think about the structures, before comparing their experiences with other students. If necessary, give them one or two examples about you.

7b This would work well in small groups.

8 Use the completed sentences as revision asking why the various tenses were used in each sentence or for alternative endings.

Photocopiable activity

Photocopiable activity 1B (p. 127) would work well after any of Exercises 6, 7 or 8. It is an information exchange activity giving further practice of language used to describe past and present habits.

▶ **Student's Resource Book page 7**

Writing pp.14–15

1 Get students started by describing who you might write a formal letter to, such as a bank, and eliciting one example of who you would write an informal letter/email to, such as friends or family. Paper 2 part 2 often includes an informal letter/email to a friend. Ask if anyone has ever had a pen friend, and if so how long they kept up correspondence.

2 Point out that students should establish the style of any writing task by considering who the reader is, and they should establish the purpose in order to use suitable language and complete the task.

3a Tell students that, in the exam, marks are given for task completion, so they should think about what the task requires. In this case they will need to cover three points: themselves, their family and suggesting a meeting.

3b When students are completing the paragraph plan, remind them that it is only an exam and not a real life situation. Although it is better to write true things about themselves – e.g. they will know more vocabulary about their own real hobbies – it is not necessary. In this case they should, e.g., invent a hobby rather than say they don't have one. Remind them that the aim is to demonstrate what they can do in English, not to write a true description of themselves.

4a Check that students understand why the sentences are inappropriate (they are too formal) before they attempt the task. Remind them that contractions such as *I'm* are acceptable in informal letters.

4b If students are unsure of any of the *True/False* statements get them to look again at the examples in Exercise 4a.

4d Get students to read the question again before they do the task.

5 The email should now take students only about 20 minutes to write and could be done in class or for homework.

6 Point out that there is a more complete list of points to check when editing in the Writing reference on page 196.

LANGUAGE SPOT: sentence word order

The aim of this exercise is to revise basic English sentence structure and word order, in particular with adverbs of frequency and other adverbials. The sentences are typical of what students might want to write in the writing task for this unit, so it could be done at any time during the writing lesson, or at the end of it, or at another appropriate moment during Module 1.

▶ **Student's Resource Book page 9**

Module 1A Key

Reading pp.10–11

2a 1 C; 2 A; 3 B

3b 1 C; 2 A; 3 B/C; 4 C/B; 5 B; 6 A; 7 C;
8 A/C; 9 C/A; 10 B; 11 C; 12 C; 13 B

3c 0 *they need to keep doing it over and over again until they get better at it.*
2 *deciding on the logistics of how we are going.*
3/4 B *time spent playing with them, talking and listening,* C *more people doing things together as a family.*
5 *They are expected to achieve more and more younger and younger*
6 *It's important that they (parents) don't push them into activities … that's damaging.*
7 *I feel uneasy about about letting her go off on her own*
8/9 A *If they are allowed to … But there has to be a balance.* C *If my son had his way, he'd be on his Wii …*
10 *I encourage my kids to play the piano, but only to amuse themselves.*
11 *since I separated from my husband it's not easy to keep them constantly entertained*
12 *maybe as adults we are scared of the world they're growing up in*
13 *the rivalry between parents at school*

4 Chill out = relax; packed off = sent; keep up = practise

Language development 1 pp.12–13

1a 1 wife; 2 husband; 3 grandfather; 4 schoolgirl; 5 grandfather; 6 older girl

1b A 1 a temporary situation: He*'s staying* with the family at the moment.
2 a changing situation: His children *are growing up fast!*
B an annoying or surprising habit: She*'s always* making long calls on the phone.
C a regular event: 1 She *usually goes out* in the evening.
2 a long-term situation: She *lives* in a small house … .
D characteristic behaviour: He*'ll sit and doze* in an armchair all evening.

2a 1 Do you live; 're living; 're looking for
2 do you get on; 'll tell/tells
3 Does anyone annoy; 's always taking (always takes)
4 do you go out; go out; 'm studying; 'm only going out
5 Do you like; 's getting

3a 1 S; 2 S; 3 S; 4 A

3b A understand, know; B have

4 1 I'm having *have* two brothers. S
2 Jan*'s having* has a shower A
3 What is it meaning *does it mean*? S
4 Marina thinks *'s thinking* about A
5 We are not owning *don't own* our house S
6 The house look*s* old S
7 What do *are* you look*ing* at? A
8 Phil*'s seeing* sees a client A

5a Past habits: *used to take; would teach*
Past state: *used to live*

5b 1 Many times 2 Many times 3 *used to, would*
4 *live, would*

5c A *used to/would, would*
B *used to, used to;* C *lived, taught*

6 1 forgot
2 lived/used to live; had/used to have
3 always went/always used to go/would always go; had/used to have/would have
4 was/used to be; worked/used to work/would work; retired

7 Answers will vary.

8 1 c; 2 e; 3 f; 4 a; 5 d; 6 b

Writing pp.14–15

1 An email to a new pen friend would usually contain personal information about family, lifestyle, interests, routines, aspirations, etc.

2 b

4a 1 It would be great to meet you sometime.
2 I live in a small town …
3 We get on (well) …
4 Next time I write, I'll send a photo.
5 … we would always go on holiday …
6 She looks like me, but she can be a bit talkative.
7 I hear you're looking for a pen friend.
8 Do you ever get the chance to visit my country?
9 I'm writing because …
10 Let me tell you about my family.

4b 1 T, 2 F, 3 F, 4 F, 5 T, 6 T

4c 1 Any of the expressions in 'Giving a reason for writing' or 'Talking about the future'.
2 It would be great to meet you sometime.
3 We get on (well) …
4 Do you ever get the chance to …?
5 Let me tell you about my family
6 I hear you're looking for a pen friend.

4d *Dear pen friend* would not be appropriate – students should never begin a letter with *Dear friend* or *Dear pen friend*.
Dear Mrs Watson is too formal.
Dear Sue, i.e. using the other person's first name, is an appropriate opening for an informal letter.

I hope to hear from you at your earliest convenience. is too formal.
Looking forward to hearing from you. is fairly 'neutral' and would be appropriate.
Well, that's all for now. Do write back soon. is possibly too informal for a first letter to someone you don't yet know, but could be used in subsequent letters to a pen friend.
Lots of love would be too informal/personal in this letter.
Best wishes is fairly 'neutral' and would be appropriate.
Yours sincerely is too formal.

5 Sample answer:

Dear Ana

I hear you're looking for a pen friend and so am I! Let me tell you a little bit about myself and my family.

My name's Ivan and I live in Prague. I used to work for a chemical company but now I'm learning to be a salesman. In the future I want a job where I can travel for my work. I've already been to a few places in Europe, but I've never been to your country.

I live at home with my parents, which is comfortable as I don't have to do much housework. My younger brother is studying at university. Although he is four years younger than me we get on quite well. We both enjoy snow-boarding and music.

What about you? Do you ever get the chance to travel? It would be great to meet you one day. Why don't you come to Prague next summer? Next time I write I'll send a photo.

Best wishes
Ivan

(172 words)

LANGUAGE SPOT: sentence word order

1 I don't always speak English very well.
2 My mother and father always eat fish on Fridays.
3 My sister's having a great time in Paris right now.
4 Usually her friends all gave her a lot of help.
5 My grandmother would always listen to music in bed.

6 Everyone enjoyed themselves very much at the party.
7 I'll send you an email on Tuesday next week.
8 Please write back as soon as you can.

Module 1B Customs and traditions

The topic of customs and traditions continues the lifestyles theme.

To set the ball rolling ...

With books closed, ask students what kinds of festivals or events they celebrate. Give birthdays and national holidays as examples of a range of possible festivals.

Ask them to discuss what makes festivals special (traditional clothes, food, processions, etc.).

Speaking pp.16–17

1 Ask students to spend a moment describing the pictures after they have matched them to the occasions.

2 Use the exercise to introduce students to the concept of collocation, the way that certain words are commonly used together, and the importance of recording and learning vocabulary by collocations. For example it will be easier to remember the difference between *blow up* and *blow out* if they learn them as *blow up a balloon* and *blow out candles*.

3a Draw students' attention to how the definitions are formed and point out that in the speaking exam such paraphrasing can be used when students are explaining something and have forgotten an important word ('I can't remember the name but it's the place where people ...')

3b Again, use the opportunity to discuss ways of recording the pronunciation of new vocabulary, including sounds and stress, and the importance of doing so.

4 The exercise focuses on words that are often confused.

5 The discussion could be done in small groups and could introduce other family celebrations, e.g. engagement, new baby, house warming, christening/naming ceremony, retirement. Clarify any new vocabulary, and in particular get students to think about word-building, e.g. *to get engaged, to be engaged, engagement*, etc.

6a Point out the speaking strategy. Remind students that in Paper 5 part 2 they will be asked to speak for a minute and compare and contrast two pictures, but not to describe them in detail. They will also be asked to respond to them personally in some way, e.g. here they have to say which celebration they would prefer to be at and why.

6b When students have decided which pictures the woman is describing, ask them what words or phrases they heard to help them.

6c Give students enough time to read the expressions before they listen for them. You could model them for the students, either before or after listening, so that they can recognise the stress patterns. Show the class the complete list of useful expressions in the Functions reference on page 215.

6d Before students do the speaking task, remind them of the strategy box and get them to think about how long they will speak on each section (similarities, differences and preference). As they speak, encourage partners to listen attentively but not to interrupt. They could also time the speaker and give feedback on his/her fluency.

7 This could be done in pairs, groups or as a whole class, and could produce some interesting stories. If any students seem to have little to say, you could prompt them to talk about any planned future celebrations, or other family celebrations that are not shown in the photos.

▶ **Student's Resource Book page 10**

Listening p.18

1 Ask students to guess what countries are shown in the photos. (A Spain, B Australia, C Scotland). Point out the first listening strategy before they discuss the questions.

2 When students have read the second listening strategy (for gist) compare it to the skimming strategy in reading. When students have matched the speakers to the pictures ask them what words/expressions they remember from each and, by combining them with the pictures, work out the gist of each speaker.

3 Before students listen again, ask them to read the last strategy box and remind them that they are listening for specific information (similar to scanning when reading), not specific words or phrases. Give them time to mark the important words in each statement before listening.

4 At this stage of the course it is probably useful to give students time to prepare what they are going to say and to have time to look up key vocabulary. However, remind them that it is a speaking activity and check that they are just making notes rather than writing out sentences in full. The discussion itself would work best in small groups.

Language development 2 p.19

The language in Exercise 1 should largely be revision for students at this level, but it is important to check that they have a good grasp of these basics. Ask students to look at the photo and ask if anyone knows anything about the carnival.

Background

Burns Night, celebrated on 25 January in Scotland and by Scottish people all over the world, celebrates the life and works of Robert Burns (1759 – 1796), Scotland's favourite poet and songwriter. It includes speeches, reciting some of his work, drinking whiskey and of course eating haggis.

1a/b Students should do this in pairs, or at least discuss their answers in pairs, before checking in the Grammar reference. Discuss and clarify any points students are not sure about.

1c Students may need access to dictionaries for this task. If so, encourage them to work out the correct form of the words before they look up the meanings. Again, get them to compare answers before checking them as a whole class.

2 Give students plenty of time to study the information in the box before attempting the exercise. Point out to students that to do well at FCE level it is not enough just to use basic comparative and superlative structures, and they should be able to demonstrate use of these modifiers when using adjectives and adverbs.

3a Remind students to modify their comparisons as they write them.

3b Discussion could be in pairs or small groups, with brief class feedback.

▶ **Student's Resource Book page 11**

Use of English 1 p.20

1a As this is the first time students encounter Key word transformations, and they are an area of the exam that students often find problematic, it is important to go through the examples carefully with the class. Demonstrate how the example sentences express the same idea in two different ways and take time to work through the strategy box and examples before starting the exercise.

1b Ask concept questions to check students' understanding of the rubric, such as *Can you change the word given? Which words do you write? Can you use six words? Five words?* Explain that some of the language has not been covered in the book yet and refer them to the contents map to show them when it will be covered.

3 When students have discussed the questions you could discuss strategies for further practice in areas they found difficult, such as using the Student's Resource Book, referring to grammar practice materials, the school study centre, etc.

Use of English 2 p.21

1 Check that students understand *hospitality* (friendly behaviour towards visitors) before they discuss the question.

2a With all text-based questions, students should understand the gist before attempting to complete the task. Give students a minute to first skim the text then scan it to find the answers to the three questions.

2b It would be useful to stop after students have answered the first one or two questions and go through them with the whole class before students go on and complete the exercise. Remind them to use the Help clues where they have difficulty.

2c This exercise points out some of the areas that are frequently tested in Paper 3 Part 1.

2d Remind students that they will need to learn a lot of vocabulary during the course and discuss with them ways to use a vocabulary book to help them.

Language development 3 p.22

This section is designed to familiarise students with the concept of collocation. They will need encouragement throughout the course to notice collocations as they occur and to record them.

LOOK When students have found the five collocations it might be useful to elicit the opposites for some of them, e.g. *heavy meal – light meal,* to further demonstrate how collocation works.

1 Students may be unfamiliar with this type of diagram, which is sometimes known as a spidergram. If so, spend a little time explaining how they can be a useful memory aid, as they help learners with strong visual memories and may help to categorise vocabulary in a similar way to the brain.

2a Although some other adjective + noun combinations might be possible, e.g. *strong clothes, wide heels,* they are not common and therefore cannot really be regarded as 'strong' collocations.

```
Photocopiable activity
Photocopiable activity 1C (pp. 129–130) gives
practice of these, and more adjective + noun
collocations.
```

3 This might be a good point in the course to show students how phrasal verbs are listed in dictionaries. (e.g. in *Longman Exams Dictionary*, 'pick somebody ↔ up' where ↔ is used to mean the object can come before or after the participle means the verb is separable. Compared with 'pick on somebody' = inseparable.)

4a Emphasise that students should learn the phrasal verbs with the nouns they collocate with, e.g. *turn the heat up, keep costs down.*

5 It would be useful to revise some of the phrasal verbs in a future lesson. One good way of doing so is to play 'Noughts and crosses'. Divide the class into teams. The object of the game is for one team to complete a row of three squares (vertical, horizontal or diagonal) in a grid with their symbol, either 'noughts' (0) or crosses (X). Draw a square on the board and divide it into nine smaller squares by drawing two horizontal lines and two vertical lines inside it. Write one phrasal verb into each square. Teams take it in turns to choose a verb and put it into a sentence which shows the meaning. If it is correct, they can put their symbol in the square. The first team with three squares in a row wins.

▶ **Module 1 Test: How much do you remember? TRB page 174**

Module 1B Key

Speaking pp.16–17

2a take photos; cut the cake; blow out the candles; propose a toast; unwrap the presents; walk down the aisle; send out invitations; blow up balloons; make a speech; be given a certificate; exchange rings; rent a marquee

3a/b 1 'registry office; 2 'bridesmaid;
3 the 'best man; 4 'witnesses; 5 re'ception;
6 'honeymoon; 7 anni'versary

4 1 get; registry office; got; bridesmaids; reception; honeymoon; 2 hold; send out; guests; dress up

6b 1 C then A in that order
2 She prefers the birthday party ('I think I'd prefer the birthday party ... as it's more relaxed and probably more fun than ...')

6c Similarities:
Both of ... are
They both seem to be ...
In this one ... and this one ...
Differences:
The main difference between ... and ... is
... this one is ... whereas ... .
Likes, dislikes, preferences:
I would like ... but ...
Although ... I'd like ... because ...
I think I'd prefer ... as ...

Listening p.18

2 1 1 B; 2 A; 3 C
2 1 c; 2 b; 3 a

3 Important words in each statement:
A mealtimes important
B people kind
C cost of living lower
D climate not as imagined
E don't feel belong anywhere
F feel isolated
G wish got into the culture
Speaker 1 C (*you can get away with living on very little*) / F (*it feels a long way away*)
Speaker 2 A (*Their priorities are different – people ... sit down ... together*) / G (*I didn't become as fluent as I would have liked*)
Speaker 3 B (*would do anything to help you*) / E (*I feel strange when I go back to Russia and yet don't feel British either!*)

Language development 2 p.19

1a 1 Burns Night is one of ~~most~~ the most important nights in Scotland.
2 For many Scots, Burns supper is the ~~most~~ ~~good~~ best event of the year.

3 Usually ~~more late~~ the later it gets, ~~more noisy~~ the noisier it gets.
4 The speech before the toast was ~~funnyiest~~ the funniest I have ever heard.
5 The music was ~~more loud that~~ louder than last year.
6 The celebration was ~~more lively~~ the liveliest one I've ever been to.
7 Outside it was just as chilly ~~than~~ as last year.
8 Next year I'll leave ~~more early~~ earlier. I couldn't get hold of a taxi.

1c 1 more enthusiastically; 2 the most popular;
3 more widely; 4 better-known; 5 bigger;
6 wider; 7 as enthusiastic; 8 liveliest; 9 most sensational; 10 more commercialised

2 1 by far the largest; 2 much more crowded;
3 not quite as long; 4 a lot more colourful;
5 far spicier; 6 easily the mildest; 7 just about the worst

Use of English 1 p.20

1a not nearly as old as; apart from
Area of grammar: comparison of adjectives; Area of vocabulary: preposition phrases

1b 1 aren't as/so widely read
2 a much better swimmer than
3 turned it down
4 much less popular than

2 5 is more difficult to study
6 always borrowing my things without
7 been good at
8 only a little more slowly

3 vocabulary: 3, 7
comparative or superlative structures: 1, 2, 4, 5, 8 tense forms: 6

Use of English 2 p.21

2a 1 They washed their feet.
2 An object in the house that the guest has admired.
3 Because they might be too embarrassed to refuse food when it is offered.

2b 1 C world – collocates with *ancient* and concerns people
2 A look – phrasal verb *look after*
3 D journey – must be countable – c.f. *travel* (uncountable) and collocate with *long*
4 B survived – continued to this day
5 D particular – specified one of a number
6 A typical – normal/common
7 C required – passive, the tradition calls for it
8 A off – *breaks off*, removes
9 B foreign – from abroad
10 D heavy – collocates with *meal*
11 A keeps on – continues

12 B turn – phrasal verb *turn s.th. down*, to refuse s.th.

HELP Question 1 *world*
Question 2 *look after*
Question 6 *typical*
Question 10 *heavy*
Question 12 *turn down*

2c **2** • the correct word from a set with similar meanings: 4, 6, 7
• phrasal verbs: 2, 8, 11, 12
• adjective + noun combinations: 1, 3, 9, 10

Language development 3 p.22

LOOK ancient world (opposite: modern)
long journey (opposite: short)
old customs (opposite: new)
special cloth (opposite: ordinary)
foreign guests

1 apples; milk; look; grapes

2a strong: <u>influence</u>, possibility, feelings, argument
wide: variety, grin, choice, gap
plain: English, clothes
high: heels, number, speed

2b **1** strong feelings; **2** plain English; **3** wide grin;
4 high speed; **5** wide choice/wide variety;
6 strong influence; **7** High heels;
8 strong possibility

3 **1** literal/obvious meaning
2 idiomatic

4a **1** up; **2** down; **3** down; **4** up; **5** down; **6** up
4b **1** d; **2** f; **3** e; **4** g; **5** c; **6** h; **7** b; **8** a
4c a – 8; b – 5; c – 7; d – 6; e – 2; f – 3; g – 4;
h – 1

Teacher's Resource Book Module 1 Test: How much do you remember? p.174

1 1 C; 2 B; 3 B; 4 A; 5 C

2 1 use; 2 like; 3 would (could); 4 between; 5 Is

3 1 inhabitants; 2 personality; 3 international;
4 outskirts; 5 talkative

4 1 He *always forgot/was always forgetting to lock* the back door.
2 Jane's cooking *is not nearly as good* as John's.
3 Shall *I pick you up* at 8.00 p.m.?
4 I don't have *(quite) as many books as* he does.
5 My boss *is always interrupting me* when I speak.

Module 2 Careers

Module 2 includes topics such as growing up, schools/education and work.

To set the ball rolling ...

Elicit the difference between the words *job* and *work* (*job* – countable – the specific thing that you do for a living; *work* – uncountable – the general concept) and between *job* and *career* (*career* – a job or profession that you plan to do for several years).

Lead-in p.23

Elicit the names of the jobs shown in the photos. (In the UK *lawyers* are divided into *solicitors* who give legal advice and prepare documents and *barristers* (shown in the picture), who represent people in court.) Ask students if they would like to do any of the jobs shown, and to give reasons why/why not.

Then get them to discuss the lead-in questions.

Module 2A Work

Reading pp.24–25

1 Before looking at the photos ask students, with books closed, if they know of anyone that has quit a job to start their own business and why they did so. Having asked the class the two questions in Exercise 1, you could add a third – Why do you think the company is called Innocent?

2 Students should first read the strategy box giving more advice on skimming. Choosing a suitable heading demonstrates a general understanding. From skimming the text, students should be able to understand the focus and scope of each paragraph.

3a Start by looking at the strategy box and the concept of reading for detail. In the technique for answering multiple-choice questions highlighted here, students should look first at the question and then try to find the answer in the text without looking at the choices. This is because seeing the incorrect answers can affect students' opinions.

3b Remind students that in the exam there will be eight questions with four possible answers to each.

4 Students are likely to encounter words with which they are unfamiliar. If the words are in an important part of the text, students should use the reading strategy to deduce the meanings. If students find it hard to guess the meanings of the underlined words in the text, give them the following

definitions and ask them to match them.

1 encouragement to work harder
2 very little
3 people who can't stop working too hard
4 keep something in order to sell it
5 tell your employer officially that you are leaving your job
6 unusual behaviour or appearance
7 something put in food (to make it taste better or to preserve it)

Get them to find other new words and use the strategy to guess the meanings. Use the opportunity to advise students on how to organise their vocabulary books. They often need a lot of encouragement initially.

5 Finish the exercise with a discussion asking questions such as

1 Would you prefer to have your own business or work for someone else?
2 What are the benefits of and drawbacks of setting up your own business?
3 What type of business would you like to have?

> **Photocopiable activity**
> Photocopiable activity 2A (p. 131) could be done at this point. It is a group discussion on various aspects of a variety of jobs.

▶ **Student's Resource Book page 14**

Language development 1 pp.26–27

With books closed ask students for ways of finding jobs (asking around, job centres, advertisements, relatives) and the process of getting them (see an advertisement, write a letter of application, attend an interview).

Discuss students' experiences of applying for jobs and attending interviews.

1a Get students to discuss the question in pairs. Note the spelling variation; program (USA), programme (UK). Point out that either is acceptable in the exam as long as there is consistency.

1b If students are not familiar with the names of the tenses, give them some examples before they do the exercise.

1c This is to draw students' attention to the different use of the tenses and is preparation for completing the grammar summary. You may want to let students discuss the questions in pairs before class feedback.

2a Students should do the exercise on their own and check in pairs before referring to the Grammar summary to check their answers. It would be helpful to compare/contrast the two perfect forms of *go* at this stage (e.g. *He has gone to the USA / He has been to the USA*) with suitable concept questions (e.g. *where is he now? Has he returned?*)

3e *for* and *since* are frequently tested in the FCE exam. One way to give further practice is to give each student two pieces of paper, one with the word *for* and the other with the word *since*. Then call out a list of time expressions, e.g. *six months, last month, October, Friday, five days, five o'clock, Christmas,* and as you say each one students hold up the correct piece of paper. To make it a game you could award points for correct answers.

4 Remind students that this type of checking and correcting is important with their own written work. Get them to justify their answers.

5b This is an opportunity for less controlled personalised practice of the structures. Encourage students to try and write interesting true sentences, but to use their imagination if they can't think of anything true to write.

6 This could be done with a competitive element. E.g. students could work in pairs and see which pair is the quickest to find and correct the eight mistakes.

···
: **Photocopiable activity** :
: Photocopiable activity 2B (p. 132) would work well :
: here. It is a roleplay with candidates being :
: interviewed and selected for a job. :
···

▶ **Student's Resource Book page 15**

Writing pp.28–29

1 Point out to students that in Paper 2 Part 2, they may be asked to write either an informal letter or a formal letter.

2 In the exam, as with all writing, the writer needs a clear focus on the reason for writing. Students should consider these four questions for every piece of writing they do now.

3a Again emphasise that the planning stage is vital if students are to include all the important information within the word count and use a range of structures/vocabulary.

3b Encourage students just to make notes at this stage, not to start writing the actual paragraphs.

4a Point out that the only problem here is the level of formality. All the sentences contain good English and interesting phrases.

4c Although addresses should not be added, there should be a suitable opening and closing.

5 Now that students have done detailed work on the planning of the letter, the writing should not take more than 20 minutes.

6 Checking should take another ten minutes. Remind students that contractions and direct questions are not used in formal letters.

When they check the number of words, teach them at this stage to calculate the average number of words per line and then just count the lines. By the time of the exam they should have a good feel for the right number of words in their handwriting, and therefore won't need to waste time counting every word.

▶ **Student's Resource Book page 17**

Module 2A Key

Reading pp.24–25
2 1 d; 2 b; 3 a; 4 e; 5 c

3b 1 b
2 c – *without the use of additives their idea wouldn't work*
3 a – *made from 100% fresh fruit and nothing else*
4 a – *new product ideas … are rejected if they are too far from their main focus*
5 c – *focus on making their employees feel valued*
6 b – *its approach to business is attractive to those who are disillusioned with …*

4 resign – tell your employer officially that you are leaving your job
additives – something put in food (to make it taste better or to preserve it)
stock – keep something in order to sell it
quirkiness – unusual behaviour or appearance
minimal – very little
incentives – encouragement to work harder
workaholics – people who can't stop working too hard

Language development 1 pp.26–27
1a Yes. Good English and some experience of working with children.

1b past simple: helped; spent
present perfect simple: have often been; have learned; haven't worked

1c No; No; Yes, last year; Yes, two years ago

1d A 1 I have often been to California
2 I have learned a lot of English over the years
3 I haven't worked at a summer camp before
B 1 Last year I spent two months on an internship program.
2 Two years ago I helped at a children's charity.

2a **1**
A: Have you ever lived abroad?
B: Yes, I have.
A: Where did you live?
B: In Dublin.
A: When did you go there?
B: In 2002.
2
A: Have you ever worked in an office?
B: No, I haven't.
3
A: Have you ever been to the USA?
B: Yes, I have.
A: When did you go there?
B: Last year.
A: Why did you go there?
B: To study English.
4
A: Have you used English in your work before?
B: No, I haven't.

3b present perfect simple: have lived; have just taken; haven't had
present perfect continuous: have been studying; have been taking part

3c **1** Yes; **2** Yes; **3** 1; **4** Yes; **5** Maybe. We don't know.

3d A I have lived in Lima since 2006.
B I have been studying for a degree in education for two years.
C I have just taken my second year exams.
D Recently I have been taking part in a series of workshops.

3e **1** for; **2** since; **3** for; **4** since; **5** for; **6** since

4 **1** ✓ Recent activity.
2 Incorrect. Recent finished action. Should be *I've had some good news.*
3 ✓ Recent activity.
4 ✓ Recent finished action.
5 Incorrect. Recent finished action. Single action, not a repeated action. Should be *Emma's fallen over.*
6 Incorrect. Recent repeated activity. Should be *We've been using the stairs all day.*

5a **1** 've/have been
2 haven't written
3 haven't been waiting
4 've/have been working
5 haven't had
6 felt
7 've/have made (viewed as a recent finished action)
OR 've/have been making (viewed as a recent activity, maybe unfinished)
8 've/have been trying
9 've/have found
10 've/have been staying

6 I ~~have been~~ *was* born in Peru 26 years ago and I've lived here all my life. I ~~am~~ *have been* married for two years but we don't have any children yet. I've been working in a bank ~~since~~ *for* four years and I enjoy it a lot. In my spare time I'm trying to improve my English – I've had private lessons ~~since~~ *for* six months. I also love reading. Last year I ~~have~~ tried to read a novel in English. I ~~go~~ *have been going* to the mountains for my holidays ~~during~~ *for* six years because I love walking. ~~I've also gone~~ *I also went* to Brazil two years ago to stay with some friends.

Writing pp.28–29
1 formal: c, d, e; informal: a, b, f

2 1 The Lifeguard Manager
2 to apply for a job
3 personal information: swimming ability/knowledge of first aid/ability to work with people, suitability, availability
4 positive, enthusiastic

3a **Paragraph 1** – Where you heard about the job (your name comes at the end)
Paragraph 2 – age, where you live, education, work experience, what kind of person you are.
Paragraph 3 – suitability
Paragraph 4 – availability (referees would normally be given in the accompanying CV)

4a appropriately formal: 2, 6, 10 too informal: 1, 3, 4, 5, 7, 8, 9

4b 1 – I would like to apply for the position of beach lifeguard assistant which I saw advertised in the student newspaper.
3 – At present I am studying at university and I am a strong swimmer.
4 – I regret I have had no experience of this kind of work but I am a good swimmer.
5 – I very much enjoy working with people.
7 – I think I would be a suitable candidate for this job because …
8 – I would be happy to provide references and attend an interview.
9 – I hope you will consider my application.

4c Opening: *Dear Sir or Madam* As the name of the manager is unknown, this is the only suitable opening.
Closing: *Yours faithfully* This is the best ending when no name has been used at the beginning. In British English, if there is a name at the beginning, e.g. *Dear Ms Smith, Yours sincerely* is usually used at the end.

5 Sample answer:

Dear Sir or Madam

I am looking for outdoor work during the summer holidays and I would like to apply for the position of hotel lifeguard assistant which I saw advertised in my university's student newspaper.

I am 20 years old and at present I am studying Physical Education. I am a strong swimmer and have recently had first aid training. I very much enjoy working with people and for the last two summers I have been working as an assistant ranger in a National Park, where I had to provide information to the public about using the park and provide emergency assistance to park users. Now I am looking for something different.

I think I would be a suitable candidate for the position because I have been described as calm in a crisis and someone who works well with others.

I am available for the whole of August and would be happy to attend an interview at any time. I look forward to hearing from you at any time in the near future.

Yours faithfully

Michael Charles

Michael Charles

(178 words)

Module 2B A learning experience

This module continues the theme of careers, focusing on the topic of education.

To set the ball rolling ...

With books closed, put students in pairs or groups to talk briefly about the school(s) they went to. Give suitable prompts if necessary, e.g. *State or private? Single sex or mixed? Strict or relaxed?*

Speaking pp.30–31

1 Start by getting students to identify the types of schools in the pictures. This will help with the vocabulary in the questions. Give students a few minutes to think of points before they speak.

2 Some of the words might match more than one picture.

Background

Continuous assessment is a way of judging a student's work by looking at what they have achieved during the year in tests, essays and projects rather than by testing them in a final year exam. It is said to give a more complete picture of a student's ability and understanding as they are free from time pressures. However, with students increasingly using the Internet to research assignments, many institutions are considering returning to the use of exams.

3 Check students know the pronunciation of the items and remind them how to mark the stresses (e.g. phi'losophy, phil<u>o</u>sophy, philŏsophy). A list of school subjects is a useful lexical set under the topic of education. A spidergram in a vocabulary book would be a good way to record them.

Background

Many school subjects are now abbreviated. PE = physical education, ICT = Information communications technology, DT = Design and Technology. Others include RP = Religion and Philosophy, PSHE = Personal, Social and Health Education.

4 Point out that students should notice the collocations as they do the exercise (e.g. *sit/pass/fail exams, attend lectures*).

6a At this stage students should not discuss the list. They will do this later.

6d Students should read the speaking strategy first. Give them time to look at the list again and to prepare before the discussion. Monitor and check that they are using the language for giving opinions, agreeing and disagreeing, and give feedback on this afterwards.

7 Give students time to look at the statements and think about them first. Remind them to use the functional language as they discuss the points, and again provide feedback on this afterwards.

Listening p.32

1a Start by getting students to describe the picture, which represents the start of university life. Students read the strategy box before discussing the two questions.

1b As with multiple-choice reading, the advice is to read only the question before they listen and to match what they hear to the choices. Encourage students to predict what they might hear.

3a Students should first read the listening strategy. Before they listen, remind them that opinions might be expressed in different words from those written in the options.

4 Students could also discuss their opinions on whether it is good to work while studying.

5 Remind students of the need to learn the collocations as a phrase. Get them to make sentences of their own using the collocations.

▶ **Student's Resource Book page 18**

Use of English 1 p.33

1 This is just intended as a quick introduction to the topic of the text. Don't spend long on it, and don't expect students to come up with too much detail!

Background

Albert Einstein (1879–1955) was born German but became a Swiss citizen in 1901. He emigrated to the USA in 1933. His theory of relativity was just one of many great theories. When the first atom bomb was used, he said that if he had known what his discoveries would be used for, he would have been a watchmaker. After the Second World War he campaigned against nuclear weapons.

2a Remind students that the purpose of the three questions is to get a general understanding of the text, and that they should only spend a minute or so looking at the article to find the answers.

2b First go through the task strategy with the class. Elicit ways of identifying whether the missing word is a noun, article, verb, pronoun, etc., e.g. *What word follows the gap? What type of words are followed by –ing forms?*, etc. When students first work through the text, point out that they don't have to work through in order; harder ones can be left until others have been filled in, by which time they might seem easier.

2c It might be useful for students to discuss these questions before giving them the answers and explanations.

3 Another question to discuss could be:
Do you think that, generally speaking, school/university exams are a good indication of how successful someone will be?

Language development 2 p.34

LOOK It might be useful to elicit some uses of articles with books closed before students read the grammar box.

1a Do the first question as an example with the whole class, asking suitable concept questions for each part. For example, sentence 1:

- How many *best courses* can you have? *The* is often used with superlatives.
- … *the one* – do we know which one?
- *the economics* – what type of word is *economics*? (a subject of study)
- *The teacher* – do we know which teacher?
- *a good progress* – is *progress* countable or uncountable?

Encourage students to work through the other sentences in the same way.

1b Students should work through the gapped text with the same systematic approach. Note how *college* is used in different ways in the text, illustrating different uses of articles; students wanted *a* college (indefinite), the attitude of *the* college (definite), to go to Ø college (fixed expression).

2 Give students time to read through the grammar box before doing the exercise.

Photocopiable activity
Photocopiable activity 2C (pp. 133–134) would work well here. Students complete the missing articles in a story and retell it to a partner.

▶ **Student's Resource Book page 19**

Use of English 2 p.35

1 Start by asking the students to describe what is happening in the picture.

2a As with other Use of English tasks, it is important for students to have a general understanding of the text before attempting the task.

2b Students should read the task strategy and the rubric carefully before starting the task. Look at the example and do question 1 together to help students with the strategy. In 0, the word must be either an adjective or a participle as it follows *It's*. The adjective which has the form of the present participle, *frustrating*, is formed by dropping the *e* and adding *–ing*. The word in 1 must be a noun as it follows the article *a* + an adjective and proceeds *for*. Point out that each text usually contains at least one negative requiring a prefix.

2c These questions focus students on the strategy and introduce expressions such as suffix and prefix, which students may not be familiar with.

3 You could also ask students whether they think listening to music helps people study or when the best time to revise something is.

Language development 3 p.36

LOOK This is the first time suffixes are dealt with in the book. Emphasise that many types of words are formed by adding suffixes and that this section only looks at adjectives. Give students advice on recording suffixes in a vocabulary book. Suggest that each time they learn a new word they also record the related words formed with suffixes. (e.g. suit; suitable, unsuitable, suitability, suitably)

1a As you check the answers, point out changes in stress as the nouns change to adjectives (<u>cou</u>rage – cou<u>ra</u>geous; <u>dra</u>ma – dra<u>ma</u>tic; all adjectives ending in -ic are stressed on the preceding syllable).

2a Students could either do this with a partner or by using dictionaries. If they use dictionaries, demonstrate how phrasal verbs are listed in the dictionary.

2b Do the first question with the class to ensure they are thinking about both the correct verb and the correct tense.

▶ **Module 2 Test: How much do you remember? TRB page 175**

▶ **Exam Practice 1: Papers 2 and 4 TRB page 176**

Module 2B Key

Speaking pp.30–31

3 2 mathema'tician, his'torian, engi'neer, 'scientist, soci'ologist, 'dramatist, phi'losopher, 'linguist, e'conomist
3 a DT; **b** PE; **c** ICT

4 1 paid; skipped; failed; re-sit; passed; apply 2 did; get; study; attends; revises

6b Most important factors:
• small classes – individual attention
• being near home – more free time and friends live nearby
• uniform – important that they all wear the
• same clothes
Least important factor:
• lots of equipment – doesn't matter at this age

6c **Giving opinions:**
Well, <u>for</u> me, one of the most important <u>things</u> is …
I just <u>don't think</u> it matters … .
The <u>least</u> important factor for me is … .
Strong agreement:
That's <u>true</u>.
I agree <u>absolutely</u>.
I couldn't <u>agree</u> <u>more</u>.
Tentative agreement:
I <u>think</u> so.
Disagreement:
I agree <u>up</u> to a <u>point</u>, but … . I
Do you <u>think</u> <u>so</u>?
Actually, I think it's <u>more</u> <u>important</u> … .

Listening p.32

3a 1 B; **2** A; **3** C; **4** C; **5** B

5 1 d/g; **2** h/i; **3** f; **4** b; **5** a; **6** e; **7** c

Use of English 1 p.33

2a 1 Science.
2 He didn't like exams or going to classes.
3 He worked in the Swiss patent office.

2b 1 a – student = singular countable noun
2 all – *nearly* + *all*
3 what/as
4 neither/nor – linking two negative ideas
5 Despite/After – before *-ing*
6 the – name of a unique institution
7 Although/Though – contrast
8 because – expresses reason
9 a – school = singular countable noun, one of many
10 both – good at two things
11 was – before past participle in passive structure
12 the – a particular, defined history

2c **1**
articles – 1, 6, 9, 12
connecting expressions – 4, 5, 7, 8
2 passives 11

Language development 2 p.34

1a **1** The best course was the one I did on ~~the~~
economics. The teacher was very good and I
made ~~a~~ good progress.
2 Nina's studying ~~the~~ German at evening classes
in ~~the~~ London.
3 My brother is 19. He's at ~~the~~ university in ~~the~~
Africa and wants to become *an* English teacher
because it would give him *a* good opportunity
to travel.
4 When we were in Japan we noticed that most
Japanese students work harder than the
American students I met in *the* USA.
5 I go to college by ~~the~~ train. Unfortunately, the
train is often late.

1b **1** Ø – students in general
2 a – one of many
3 Ø
4 the – superlative
5 the – defined noun
6 the – referring to something known
7 the – still connected to the superlative in 4
8 the – defined
9 the – known buildings
10 The – only one
11 a – college = singular countable noun
12 Ø – in general
13 a – as 11
14 a – timetable = singular countable noun
15 Ø – fixed expression
16 Ø – in general
17 Ø – fixed expression

2 **1** some – a large amount of
2 any – negative, before uncountable noun
3 anything – negative
4 some – positive, before uncountable noun
5 anything – negative
6 some – positive, before uncountable noun
7 hardly any – almost no
8 some – in a question, hoping for a
positive answer
9 some – positive, before uncountable noun
10 anything – it doesn't matter what

Use of English 2 p.35

2a **1** Trying to remember things
2 Use all senses, so listen to as well as read the
information. Study at the right time (before
bed) and in the right atmosphere (peaceful).

2b **1** disadvantage; **2** countless; **3** helpful;
4 information; **5** silently; **6** combination;
7 written; **8** unlikely; **9** possibility; **10** peaceful

2c **2** nouns – 1, 4, 6, 9
adjectives – 2, 3, 7, 8, 10
adverbs – 5
3 2, 3, 4, 5, 6, 9, 10
4 1, 8

Language development 3 p.38

1 **1** harmless; **2** natural; **3** courageous;
4 childish; **5** helpful; **6** passionate; **7** dirty;
8 horrible; **9** dramatic; **10** lively

2a **1** g; **2** a; **3** h; **4** c; **5** j; **6** i; **7** b; **8** d; **9** e; **10** f

2b **1** turned up (to suddenly appear); **2** staying on;
3 carry out; **4** got down to; **5** Go over;
6 handed in; **7** keep up with; **8** pick up;
9 get (his meaning) across; **10** work out

Teacher's Resource Book
Module 2 Test: How much do you remember? p. 175

1   1 C; 2 B; 3 C; 4 A; 5 D

2   1 hearing; 2 does; 3 has; 4 the; 5 some/many

3   1 irresponsible; 2 disability; 3 dirtiest;
4 flexible; 5 strength

4   1 Paul *has been playing tennis for* three years.
2 Susan *has liked jazz since* she was a teenager.
3 There *is hardly anything to do* at the weekends.
4 Nina's looking for a *more suitable* job.
5 I *am available to attend/am available for* an interview at any time.

Teacher's Resource Book
Exam practice 1 p.176

Paper 2 Writing

Style: Informal letter – avoid formal expressions.
Content:
Tell your friend where you went, who you went with, what you ate and how enjoyable the picnic was. Include one or two interesting things that happened and say how your friends reacted.

Paper 4 Listening

Part 4 1 C; 2 A; 3 C; 4 A; 5 B; 6 C; 7 B

Module 3 The world around us

Module 3 includes topics such as cultural heritage, the environment, weather and animals.

Lead-in p.37

With books closed, get students to think of three man-made and three natural things which they see around them on a normal day. Compare ideas as a class. Then ask them to look at the two photos, and say which place they would prefer to visit and why. Explain *World Heritage sites* briefly (see 'Background' below). Get students to discuss the questions together, followed by class feedback.

Background

World Heritage sites are a list maintained by UNESCO (the United Nations Educational, Scientific and Cultural Organization) of over 730 'natural and cultural properties of outstanding universal value, protected against the threat of damage in a rapidly developing world.'
The Kremlin and Red Square, Moscow, were chosen as World Heritage sites because the Kremlin is 'inseparably linked to all of the most important historical and political events in Russia since the 13th century' and 'on Red Square, the Saint Basil Basilica is one of the most beautiful monuments of Russian Orthodox art.'
The Galapagos Islands, in the Pacific Ocean 1,000 km off the coast of Ecuador, were chosen because they are 'a unique living museum and showcase of evolution … unusual animal life – such as the land iguana, the giant tortoise and the many types of finch – inspired Charles Darwin's theory of evolution following his visit in 1835.'

For the complete list of sites see http://whc.unesco.org/en/list

Module 3A Our cultural heritage

To set the ball rolling ...

With books closed, ask students what they know about London and its history.

Reading pp.38–39

2 Remind students of the difference between skimming and scanning. Ask them first to skim to get a general idea of its content. If necessary, set a time limit of about 1¹/₂ – 2 minutes. They then scan the text to answer the questions in 1.

3a As this is the first time students have encountered gapped texts, spend some time going through the rubric and strategy box with them. Point out that the sentences must fit logically with both the preceding and following paragraphs and also grammatically. The example demonstrates this.

4 Give students time to think about the questions before they discuss them in small groups, then as a whole class.

5 Multiple matching often requires the recognition of near synonyms. Encourage students to build their vocabulary by recording near synonyms.

▶ **Student's Resource Book page 22**

Language development 1 pp.40–41

1a Ask students if they know what the three sites are and where they are.

Background

The Taj Mahal, near Agra in India, was built by the Mughal emperor Shah Jahan in memory of his wife, Mumtaz Mahal ('Chosen One of the Palace'), of which the name Taj Mahal is a corruption. She died in 1631, and the building was commenced around 1632. It took 22 years to complete and cost 40 million rupees (830,000 US dollars).
The Statue of Liberty stands in New York Harbor. It is 92 metres high and made of copper sheets over a steel frame. Begun by the French sculptor Frédéric-Auguste Bartholdi in 1875, it was dismantled in 1885, shipped to New York and reassembled.
Marrakesh was founded in 1071–1072. The lively medina contains an impressive number of architectural masterpieces, including the walls and the monumental gates, the Kutubiya Mosque with its 77-metre-high minaret, the Saadian tombs and characteristic old houses.

1b After they have read the text, ask students if they know any other World Heritage sites, perhaps in their own country.

2b You might want to go through these questions one by one with students. If necessary, use further examples to highlight the difference between the adverbs *hard* and *hardly: He works hard* = He works a lot. *He hardly works* = He doesn't work very much at all, he does almost no work.

25

3a Students could work on their own or in pairs, then check by looking in the Grammar reference on page 184.

3b Remind students that World Heritage sites can be cultural and/or natural and should be of 'outstanding universal value'. It would be interesting for students to check whether their chosen place is already a World Heritage site – they may not even know that it is!

4 Tell students that this language is frequently tested in Paper 3, and that it can make their writing and speaking more interesting in Papers 2 and 5.

5 This is an opportunity for less controlled, personalised practice of the language, probably best in small groups followed by class discussion.

6 Correcting is a vital element of writing and students should be encouraged to check their own writing, looking for typical mistakes such as these.

Photocopiable activity

Photocopiable activity 3A (pp. 135–136) could be used here. It is a structured debate on the pros and cons of tourism.

Photocopiable activity

Photocopiable activity 3B (pp. 137–138) gives further practice of adjectives and adverbs.

▶ **Student's Resource Book page 23**

Writing pp.42–43

1 If necessary, for question 1 you could suggest two or three cities locally for students to choose from, outlining briefly what attractions each one has.

2 Emphasise that it is very important for students to think about these four questions in all their FCE writing, and the transactional letter in particular.

3a Remind students that their writing needs to be well organised. A good plan should include both the organisation of key points into paragraphs, and language (vocabulary and structure) to include at each stage. A good composition should contain a range of structures and vocabulary relevant to the topic.

4a Explain that a good opening is important. It makes the reader want to read on, and in the exam it will make a good first impression on the examiner.

4b Elicit what kind of language makes a letter informal. E.g. contractions, informal vocabulary such as *great, thrilled, loads,* and phrasal verbs such as *put you up*.

4c Explain that the expressions match the points in the paragraph plan and are informal. Students could compare in groups or as a whole class to establish the range and use of the structures.

4d Get students to discuss these in pairs and encourage them to give reasons for their choices – again, it is a question of the level of formality in the sentences.

5 As students now have a detailed paragraph plan and expressions to use, the writing should take only about 20 minutes. In the exam, if students aim to spend 15 minutes planning and 20 minutes writing, they will have ten minutes to check their work.

6 Encourage students to get into the habit of systematic checking. They should use the checklist in the Writing reference on page 196. In addition, they should check for errors with particular language areas that they have problems with.

LANGUAGE SPOT: punctuation

Although poor punctuation is not specifically penalised in the exam, the overall impression mark may be adjusted if communication is impeded. Students could use the Punctuation section of the Writing reference on page 207 to help them with any they are not sure about, and/or to help check when they have finished.

▶ **Student's Resource Book page 25**

Module 3A Key

Reading pp.38–39

3b 1 D

2 E *Romans hoped – these dreams, rebellion launched   defeated Boudica, Londinium burnt to the ground – rebuild the city*

3 G *a downward turn – but too good for its decline to continue – soon began to expand again*

4 C *Henry 8th – During his reign, Thames became focal point – it was also the period of the first theatres*

5 F *household pets killed – this meant ... this disaster – Although the next calamity*

6 B *living conditions were dreadful – diseases were common*

7 A *luxury hotels and department stores sprung up – this new period of wealth; another attack, London ruined – this time it was bombs*

5 1 cutting edge; **2** injecting; **3** put off; **4** hygiene; **5** wipe out; **6** calamity; **7** stink; **8** snowball

Language development 1 pp.40–41

1a The Taj Mahal, the Statue of Liberty and the Islamic centre of Marrakesh

1b They are all UNESCO World Heritage sites.

2a Adjectives: natural, cultural, best-known, lively, impressive, fascinating, bleak, worrying, political, full
Adverbs: fast, hard, actively, extremely, hardly, well

2b 1 fast, hard, well; **2** lively; **3** hard, hardly.

3a 1 easy – *be* + adjective

2 incredibly – adverb before an adjective (*well-preserved*)

3 fast – adverb after *spoke*. *too quickly* would be possible.

4 classic – adjective describing the noun *site*

5 late – adjective; hard – adverb = a lot

6 surprising – adjective describing *sites*; imaginatively – adverb before an adjective (*created*)

4 1 D – a remarkably + adjective + noun (*quite a simple idea*)

2 C – quite + a + adjective + countable noun (*a pretty/very fast car*)

3 A – a little + adjective (*a little/bit of* + noun)

4 C – very + gradable adjective

5 B – rather + a/an + adjective + noun (*a/an + fairly/rather/extremely/pretty* + adjective + noun)

6 D – very + gradable adjective (*gorgeous/wonderful/marvellous* = ungradable adjective)

7 B – absolutely + ungradable adjective (*very/extremely/remarkably* + gradable adjective)

6 1 ... a ~~very~~ huge statue ...

2 ... the new theatre is ~~very~~ fantastic.

3 ... to be ~~smart~~ *smartly* dressed.

4 ... are working very ~~hardly~~ *hard* to restore ...

5 ... the streets are sometimes *a* bit noisy ...

Writing pp.42–43

2 1 An old friend.

2 To give information and suggestions.

3 Four – trains, accommodation, what to see, clothes.

4 Informal – she is an old friend and the style of her letter is informal.

3a Five paragraphs.

3b **Paragraph 2:** Travel instructions: Hourly train connections.
Paragraph 3: Places to go: 1 Lovely park.
2 Medieval castle.
Paragraph 4: Clothes: Shorts. T-shirts.

4a B. It is less formal.

4b Formal language in A:
Thank you very much ...
... your letter of 10 July ...
... your visit to my home town ...
... I am writing to invite you to stay with me at my house.
Informal language in B:
It was great to hear from you ...
I'm thrilled you're coming ...
I hope you'll stay with me ...
I've got loads of room to put you up now I've unpacked!

4d 1 A – All the language in A is informal, whereas all of B is extremely formal.

2 B – This is less formal (contraction, use of continuous not simple) and makes it clear they have met before, whereas in A *meeting you* makes it sound as if they are going to meet for the first time.

3 B – Again, this is less formal, with contractions and *Let me know*.

4e *Love* if they are very good friends, or *Best wishes*

5 Sample answer:

Dear Sue,

It was great to hear from you and I'm really excited that you're coming to visit me. You and Tom don't need to stay in a hotel – you can both stay at my house.

It's quite easy to get here from the conference centre as there's a fast train every hour and it's only about 20 minutes away. If you call me I'll pick you up at the station.

My town's fairly small so there isn't much to do but you really must visit the castle, which is incredibly old. There's quite a large park, which is a lovely place for a picnic in the summer.

It tends to be very hot here in July, so just bring a few casual clothes such as shorts and T-shirts.

Let me know if there's anything else you'd like to know – just call or email. I can't wait to see you again.

Love

Daisy

(154 words)

LANGUAGE SPOT: punctuation

Chester itself is a very pretty town. It dates back to Roman times, so there are a lot of fascinating ruins and lovely architecture which I'm sure will interest you. The Roman amphitheatre is well worth a visit with its guides dressed up as Roman soldiers. There is also a cathedral and a church, and there are red sandstone walls all round the town. It takes about an hour and a half to walk around them but it's a lovely walk. Henry James, the American writer, wrote about how much he loved the walls. You'll also find a river in Chester where you can go for a boat trip or have a picnic. If you have time to go shopping, there are lots of wonderful shops.

Module 3B Our natural heritage

The 'world around us' theme continues in this unit with the topics of animals, natural phenomena and weather.

Speaking pp.44–45

To set the ball rolling ...

With books closed, go round the class, with students naming an animal beginning with the next letter of the alphabet, (e.g. ant, bee, crocodile, dog, elephant, frog, goat, hamster …) with those who can't think of one quickly dropping out until one winner remains.

1a Get students to identify the animals illustrated. Many students are confused by the difference between mice and rats (mentioned in the text on London). Ask students to think of other words ending in -f that change to -ves in the plural.

1b-e Use the illustrations to get examples of the words listed and then elicit other suggestions.

2 Sorting new vocabulary into lists is a good way to process the language and helps to remember it.

3 Elicit the parts of the animal used in each verb (e.g. bite – teeth; peck – beak; scratch – claw)

4 Allow a certain amount of individual interpretation here.

5 You could add *What animal would you most like to be and why?*

6 There may be some discussion about exactly what each person's job is, which gives you the opportunity to teach some useful vocabulary. The man in the photo on the left could be a farmer or a shepherd. The woman in the photo on the right could be a vet, a veterinary nurse or a veterinary assistant. In British English, *vet* is the most common word; *veterinary surgeon* is more formal. In American English, *veterinarian* is more common.

7 This activity aims to train students to compare and contrast the pictures, rather than simply describe each one separately, a common mistake in Paper 5 Part 2.

8a Point out that the instructions usually have two parts: First 'compare and contrast' and then 'say …' (i.e. give a personal reaction of some kind).

8b As students listen, they should think about what the student says compared with what they said in Exercise 2.

8d Get students to discuss the questions in pairs. Play the recording again if they can't answer the questions. Point out that in Paper 5, if students don't know a word, they should explain it in another way, just as the student does on the recording. They will be given credit for this by the examiner. If they make no attempt to explain a word they don't know, they could lose marks.

9 Students should read the task strategy first.

10 Encourage students to discuss their own and each other's performance in the task.

▶ **Student's Resource Book page 27**

Listening p.46

1a First ask students to describe the photo. Elicit/Check the words *jaguar* and *rainforest*. Let students discuss the questions in pairs, then explain that they will hear the actual answers on the recording.

2a Get students to do this in pairs. It is important that students think about what kind of word could go into each space. Look at the example with them, and perhaps do number 2 together, to make sure they know what to do.

2c Point out that Exercise 2b is similar to Paper 4 Part 2, in which three words is normally the maximum necessary. Numbers can be written as numbers or words; e.g. question 1 could be *5.30* or *half past five*. In question 4, *a hundred and seventy kilometres* would obviously be more than three words, and this would not usually occur in the exam. Note also that in question 4, an abbreviation such as *km* would be acceptable. The most important thing is to show the examiner that they have understood the material on the recording.

After checking all the answers, ask students if they would like to do the job that Nick Gordon does, and why.

Use of English 1 p.47

1 This is to generate interest in the topic of animals' unusual abilities – you might want to reassure students that they don't need to know facts like these for the exam! Use the photo to teach *cricket*. Students should discuss the questions in pairs before turning to page 209 to check their answers.

2a Students should always look at the title of a Use of English text, as it will give them a clear indication of the content.

2b Again, students should always read any text for a general understanding before they start the exam task.

2c If you think it necessary, do the first one or two gaps with the whole class so that they can see the process of deciding what the missing words are.

2d This focuses students on choices they made and highlights typical areas tested in this part of the exam.

Language development 2 p.48

Look Point out the section in the Grammar reference on verbs of the senses, which can be followed by an infinitive without *to* or an *-ing* form.

1a This is a brief lead-in to the grammar exercise.

2a These three verbs are commonly tested at FCE.

2b Get students to check in pairs then perhaps look at the Grammar reference to check their answers.

3a Ask students what they know about the phenomenon.

> ### Background
>
> The Northern Lights is the popular name for the *aurora borealis*, which occurs when solar particles enter the earth's atmosphere over the north pole and react with gases, causing them to emit light. In the southern hemisphere, the corresponding phenomenon is known as the Southern Lights or *aurora australis*.

3b If students find any of the verb + preposition combinations hard, encourage them to note them down to learn.

4a Encourage students to write true sentences.

> #### Photocopiable activity
> Photocopiable activity 3C (pp. 139–140) would work well here. It is a card game in which students have to connect two verbs together correctly.

▶ **Student's Resource Book page 28**

Use of English 2 p.49

1 Any students who have seen the film will be familiar with Groundhog Day. Get them to explain it briefly to the others.

> ### Background
>
> In the fantasy comedy film *Groundhog Day* (1993) a weatherman, fed up with reporting on the Punxsutawney story every year, suddenly wakes up and finds himself in a world where every day is 2 February, and all the events of that day are repeated daily.

2a Give students a limit of one minute to read the text, ignoring the spaces.

2b Remind students to use the strategy on page 20 and the Help questions if they need to.

2d Weather collocations are practised further in Exercise 3a on page 50. Knowledge of collocation is tested in various parts of the exam. Encourage students to note down collocations as they hear them rather than only writing down individual words.

Language development 3 p.50

1 This could be in pairs or small groups, followed by class discussion. Get students to expand their answers and to support them with reasons.

2a Make it clear that some words may go into more than one category. E.g. *hurricane* could go with wind or storm; *snow* and *hail* could go with rain or storm. Encourage students to discuss them together; if they give reasons for their answers, it will help them to understand the meanings of the words. Use the short definitions in the Key on TRB page 32 to help clarify meaning.

2b If there is time, students can make sentences of their own using the other items from the exercise.

3a If students have already done Exercise 2d on page 48, remind them of the collocations they found then.

3b Get students to think of the context of each sentence before completing it.

4a There may be more than one possibility, but students should look for the strongest collocations.

5 Check that students understand all the vocabulary in the questions. Obviously there are no 'right' answers here, but encourage students to give reasons for their choices.

▶ **Module 3 Test: How much do you remember? TRB page 177**

Module 3B Key

Speaking pp.44–45

1a A butterfly/butterflies; B goat/goats; C lizard/lizards; D goldfish/goldfish; E wolf/wolves; F sea lion/sea lions; G mouse/mice; H parrot/parrots

1b farm – goat; jungle – parrot; forest – wolf; house – goldfish
Others: mouse – house/fields; sea lion – sea/beach; butterfly – garden/countryside; lizard – desert/forest/house

1c insect – butterfly; rodent – mouse; reptile – lizard; sea animal – sea lion; domestic pet – parrot/goldfish/mouse

1d tail – mouse; wings – butterfly; claws – wolf; whiskers – mouse; beak – parrot; hooves – goat; fur – wolf; fins – goldfish

1e squeaks – mouse; howls – wolf; screeches – parrot

2 Domestic pets – guinea pig, tortoise, spider, rabbit, hamster
Farm animals – sheep, calf, bull
Wild animals – bear, whale, giraffe, penguin, leopard, rabbit, squirrel, jaguar, moose, beaver, dolphin, spider
Birds – pigeon, vulture
Insects – bee, beetle (NB A spider is not an insect)

3 Examples: bites – dog; pecks – bird; stings – bee/wasp/scorpion; scratches – cat; hibernates – bear; nests – most birds; becoming extinct – some whales/some sharks/pandas

4 Examples: aggressive – crocodile; elegant – snake; proud – lion; fierce – tiger; cunning – fox; agile – jaguar; affectionate – cat; useful – donkey; intelligent – dog

8a … is difficult about these jobs.
8c Personally, I … / … if I had to choose …
8d vet – a kind of doctor who looks after animals … a doctor for sick animals.
pets – small animals who live in the home

Listening p.46

1b Nick is a wildlife photographer/film-maker. (*I was sent out to the Amazon … to make a TV documentary about monkeys and birds.*)
He liked: the heat, the humidity, the snakes, the insects, the animals, the people.
He didn't like: the loneliness, sweating so much, getting bitten by the insects, the feeling of claustrophobia caused by lack of daylight. (*You pour sweat … . The insects … you're bitten all the time. … claustrophobic … no real daylight … It's lonely.*)

2a 1 a time
2 two colours
3 a countable noun – get a … of sth.
4 measure of area
5 adverb – describing how jaguars move
6 noun – something edible but unusual
7 noun – describing a feeling
8 noun – something researchers fix to an animal
9 noun – something or someone that kill jaguars
10 two animals

2b 1 half past five/five thirty/05.30; 2 (deep) yellow; black; 3 photograph;
4 170/kilometres/kilometres/km; 5 quietly;
6 spider; 7 (great) respect; 8 radio collars;
9 (cattle/sheep/livestock) farmers; 10 domestic cats; dogs

2c 1 No more than three words.
2 Yes. All the words needed are used by the speakers.

Use of English 1 p.47

1a See Coursebook page 209

2a **Possible answer:** animals can help us to predict when an earthquake is coming.

2b 1 Fish jump onto land; mice seem dazed and are easy to catch.
2 They evacuated a city and saved many lives, after the strange behaviour of some animals alerted the authorities to a major earthquake.
3 Some animals' senses are very sensitive, so perhaps they can detect seismic activity before an earthquake.

2c 1 have – present perfect with plural subject (people)
2 them/themselves – plural object or reflexive pronoun (fish/mice)
3 to – *begin* + to – infinitive
4 by – past passive + *by* + agent
5 more – compares with previous sentence
6 of – after *many*
7 had – past perfect
8 too – *too* + adjective + to do sth.
9 the – city (Haicheng) referred to earlier
10 in – *succeed* + in + *-ing*
11 Since – present perfect and a point in time, *then*
12 for – *prepare* + *for* sth.
13 It – subject
14 which/that – relative clause
15 be – infinitive after *would*

HELP Question 1 present perfect
Question 7 before
Question 9 the
Question 13 It

2d articles – 9
auxiliary verbs – 1, 7

verb + verb patterns – 3, 10
verb + preposition – 4, 12

Language development 2 p.48

LOOK main verb + infinitive with *to*: … *scientists begun to receive reports* …
main verb + infinitive without *to*: People **have seen fish jump** out …
preposition + -*ing* form: … leaders had *succeeded in saving* …
adjective + infinitive: … *too frightened to enter buildings*/… *may be able to detect* the seismic activity …
noun + infinitive: … **a pity to ignore** the signs …

1a 1 The moon passes exactly in front of the sun and blocks out its light.

1b 1 to settle; 2 sleeping; 3 fly; 4 noticing;
5 solving; 6 go; 7 not bringing; 8 feel;
9 to talk; 10 not to drive

2a 1 a He remembered that he needed to wear them, and then put them on.
b He remembered that he had worn them at some point before then.
2 a She experimented with using one to see if it would work or was a good idea.
b She physically attempted to do it. Maybe she didn't succeed.
3 a He stopped doing something (e.g. driving) in order to look at the lights.
b He was looking at the lights and then he didn't look at them.

2b 1 to buy; 2 to get; 3 drinking; 4 to post;
5 calling; 6 adding

3b 1 of seeing; 2 to going; 3 in getting; 4 on putting up; 5 for not helping; 6 to go; 7 to her going; 8 on walking; 9 her from doing;
10 of getting lost

Use of English 2 p.49

2a 1 The groundhog 'Punxsutawney Phil' comes out of his hole and people make weather predictions based on his behaviour.
2 The 1993 film *Groundhog Day* has made the event better-known in recent years.

2b 1 B – *come out of a sleep* (*get up* is intransitive)
2 C – *clear* collocates with *sky*
3 B – *severe* is the only adjective here that collocates with *weather*
4 C – *early* collocates with *spring* and contrasts with *six more weeks of winter*
5 A – *gather in* a place (*combine with, crowd into*)
6 B – *a large number of* + plural noun
7 D – *just around the corner* – idiom = soon
8 B – *hard* collocates with *winter* to mean *severe/cold*

9 C – *heavy* collocates with *snow*
10 A – *of the same name* is a fixed expression
11 D – *turn s.b. into s.th.* = to make somebody become something different
12 A – *turned up* = arrived
13 B – *although* followed by a clause
14 A – *hope for* + noun (*hope to* + infinitive)
15 C – *last for* + a period of time

2c words that go together – 2, 3, 4, 8, 9
the correct word from a set of similar meanings – 4, 5, 6, 10, 15
fixed expressions – 7, 10, 14
phrasal verbs – 1, 11, 12
linking words – 13

2d clear sky; severe weather; cloudy day; early spring; long, hard winter; heavy snow; good weather

Language development 3 p.50

2a **rain:**
drizzle (light rain)
hail (frozen rain)
shower (a short period of rain)
snow (soft flakes of frozen rain)
downpour (a lot of rain in a short time)
wind:
breeze (a light wind)
gust (a sudden, short, strong wind)
hurricane (a violent storm, especially in the Western Atlantic; we often associate hurricanes with strong wind)
gale (a very strong wind)
storm:
hurricane (a violent storm, especially in the Western Atlantic; we often associate hurricanes with strong wind)
thunder (a loud noise in the sky)
lightning (light in the sky caused by electricity)

2b **1** lightning; **2** gusts; **3** hail; **4** Hurricanes; **5** snow

3a **1** c, e, g; **2** b, c, e, g; **3** a, f; **4** b, c, e, g; **5** f; **6** a, b, e, f; **7** d; **8** f; **9** e; **10** e; **11** a, f

3b **1** high/strong; **2** heavy; **3** gentle/light; **4** loud; **5** heavy; **6** chilly; **7** torrential/tropical

4a **1** d; **2** c; **3** e; **4** a; **5** b

Teacher's Resource Book Module 3 Test: How much do you remember? p.177

1 **1** D; **2** C; **3** A; **4** C; **5** B

2 **1** away; **2** fancy; **3** where; **4** in; **5** to

3 **1** threatened; **2** similarities; **3** scientifically; **4** friendliest; **5** Tourism

4 **1** I *stopped smoking when I was/reached* 26.
2 Do *you remember paying/if/whether you paid* that bill?
3 Dan's office *is fairly close to/near (to)* his house.
4 There *were hardly any tourists in* the city five years ago.
5 The children had been *looking forward to going to* the zoo for ages.

Module 4 Challenges

Module 4 includes topics such as fundraising, adventurous people race and various aspects of sport.

Lead-in p.51

A challenge is something that tests skill, ability or strength. Get students to look at the photos and talk about what challenge the people in each picture are facing. They should then discuss the lead-in questions. For the second question, you may want to start students off by giving one or two examples of your own.

Module 4A Personal challenges

Reading pp.52–53

1 This is a quick introduction and students only need to identify what they can from the pictures, e.g. he's in the Arctic/Antarctic, he's swimming.

Background

Lewis Pugh started his love of the ocean after moving to South Africa as a boy. As well as the swims described here he pioneered more swims around famous landmarks than any other swimmer and can lay claim to having been the greatest cold water swimmer in history. When not swimming he works as a maritime lawyer in London and does motivational speaking. He says his swims are about competing against himself and his own limits, and campaigning against climate change.

2 Students could write the questions individually or in pairs. Write some of their questions on the board.

3 Before students skim the article they could refer to the strategies on page 24. They should first skim for general understanding (60–90 seconds) then scan to find answers to their questions. Explain that they may not find all the answers. Check which questions remain unanswered, and help students find those answers which you know to be in the text.

4a Elicit the best strategy for dealing with multiple-choice questions then get students to look at the strategy box. Use the technique to do question 1 together.

4b Students should compare their answers and how they arrived at them.

5a The article uses a number of phrasal verbs that students need to identify. Point out that they are not only used in informal writing.

5b Students discuss the questions in groups.

▶ **Student's Resource Book page 32**

Language development 1 pp.54–55

With books closed, write the three words *unlock*, *door*, *noise* on the board and ask students to try and combine them in a sentence.

1a Ask students to cover the second part before they read the opening sentence and compare it with their own.

1b Students uncover the next part to check their predictions.

1c Establish that the story takes place in the past. It is not important if students don't know the names of the past verb forms at this stage.

1d When students have completed the table, they should look at the Grammar reference on pages 188–189.

2 Get students to skim the text first and find out what the noise was. They could then do the exercise individually and compare answers at the end, or work in pairs to discuss their answers.

3 As students read the information in the box, check understanding of the vocabulary and concepts, such as *cross the finish line*, *fill up*. It would also be useful to compare and contrast some of them by rephrasing examples with other conjunctions and asking students if there is any change in meaning, e.g.:
By the time the police arrived, the robbers had run away.
When the police arrived, the robbers had run away.
When the police arrived, the robbers ran away.
The police arrived after the robbers had run away.

Get students to compare answers in pairs. As you go through the answers with them, ask concept questions to check understanding, such as:

1 How late was he? (Very!)
2 Did they catch the plane? (No)
3 Did she say it during the call or before? (During)
4 Did she finish the book? (No)
5 Did he see the end of the programme? (Yes)
6 Did they check during the race? (No, before)

7 Was the search before or after we arrived?
(Just after)

8 Why was I relieved? (I found the purse.)

4a Students should try to make true statements about themselves, as they are more likely to be remembered. But they could make up sentences if they can't think of any true ones.

5 Point out that there may be more than one answer and try to elicit all possible answers when checking with the class.

6 This could be set as a writing task for homework. Encourage students to use a range of tenses.

Photocopiable activity

Photocopiable activity 4B (p. 142) would work well here. It is a group work activity in which students devise a scenario and write a story from picture clues.

▶ **Student's Resource Book page 33**

Writing pp.56–57

1 With books closed, brainstorm the different types of stories before the Lead-in.

2 There are no 'right' answers here.

Question 1: The opening words given allow for the students to write any kind of story.

Question 2: Obviously, all these things will make for a good story, and students' opinions may differ as to which are more important.

Question 3: Again, this will be up to the students.

Point out how the exam rubric clearly establishes the writing task. Who is it for? The readers of a student magazine. What is it? A short story that must follow on from the opening words. The purpose? To engage/interest the readers.

3a Students should do this in pairs or small groups. Help with vocabulary where necessary.

3b Make sure students only write notes at this stage, and don't start writing the actual story yet. As they make notes, encourage them to start thinking of vocabulary and verb tenses they might use in each part. Emphasise that in such a composition they need to use a range of narrative tenses.

4a/b Point out that the level of the language is not higher in the 'better' paragraphs, just slightly fuller and more complex, making it more engaging and interesting for the reader.

4c The phrases in the box will add depth to students' narrative writing. Encourage them to use as many as possible.

4d Ask students if the gapped sentence makes sense as it is, before eliciting possible adverbs. Then compare the sentences with and without the adverbs and ask students to comment on the difference. The sentences with the adverb are more vivid.

5 Give students just 20 minutes to write the composition.

6 Allow ten minutes for this checking stage. Go through the four points here in detail.

• Have they stuck to the plan? Does the story have a strong beginning, middle and end?
• Have they used a range of different narrative tenses? And some linking words?
• Have they used a range of adjectives and adverbs to make the story more vivid?
• Is it within the acceptable range? Too long and the story could be marked without an ending.

Photocopiable activity

Photocopiable activity 4A (p. 141) could be used here. It is a discussion similar in format to Paper 5 Part 3, with students deciding on the best way to raise money for their club.

▶ **Student's Resource Book page 35**

Module 4A Key

Reading pp.52–53

4b 1 D

2 B *he'd spend as much time as he could going around the world to collect 'firsts'*

3 C *… frozen waters of the Artic near the North Pole … Four months later he went on to do the same in for the most southern part of the Antarctic.* NB Although he swam near polar bears there is nothing to say he is the only person to have done so.

4 A *… his unique ability to raise his core body temperature … in anticipation of the water*

5 A *these boundaries are just in our mind and need to be pushed away.*

6 D *he remains tight-lipped about them* (his next round of adventures)

7 A see paragraph 5

5 take to = to start to like something or someone
get on (with) = continue doing something
end up = to finish in a particular way
speed up = to become faster
put (yourself) through (something) = to make (yourself) do something difficult or unpleasant
give out = to hand something to each of a group of people

Language development 1 pp.54–55

1c was unlocking, heard, closed, ran out, tried, wasn't working, I'd been talking, had run down

1d A an action or event at a point in the past: *heard; closed; ran out; tried*

B an activity in progress at a point in the past: *was unlocking; wasn't working*

C a single action which happened before a point in the past: *had run down*

D an activity which happened before a point in the past: *I'd been talking*

2 1 ran (action at a point in the past)
2 was talking (activity in progress)
3 was arguing (activity in progress)
4 had been waiting (viewed as an activity before a point in the past)/had waited (viewed as an action before a point in the past)
5 came (action at a point in the past)
6 had been crying (activity before a point in the past – when I saw her she was no longer crying)/was crying (activity in progress)
7 told (action at a point in the past)
8 had happened (action before a point in the past)
9 was talking (activity in progress)
10 came (action at a point in the past)
11 was carrying (activity in progress)
12 was going (activity in progress)
13 was (event at a point in the past)
14 had been waiting (viewed as an activity before a point in the past/were waiting (viewed as an activity in progress)
15 explained (action at a point in the past)
16 went (action at a point in the past)
17 was laughing (viewed as an activity in progress – they were already laughing)/laughed (viewed as an action at a point in the past – they started laughing at that point)
18 started (action at a point in the past)
19 felt (action at a point in the past)
20 had reacted (action before a point in the past)

3 1 C; 2 B; 3 C; 4 D; 5 B; 6 A; 7 A; 8 D

5 1 As soon as I heard the news I phoned my sister./I phoned my sister as soon as …
2 After I'd been to see a friend, I went home./I went home after I'd been to see a friend.
3 By the time he arrived, I had waited for around an hour./I had waited for around an hour by the time he arrived.
4 When the boss resigned, the business collapsed./The business collapsed when the boss resigned.
5 I had been gardening for hours when she phoned me./When she phoned me, I had been gardening for hours.
6 While his owner was talking, the dog ran into the road./The dog ran into the road while his owner was talking.
7 By the time we got to the airport, the plane had left./The plane had left by the time we got to the airport.
8 Before I went to Russia I had never eaten caviar./I had never eaten caviar before I went to Russia.

Writing pp.56–57

4a A because it contains more interesting details and would have more impact. B sounds flat and the short sentences make it sound like a list.

4b B because it sounds more enthusiastic and really conveys what the experience meant to the writer. A sounds more flat and uninterested.

4d 1 absolutely; 2 Unfortunately; 3 at once; 4 exactly; 5 Luckily; 6 definitely

5 Sample answer:

That day, my life changed forever. Our local children's hospital needed to raise money or it would close, so I decided to take part in a six-day sponsored walk along 90km of the Great Wall of China. At the time I didn't realise what an incredible challenge it would be.

Before I went I thought that I would be walking on a flat surface but when I saw the Great Wall my heart sank. Part of the time we would be trekking up hundreds of 60cm high steps, some of the paths were 30cm wide with steep falls either side and there was nowhere else to go because we were surrounded by mountains and forests. I was terrified, and at the end of the first day my body ached all over. However, on the third day I started to love the experience. I was in one of the most amazing places on earth and the views were incredible.

Every year now I challenge myself to do something that I wouldn't normally do and this year I'm planning to cycle across Cuba!

(181 words)

LANGUAGE SPOT

1 beautiful, wonderful, warm
2 heavy, considerable
3 set off
4 exhausted, worn out
5 seldom, hardly ever, rarely
6 Eventually

Module 4B Sport

The 'challenges' theme continues with the topic of sport, including a listening on the challenge of taking up a new sport.

To set the ball rolling ...

With books closed, ask students in pairs to write a definition of *sport*. Compare definitions and ask, e.g., if all sports use a ball/are competitive/are physical. *Longman Exams Dictionary* defines sport as: *a physical activity in which people compete against each other.*

Speaking pp.58–59

1 Use the pictures to establish the name and key vocabulary of the sports.

2 Encourage students to use target vocabulary in their discussions.

3a After the students have matched the expressions, get them to look more closely at the vocabulary and the relationship between the nouns and their verbs (e.g. tackle, putt, lap are both nouns and verbs; a knock out/to knock someone out).

3b The exercise highlights words that are often confused so time should be spent examining the differences of use in each pair with students making up sentences for the alternative word. (e.g. win is intransitive – 'Brazil won', whereas beat is transitive and requires an object – 'Brazil beat France.')

In Paper 5 Part 3, the candidates speak together in a collaborative task based on a visual stimulus (usually several pictures). It is not important to come to an agreement; it is the interactive communication that matters.

4 Getting students to look at both sides at this stage will help to develop the discussion later.

5a After checking students' answers, point out that this task usually has two parts: first 'talk about' and secondly 'choose/select/decide', etc.

5c Give students enough time to read the expressions in the table before they listen again.

6 Refer students to the task strategy and remind them of the importance of turn-taking. If the class is not divisible by three, it would be better to have extra examiners with some pairs than a pair without an examiner, so everyone can have some feedback. Remind the 'examiners' that as well as giving the instructions (on CB page 209) and keeping time, they will need to be noting the two candidates' performances.

7 Try to encourage the students to be constructive rather than just polite.

Listening p.60

1 Establish a definition for extreme sports (a sport that is done in a way that has much more risk and so is more dangerous than 'normal' sports) before eliciting examples.

2a As this is the first time students encounter multiple matching in Paper 4, give them plenty of time to read the rubric and answer the questions. As you go through the task strategy, point out the highlighted points in the first two options (persuaded / advised more exercise).

3 If students find any of the words in italics difficult, e.g. *keen on*, *enrol*, remind them of strategies for guessing unknown words.

4 Encourage students to use some of the new language in the discussion.

▶ **Student's Resource Book page 37**

Language development 2 p.61

The concept of countable and uncountable nouns is not usually a problem for students, but it can be difficult for them to know which nouns are which.

1a It might be useful to show students how countable and uncountable nouns are marked in a dictionary ([C] and [U]) before they do this exercise, so they can check any that they are unsure of.

2 These are typical FCE level mistakes; remind students to check their own work for similar mistakes.

3 Get students to skim the text first and answer the question *Who was most seriously injured?* As a follow-up, you could put students in groups to discuss which sports are popular in their country, which are more popular with men and with women, and whether any dangerous sports are popular. Give an example first, such as: *In the UK a lot of people play football, but not so many play basketball and very few play baseball.*

▶ **Student's Resource Book page 38–39**

Use of English 1 p.62

1 Remind students that Paper 3 Part 4 tests students' knowledge of grammar and vocabulary by getting them to express the same idea in two different ways.

2 Remind students of the rubric and strategy for approaching Key word transformations tasks. Point out the Help clues that they can use if necessary. Pick up on any difficult vocabulary (e.g. *a lack of*).

3 This is designed to remind students of the range of structures that are tested in Key word transformations.

Use of English 2 p.63

1 Some of the more dangerous popular sports include rugby and horse-riding. Many extreme sports can be considered as new.

2a Remind students that it is good to get into the habit of using the title and a skim read to get a general sense of the text.

Background

The most famous 'traceurs' are the founder David Belle and Sebastien Foucan (who appeared in the opening scenes of the James Bond film *Casino Royale*). To many people *Parkour* and the English term *Freerunning* are the same things. However, purists insist that whereas Parkour focuses on the most efficient uninterrupted forward motion over and around objects, Freerunning has more emphasis on aesthetics, fun and creativity using more flips and summersaults. There are now groups all over the world and Parkour games for games consoles.

2c Give students examples of useful collocations that they should record. (e.g. *man-made objects*, *serious injury*, *featured on television*)

Language development 3 p.64

You could introduce the language point with books closed by putting the pairs of words *actual/current*, *old/ancient* and *great/big* on the board. Ask students if the words in each pair are the same or different and if they are different, what that difference is. They then look at the examples and explanations.

1 Check students understand that the words and definitions are in pairs. They may need to use a dictionary to check some of the words.

2 The exercise puts the vocabulary from the previous exercise into context. If time, get students to create other sentences using the words.

Background

Larry 'Buster' Crabbe (1907–1983) started his film career as a stunt double, performing dangerous swimming scenes. He went on to play various action heroes, including Tarzan, Flash Gordon and Buck Rogers. He also starred in a number of Westerns, playing Billy the Kid on many occasions. He is often compared to Johnny Weissmuller, another Olympic swimmer who famously played Tarzan. A popular performer, he made over 100 films.

```
..........................................
:         Photocopiable activity          :
: Photocopiable activity 4C (pp. 143–144) would :
: work well here. It is a board game with students :
: answering questions using adjectives that are often :
: confused.                                :
..........................................
```

3 Adjectives ending in *–ing* and *–ed* are often confused. Further help could be given with a drawing on the board of a person reading. Label the person 'interested' and the book 'interesting'. Elicit the difference before looking at the examples from the text.

4a When students have completed the exercise, ask them if they agree with sentences 1, 3, 5, 7.

5 Point out that although *take place* looks and acts like a phrasal verb, it is just an idiom as phrasal verbs are usually verb + adverb/preposition, as in *to take off*.

7 Whichever way students record phrasal verbs, encourage them to record examples or notes on usage as well as the meaning of the phrasal verbs. It would be a good opportunity to revise the grammar of phrasal verbs:
1 Parkour *took off* in the 1990s. [Intransitive]
2 He *took off* his tracksuit/*took* his tracksuit *off* before the race. [Transitive separable]
3 He *took up* acting / he *took* it *up* but not He *took up it.* [Pronoun in separable phrasal verbs goes between verb and particle]
4 Damon Hill *took after* his father. [Transitive inseparable]

▶ **Module 4 Test: How much do you remember? TRB page 178**

▶ **Exam Practice 2: Papers 2 and 4 TRB pages 179–180**

Module 4B Key

Speaking pp.58–59
1   sport   place   equipment
swimming: pool; costume, trunks, goggles
cycling: track; bike, helmet
golf: course; balls, clubs, bag, trolley, pencil
running/athletics: track; shoes/spikes
tennis: court; racket/racquet, balls, net
football: pitch; ball, boots, shin pads
baseball: field; ball, bat, gloves
boxing: ring; gloves, gum shield, headgear
skating: rink; skates
skiing: slopes; skis, boots, poles, sunglasses

3a do the backstroke – swimming
win by two laps – athletics
serve an ace – tennis
win with a knock-out – boxing
take three putts – golf
make a tackle – rugby

3b 1 results; 2 matches; 3 beat; 4 drew; 5 scored; 6 won; 7 game; 8 team; 9 half-time; 10 referee; 11 penalty; 12 shot.

5a First, talk to each other about the advantages and disadvantages of doing each of these sports. Then decide which one would be best for someone who doesn't have much spare time.

5b Running, because it's easier and quicker than the others.

5c **Starting a discussion:**
Let's begin with …
Interrupting/Showing you want a turn:
Yes, and as well as that, ...
Sorry to interrupt, but …
Involving the other person:
What would you say?
What do you think?
Bringing the discussion to an end:
Anyway, we have to decide …
So let's decide which …

Listening p.60
1a skydiving, big wave surfing, ice climbing, mountaineering, storm chasing, hang gliding, paragliding, bungee jumping, etc.

1c 1 five speakers; they will talk about their reasons for taking up a sport.

2a/b 1 C (*get people to give donations*)
2 D (*the expressions of amazement on my kids' faces*)
3 A (*I had to be talked into doing it by friends*)
4 F (*determined to show Tony that he was wrong*)
5 E (*the only way I can really unwind*)

3 1 from the word go; 2 into; 3 sign up; 4 fancy; 5 give it a go

Language development 2 p.61

1a 1 spectator (C) fan (C) excitement (U)
(*excitement* different because (U))
2 advice (U) fact (C) information (U) (*fact*
different because (C))
3 skiing (U) athletics (U) football (Both)
(*football* different because both)
4 money (U) salary (C) coin (C) (*money*
different because (U))
5 racket (C) equipment (U) glove (C)
(*equipment* different because (U))
6 temperature (C) weather (U) sunshine (U)
(*temperature* different because (C))
7 exercise (Both) tracksuit (C) trainer (C)
(*exercise* different because both)

2 1 Our trainer gives us good ~~advices~~.
2 I've heard the results. The news ~~are~~ *is*
very bad.
3 People ~~likes~~ Tiger Woods.
4 Some footballers have long ~~hairs~~.
5 It was ~~a~~ terrible weather so the match was
cancelled.
6 Beckham has very expensive ~~furnitures~~ in his
house.
7 My shorts ~~was~~ *were* very dirty after the match.
8 I had to do some hard ~~works~~ to beat the
champion.
9 The national team stayed in ~~a~~ luxury
accommodation.
10 I need ~~informations~~ about tickets.

3 1 Many – *sports* [C]
2 a number of – *hours* [C]
3 much – *time* [U]
4 several – *friends* [C]
5 any – *didn't see* (negative) + *any*
6 lots – followed by verb *to eat*
7 much – followed by adjective *better* + *luck* [U]
8 a lot of – positive
9 few – *hours* [C]
10 a few – significant number
11 a few – *sounds* [C]

Use of English 1 p.62

Lead–in 1 determiners; 2 time conjunctions;
3 present perfect

2a 1 wasn't much interest; 2 quite a nice; 3 used to
play; 4 was a lack of; 5 great deal of work;
6 people like; 7 doesn't belong to me; 8 to be
fewer

Use of English 2 p.63

2a 1 Moving around objects in towns in the fastest
most direct way possible.
2 People have started adding moves for show.
2b 1 B; 2 C; 3 D; 4 D; 5 C; 6 B; 7 A; 8 C; 9 B;
10 A; 11 C; 12 D

Language development 3 p.64

1 1 b; 2 a; 3 c; 4 d; 5 f; 6 e; 7 h; 8 g

3 *-ed* adjectives describe a reaction to something.
-ing adjectives describe the person/thing that
causes the reaction.

4a 1 boring; 2 disappointed; 3 tiring; 4 annoyed;
5 terrifying; 6 depressed; 7 interested;
8 amusing

5 In the UK, the sport really *took off* after it was
featured on television …

6 1 took up; 2 took off; 3 took over; 4 took
after; 5 took to

Teacher's Resource Book
Module 4 Test: How much do you remember? p.178

1   1 C; 2 B; 3 A; 4 B; 5 D

2   1 by; 2 in; 3 had; 4 much; 5 to

3   1 untreatable; 2 sensible; 3 boring;
4 informative; 5 invaluable

4   1 The course was cancelled because *of a/the lack
of* people.
2 Nick *had been working since/had been at work
since* 6.00 a.m. that day.
3 Ann *was watching TV at* 9.00 p.m.
4 He *had left by the time* I arrived at his house.
5 She got married *as soon as she (had)* left
university.

Teacher's Resource Book
Exam practice 2 pp.179–180

Paper 2 Writing
1
Style:
Formal letter.
Content:
1 Say that you want a course.
2 Ask about the level of the classes and whether you
need your own instrument.
3 Find out about the timing and length of lessons,
and how to pay.
4 Ask about the price of practice rooms.

Paper 4 Listening
Part 3 1 D; 2 E; 3 A; 4 F; 5 B

Module 5 Discovery

Module 5 includes texts on human science, talking about the future, museums, inventions, discoveries, computers, robots and explorers.

Lead-in p.65

Start off by eliciting what scientific advances the photos show (genetics/gene therapy/gene manipulation; vaccination/immunology, etc.), before students discuss the questions in pairs or small groups.

Module 5A Human science

> **Photocopiable activity**
>
> Photocopiable activity 5A (p. 145) is designed to be an introduction to the unit and will help to pre-teach some of the vocabulary. It is a quiz about the human body.

Reading pp.66–67

1a It would be a good idea to check the pronunciation of the fields of science before students do the exercise. All are stressed on the second syllable except archae'ology.

1b The title of the article makes it quite clear what students are going to read. The sub-headings A–D are harder and might throw up a number of possibilities, which would generate interest in the text.

2 Set a suitable time limit, e.g. two minutes, so that the skimming doesn't become detailed reading.

3a The reading task in Module 1 gave students an introduction to multiple matching tasks. This activity is much more like the exam in terms of text length, options and number of questions. Refer students to the task strategy. Point out that only when they have skimmed the article will they be able to predict which part to look in for each question. It would be useful to set the students a suitable time limit (e.g. 15 minutes) to do the task, so that they become aware of the time available in the exam, although you could give them a few minutes more at this stage if necessary.

4 Additional questions could include:

Have you ever studied any of these subjects? Would you like to?

▶ **Student's Resource Book page 42**

Language development 1 pp.68–69

1a Look at the first sentence and elicit that *I don't feel well* is in the present and *I'm going to be sick* is the consequence in the future. See if students can think of any other possible situations, e.g. someone on a roller coaster or someone who has seen/eaten something disgusting.

1b Encourage students to look at the sentences in their contexts and not just identify future forms that they may already be familiar with.

1c When students have completed the table, give examples of how a decision might become an arrangement. E.g., you read a restaurant review and think it sounds good, so you decide: 'I think I'll take X there'. Later, when someone asks what your plans are for the weekend: 'I'm going to take X to …'. Then after you ring and book the table you could say 'I'm taking X to …'

Time clauses
Refer students to sentence 4 in Exercise 1a: *If you tell her, she'll tell everyone.* Remind students that although the first part uses the present tense, the sentence refers to the future. The time clauses here work in the same way.

2 Get students to compare and explain their answers.

3b When students have matched the forms to their uses it might be useful to compare the structures with those practised in earlier units:

The present continuous refers to an action in progress now. The past continuous refers to an action in progress at a point in the past. Hence the future continuous refers to an action in progress at a point in the future.

The present perfect refers to an action before now. The past perfect refers to an action before a point in the past. Hence the future perfect refers to an action before a point in the future.

4 Students should complete the predictions with positive verb forms. They have a chance to agree or disagree in 5b.

5a When students have completed the exercise, show how the 'certainty' language is often stressed, e.g. *We **may** have … but I **doubt** it.*

5b As students give their opinions on the predictions for 2100, encourage some discussion leading in to the questions in 5c.

6 Give students time to think about the statements and make a few notes before they discuss them in groups.

7 The text contains mistakes typically produced by FCE students. Point out that all the errors are with verb tenses. Checking through a piece of writing systematically, in this case just checking the tenses, is an important strategy in the exam.

:::
Photocopiable activity

Photocopiable activity 5B (p. 146) would work well here. It is designed to get students using all the tenses covered here while talking about their futures.
:::

Writing pp.70–71

1 Check that students know the difference between a museum and a gallery. A museum contains objects that are scientifically or culturally important, possibly including art objects. A gallery specifically contains works of art. Suggested answers for question 2 would be the points in handwriting in the exam task below on page 70.

2 This is the second time that students practise a transactional letter/email, Paper 2 Part 1 (see Module 3). Elicit some of the key points:

• The transactional letter/email might be formal or informal.

• The overall aim is to achieve a positive effect on the reader. This is done through organisation, layout, and cohesion as well as accuracy of language.

• Candidates must include the key points from the input if they are to achieve good marks.

3a Remind students that a logical strategy is to think first about what to include, then in what order, and finally how to divide it into paragraphs.

4a The expressions can be used in any formal letter of this type. Look at the grammar of each expression by eliciting the next word in each case, e.g. *grateful if, possible to, arriving at – time / on – date / by – means of transport.*

LANGUAGE SPOT: polite questions

Polite or indirect questions are a feature of more formal writing. Compare the efficiency and directness of the form *Where's the café?* with the more polite forms.

▶ **Student's Resource Book page 45**

Module 5A Key

Reading p.66–67

1a **1** astronomy; **2** archaeology; **3** psychology; **4** linguistics; **5** genetics; **6** forensic science

3a **1** D (*amusing anecdotes …*)
2 A (*even if you don't have a scientific background*)
3 B (*an ideal birthday present*)
4 D (*examples of language taken from various sources*)
5 A (*… people believed that family traits were carried in the blood. Today we know that they were wrong*)
6 D (*his personal belief*)
7 C (*… gets better and better with age …*)
8 B (*… scientific studies … thirty minutes after birth …*)
9 C (*… main objective is to encourage the greater public understanding of scientific ideas.*)
10 A (*… up-to-date with the latest influential theories.*)
11 C (*… television audiences in mind (a tie-in series has just begun on BBC1) …*)
12 B (*… packed with eye-catching photos … *)

3b **1** In A his earlier books were on other subjects and therefore this book doesn't follow on.

Language development 1 pp.68–69

1a **Suggested answers:**
2 Two colleagues or friends are trying to arrange to meet tomorrow, but the speaker can't because he/she has a driving test.
3 One friend to another. The speaker has bought something, such as a radio, and has found that it doesn't work.
4 One friend to another. They have a secret, and the speaker doesn't trust the third person not to reveal the secret if she is told about it.
5 Friends, or husband and wife. They are going to the cinema or theatre, and the speaker is waiting for the other person who is still getting ready.
6 Two strangers at a supermarket or station. One is offering to carry the other's heavy bag.

1b **1** 'm going to be; **2** 'm taking; **3** 'm going to take it back; **4** 'll tell; **5** starts; **6** 'll carry

1c **A** Planned, a definite arrangement (e.g. in a diary): *I'm taking my driving test.*
B Planned, fixed event (e.g. a public timetable): *It starts at eight.*
C Planned, decided earlier (intention): *I'm going to take it back.*
Prediction: we notice something in the present that will make something happen: *I'm going to be sick.*
D Unplanned, decided now (e.g. an offer, a promise): *I'll carry it.*
Prediction: we expect something to happen (it is our opinion or we have experience of it): *She'll tell everyone.*
Time clauses
3 Are you going to have a drink before the show ~~will~~ star**ts**?

2 1 will be; **2** 'm going to visit; **3** get; **4** starts; **5** 'll cook; **6** 'm having lunch; **7** 's going to have; **8** go

3a Future continuous: *will be having*
Future perfect: *will have established*

3b Complete by a point in the future: *will have established*
Still in progress at a point in the future: *will be having*

4 1 will have found
2 will be travelling
3 will have discovered
4 will be living
5 will have taken over; will be providing
6 will be making; will be going

5a Very certain: 1
Fairly certain: 3, 5
Not very certain: 2, 4

7 After I ~~will~~ finish the last year of university I am definitely going to have a long holiday. I expect I ~~am going~~ *will go* with my friend, Luis, to a place where we will ~~be doing~~ *do* lots of sport and relax~~ing~~ in the sun to recover from all our hard work.
But before that there is a lot of work. My exams ~~will~~ start on the 15 June and they ~~are lasting~~ *last* two weeks. The results will not ~~have been~~ *be* here before the end of August, so I ~~am having~~ *will have* a long time to wait. For the next month I will *be* study***ing*** for two hours every evening and I ~~am not~~ *won't be* going out during the week.

Writing p.70–71

2 1 The museum's groups organiser.
2 You are interested in organising a group visit to the museum.
3 Who you are, your intention and the four questions.
4 Formal (no direct questions, contractions, etc.).

3a 1 introducing myself
2 saying why I'm writing
3 asking about booking
4 asking about numbers
5 asking about eating
6 conclusion

3b **Paragraph 1**: introducing myself; saying why I am writing
Paragraph 2: asking about booking; asking about numbers
Paragraph 3: asking about eating
Paragraph 4: conclusion

4b **Opening:** I am the secretary of my college Science Club. I saw your advertisement for the exhibition 'The Next 100 Years' and I was wondering if I could ask you some questions about it.
Closing: I look forward to hearing from you.

4c Yours faithfully

5   Sample answer:

Dear Sir or Madam

I am the secretary of my college Science Club. I saw your advertisement for the exhibition 'The Next 100 Years' and I am interested in organising a group visit. I was wondering if I could ask you some questions about it.

I would be grateful if you could let me know whether we need to book, and if so, how far in advance do we need to say that we will be coming? Our group is quite large, so I would also like to know if there is a maximum size for a group.

Since we will probably be coming for the whole day, I would like to know if there is anywhere to buy snacks, or if there is a picnic area where we can eat our own food.

I look forward to hearing from you and visiting your museum.

Yours faithfully

Toni Hidalgo (Ms)

(147 words)

LANGUAGE SPOT: polite questions

1 Do you think you could tell me where we can/could leave our bags?
2 Could you tell me whether there is a toilet on this floor?
3 I would be very grateful if you could tell me how much we will have to pay.
4 I wonder if you could tell me when the museum closes?
5 Could you please tell me where the cloakroom is?
6 I would be grateful if you could tell me what time the museum closes.
7 Could you tell me whether we can pay by credit card in the museum shop?
8 I wonder if you could tell me who is in charge?

Module 5B Invention

To set the ball rolling ...

With books closed, ask students the difference between a discovery – something that existed but was not known before, such as penicillin – and an invention – something new that did not exist before, such as the telephone. Ask them to name the most important invention in their lives.

Speaking pp.72–73

1a Students might need some help with the difference between an appliance (a larger piece of electrical equipment used in the home), a gadget (a smaller cleverly designed useful machine or tool) and a device (a machine or simple tool designed to do a special job)

1b/c The focus is on whether the words are stressed on the first or second syllable.

2 Matching the words and phrases to the items in Exercise 1 will help students to remember them.

3 You could also ask what students think computers will be used for in the future.

4 It could be the most important for them personally or for people in general.

5a Here, students see how Part 3 leads into Part 4, when the examiner joins in and it becomes a three-way discussion. Once you have checked students' answers, tell students that it is important in Paper 5 that they know what to do in each part. If they have any doubts, they should check with the examiner. They will not be penalised for this at all. The candidate in the recording summarises the examiner's instructions, which is a good way to check you have understood.

6a These are typical Part 4 questions, extending the topic from Part 3. Students could consider why some are easier to answer than others, e.g. is the language difficult, or would they find it hard to come up with ideas and opinions?

7 If the class is not equally divisible by three, have one or two groups of four, so that each group has at least an examiner and two candidates.

8 Students should discuss their own and the others' performance.

▶ **Student's Resource Book page 47**

Listening p.74

1 Ask students what the cartoon shows (MP3 player, portable games console, hands-free phone, portable DVD, mobile phone) before they discuss the questions.

2a Point out the task strategy. Emphasise the importance of studying the notes as carefully as possible before listening. The more they are able to predict the type of words in each gap. the easier it will be to hear the missing information.

2b Students should discuss whether their answers fit logically and grammatically and should compare the spelling of more difficult words.

3 Remind students what collocation means before they do the exercise. Following the exercise highlight the form of the verbs used (e.g. gerund after the prepositions *from* and *to* in questions 2 and 3). Get them to highlight each collocation and discuss how they should record them in their vocabulary books (e.g. *to take something/one for granted*).

4 The discussion could be done in pairs or small groups which then feedback to the whole class.

Use of English 1 p.75

1 To remind students of the concept of Key word transformations, you could start, with books closed, by putting the first sentence (*I can't speak Mandarin Chinese*) on the board and eliciting an alternative way of saying it.

2 Get students to read the task strategy and remind them of essential points (use 2–5 words, don't change the word given, etc.).

3 The follow-up highlights a number of areas of grammar that could be tested and that students might want to do more practice in if they had problems.

Language development 2 p.76

LOOK As you go through the box with students, you could use simple drawings on the board to illustrate differences, e.g. *He hurt himself* – a man sitting on a chair with an arrow pointing down to indicate *fell off*. *He hurt his sister* – a man and a woman with an arrow pointing from the man towards the woman to indicate *bumped into*. *They talked to each other* – two people facing each other, with speech bubbles. *They talked to themselves* – two people with speech bubbles, but further apart, not facing each other, and with a line between to indicate that they are in separate rooms and talking to themselves!

1a Students could discuss their answers in pairs, referring to the box, before class feedback.

1b Point out that students will need to use object pronouns here, as well as language from the box.

2 After question 1, as a contrast you could ask *What things do you prefer to do by yourself?*

3a Look at the box with students before they start the exercise, pointing out that the word order in *B Question word + clause* is as in a statement, not as in a question. The first example is from the Use of English text on page 76.

3b If students can't think of anything true to write, they should try to invent interesting sentences.

▶ **Student's Resource Book page 48**

Use of English 2 p.77

1 Set the questions as a quick competition in groups. Alternatively, set them for research homework the lesson before. Check that students know *penicillin* – today, a medicine known as an antibiotic because it kills bacteria and so helps cure infections.

Background
Sir Isaac Newton discovered gravity in 1687, stating that gravity is the force of attraction between two objects, and that greater objects, such as the earth, pull smaller objects, such as people, towards them. He is said to have discovered this watching an apple fall from a tree to the ground.
Fleming – see texts on p.77
In the first century BC, Archimedes discovered that an object placed in water 'loses' an amount of weight equal to the weight of the water that it has displaced. He is said to have discovered this when he got into a full bath and it overflowed.

2a Remind students not to focus on the gaps. They should only need a minute or so to do this exercise. Students might need help with the words *mould* and *germs*.

2b Get students to do the exercise alone and then compare answers.

3 Repeat the process with the second text but this time you could introduce a suitable time limit (10 minutes). When they have finished, ask them which of the three discoveries in Exercise 1 is the most important.

Language development 3 p.78

1a Nouns can be formed from verbs or adjectives. This exercise focuses on nouns formed from verbs. When students have checked the meanings, ask them to think about the stress in each word.

2a Before students do the exercise, ask if they know of any famous explorers.

3a This exercise focuses on nouns formed from adjectives.

4 Encourage students to guess the formation of nouns not given in the tables by comparing them to similar words, e.g. *describe/description* is similar to *decide/decision*.

5a Point out that the phrasal verb is before question 9 in the second Use of English text.

5b Students could use their dictionaries to check.

6 Remind students to put the verbs in the correct form. You could provide personalised practice by giving students sentence stems to complete, e.g.:

1 The best idea I've come up with is/was … .

2 I once tried … but it didn't come off.

3 Once when I was looking for … I came across … .

4 Recently I came up with … .

Photocopiable activity

Photocopiable activity 5C (p. 147) would work well here. It is a game of dominoes in which students form nouns by joining suffixes to verbs.

▶ **Module 5 Test: How much do you remember? TRB page 181**

Module 5B Key

Speaking pp.72–73

1b Oo (first syllable) HOUSEhold; USEful; GADget; GROUNDbreaking; LAbour-saving; REcent; LUXury

oO (second syllable) apPLIance; inVENtion; deVICE; deVELopment; unNECessary household APPLIANCE; useful GADGET; ground-breaking INVENTION; LABOUR-SAVING device; recent DEVELOPMENTS; unnecessary LUXURY

1c LAPtop; microwave OVen; FOOD blender; electric TOOTHbrush; HAIRdryer; WASHing machine; MObile; DISHwasher

2a keyboard and mouse – laptop; long-distance call – mobile; e-commerce – laptop; blogging – laptop; virtual reality – laptop; headphones – iPod; get cut off – mobile; social networking – mobile/laptop; get the wrong number – mobile; re-charge – iPod/toothbrush/mobile/laptop

2b 1 d; 2 e; 3 g; 4 f; 5 c; 6 a; 7 b

5a 1 First, *I want you to decide on the advantages and disadvantages of each one.* Then *decide which is the most important and which is the least important.*
2 *So we have to discuss <u>all</u> the photos and then say which is the most and the least useful?*

5b Yes, and neither of them speak for too long at a time.

5c 1 *So we both think that the mobile phone is the most important and the microwave and toothbrush are the least important.*
2 It doesn't matter if the candidates don't agree (in fact disagreement can lead to more interesting discussion) but they should be trying to reach a consensus.
3 *Thank you very much.*

6b 1 and 3

Listening p.74

2a 1 food shopping; 2 clothes; 3 crossword; 4 text messages; 5 computer games; 6 chatrooms; 7 spellcheck; 8 (loud) music; 9 hands-free phone; 10 book holidays

3 1 taking; 2 paying; 3 booking; 4 save; 5 do; 6 try

Use of English 1 p.75

1 1 how to speak (structures with question words)
2 cleaned the house by herself (reflexives / word order)
3 put off handing (phrasal verbs + *-ing*)

2 1 on my own; 2 no point in Tania going; 3 love each other; 4 wasn't until she left; 5 painted

this room myself; **6** don't know who to;
7 gave me most pleasure; **8** couldn't/didn't carry
on working

3 phrasal verbs 8; reflexives 1, 3, 5; structures
with question words 6; time clauses 4; noun
phrases 2

Language development 2 p.76

1a **1** I used to work ~~myself~~ abroad. – in this case
work is intransitive
2 ✓ – reflexive
3 Can you help ~~myself~~ me? – subject and object
are different people, so reflexive not possible
4 Robots can't talk to ~~each~~ one another. – *each
other* or *one another*
5 ✓
6 Have you enjoyed ~~you~~ **yourself**? – subject and
object are the same person, so the reflexive is
needed
7 ✓ subject and object are the same person, so
the reflexive is needed
8 Relax ~~yourself~~ ! – *relax* not a reflexive verb
9 I built the model **on** my own.
10 Clare and Rob met ~~themselves~~ **each other** last
year – you can't meet yourself, you have to meet
somebody else

1b **1** its own – a bird
2 themselves – a fly and an eagle
3 myself – same subject and object
4 myself – for me
5 them – robots
6 us – relates to *we* in the previous sentence, and
our in this sentence
7 themselves – without the help of others
8 me – relates to the object pronoun
9 themselves – without the help of others

3a **1** know how to use a
2 you've done what I
3 where to find the/where we can find the
4 know who to/know who I should

Use of English 2 p.77

1 **a** Alexander Fleming; **b** Archimedes;
c Isaac Newton

2a penicillin, mould, bacteria, important
2b **1** unexpected – negative adjective
2 possibility – noun
3 puzzling – adjective
4 accidentally   adverb
5 excited – adjective
6 discovery – noun
7 effective – adjective
8 infection(s) – singular or plural noun possible
here
9 scientists – plural noun
10 successfully – adverb

HELP Question 1 – no
Question 2 – *-ity*
Question 4 – adverb

2c **1** Nouns – 2, 6, 8, 9
2 Adverbs – 4, 10
3 unexpected

3 Lucy's Baby is important because of the
completeness of the remains and therefore the
opportunities it gives for research.

1 careful – adjective – before noun *work*
2 length – noun – *the* noun *of*
3 researchers – noun – subject of phrase and
plural (no *a*)
4 unusual – neg adjective – after verb *be*
5 development – noun – *the* noun *of*
6 discoveries – noun
7 highly – adverb – before adjective *significant*
8 mixture – noun – *a* noun *of*
9 criticism – noun – object of verb *come in for*
10 insufficient – adjective – before noun *evidence*

HELP Question 3 – plural
Question 5 – *-ment*
Question 10 – negative

Language development 3 p.78

1b *-ment*: development
-ure: mixture
(t/s)ion: infection
-y: discovery
-er: researcher

2a **1** b; **2** a; **3** c; **4** a
2b **1** assistance; organisation
2 existence; achievement
3 sailors; equipment
4 explorer; failure

3a *-ness*: kindness; darkness; sadness; illness
-th: length; strength
-ity: ability; generosity; equality; reality;
popularity
3b possibility

4 **1** popularity
2 descriptions
3 ability, importance
4 observations, loneliness

5a c – received
5b **1** b; **2** d; **3** f; **4** a; **5** g; **6** e; **7** c

6 **1** come up; **2** came round; **3** come out;
4 came across; **5** come about; **6** come off;
7 come up with

**Teacher's Resource Book
Module 5 Test: How much do
you remember? p.181**

1   1 B; 2 D; 3 C; 4 A; 5 B

2   **1** himself; **2** own; **3** what; **4** if; **5** where

3   **1** pride; **2** unscientific; **3** specialist; **4** equality;
    5 longest

4   **1** Jackie didn't want to do all *the cooking on
her* own.
    2 We did all the *work ourselves to keep* costs
down.
    3 Could you *let me know whether/if* you will
have a room available next month?
    4 I *will have moved house by* the end of the year.
    5 It won't be *long before someone discovers* a
cure for cancer.

Module 6 Enjoying yourself

Module 6 includes topics such as favourite books/films, art and pop music.

Lead-in p.79

With books closed, get students to compare *art* (painting, drawing, sculpture, etc.) and *the arts* (more general). Brainstorm different types of arts, e.g. music (classical, pop, folk, opera), theatre, musicals, dance (ballet, contemporary), cinema, art (modern, different periods/media), literature. Build up a spidergram on the board, then ask students what 'arts' are shown in the pictures on page 79. Get them to discuss the questions. In the first question, *important to you* could be interpreted either as something that you personally spend time on, or that you consider to be important in general.

Module 6A Music

> ### Photocopiable activity
> Photocopiable activity 6A (p. 148) could be used either as a lead-in to the unit or as follow-up to the reading. It is a questionnaire designed to find out how ambitious you are.

Reading pp.80–81

> ### Background
>
> The title of the text comes from Nirvana's classic song 'Smells like Teen Spirit' from their 1991 album Nevermind. Nirvana were one of the first grunge bands, and the singer Kurt Cobain was referred to as 'the spokesman of a generation'. His girlfriend used a deodorant called Teen Spirit and the song came about from a reference to that!

1a Students compare the list with their brainstorm. Other genres of music could be: pop, soul, punk, indie, house, etc.

1b Students need not mention every association; the exercise is just to process the new vocabulary.

2 It would help if students read the rubric in 3a before skimming. Remind students that skimming should take 60–90 seconds for a text of this length.

3b Comparing answers and giving reasons will help students to focus on the links between the text and

the questions and help you see how well the students have understood it.

4 The exercise would work well with students working together, sharing and justifying answers.

▶ **Student's Resource Book page 52**

Language development 1 pp.82–83

1a Ask students if they know any music by the bands pictured.

1b Students could also discuss the origins of each genre as a lead-in to the text in Exercise 2.

2a Students might be interested in the example of Jamaican English in the Bob Marley song where 'No cry' means 'don't cry'.

2b It would be useful to find an example of each type of clause with the whole class and to highlight their structures before students look for the rest.

3 Review what each relative pronoun refers to, such as *who* for people, *whose* for possession, before students do the exercise. Follow up with a discussion about the singers/bands mentioned.

4,5 These exercises require students to think a little more about both which type of clause to create and how to do it. Point out that way of combining information and adding detail is exactly the same when they are planning and writing compositions in Paper 2.

6 It can be difficult for students to grasp that a participle clause can be used to refer to different times. Point out that the time reference is usually clear from the second part of the clause, e.g.: *The woman singing that song is* … . *The car going round the corner was* … .

7 This exercise will require some planning, which could be done for homework.

> ### Photocopiable activity
> Photocopiable activity 6B (p. 149) would work well here. It is a game in which students use relative clauses to define vocabulary associated with the arts.

▶ **Student's Resource Book page 53**

Writing pp.84–85

1 Some discussion here on if, where and when students see bands live would be useful to generate interest in the topic and some relevant vocabulary.

4 Point out how a strong opening engages the reader and a strong ending has a positive effect on the reader.

4c One way to look at the functions table would be to go through it first as a whole class using a band that most students are familiar with, e.g. *U2* as an example.

5 Review the outline and content of the article before students choose a concert of their own to write about.

6 Remind students to check their writing thoroughly.

▶ **Student's Resource Book page 55, exercises 1–3**

Module 6A key

Reading pp.80–81

2 Jamie Cullum – jazz; Michael Bublé – swing; Katie Melua – jazz, blues and folk; Marcella Puppini – 1940s

3a 1 B *worldwide sales*
2 D *includes supermodel Kate Moss amongst her fans*
3 A *doing every kind of gig possible …*
4 D *wearing clothes and make-up in keeping with the songs they sing*
5 C *OK, it happens not to be hip and cool*
6 A *… isn't pure jazz. Pop, rock, dance, hip-hop – everything gets thrown together*
7 D *met at the Royal College of Music where they studied … piano, sax, violin …*
8 & 9 A *what I do is totally true to me;*
C *completely from my heart*
10 D *one third of one of the most interesting acts*
11 C *write a song about the wrongs of the world …*
12 D *would like the band to cross over to the pop charts*
13 A *provokes extremes of love and loathing*
14 & 15 B *kids weren't given any choice so this was my rebellion;* C *I feel there should be another option*

Language development 1 pp.82–83

1a 1 rock – Rolling Stones
2 disco – Abba
3 Punk – Sex Pistols
4 Reggae – Bob Marley
5 Soul – Gladys Knight
6 hip hop – Black-eyed Peas

2a 1 Reggae – in the 70s and 80s; punk – 70s and 80s; hip hop – 1990s and 2000s
2 New York

2b A 1 *The bands which dominated Western popular music*
2 *the one singer who had the most influence*
3 *that first emerged in the 1970s*
B *the records* (that/which) *they made*
C 1 *Elton John, whose piano based pop songs were hugely popular*
2 *Bob Marley, who had a hit with …*
3 *hip hop, which was an Afro-American …*

3 1 The singer Nelly Furtado, **whose** parents emigrated to Canada … Furtado, **who** can speak English, Spanish, Portuguese and Hindi, incorporates cross-cultural sounds …
2 The girl band Girls Aloud were discovered on *Popstars*, **which** was an international reality television programme in **which** boy bands …
3 The rock band Snow Patrol was formed in 1994 in Scotland, **where** two of its members …

so it's not surprising that the band (**which/that**) they admire most is …

4 Shakira, **which** means 'grateful' in Arabic, was born in Columbia, **where** she grew up … In almost every country in **which** it was sold.

5 Justin Timberlake was one of several singers (**who/that**) were discovered on the TV show *The Mickey Mouse Club*, **which** first began in the 1950s. Other singers from the show **that/who** went on to become …

6 Oasis, **whose** major influence was the Beatles, was one of several bands in the 1990s to **which/whom** the media gave the label *Britpop* … Zak Starkey, **whose** father, Ringo Star, was drummer for the Beatles.

4 1 I saw a poster which/that was advertising a gig for a new rock band.
2 I phoned the box office, which was in London.
3 There was an answering machine which/that was telling me to call another number.
4 I spoke to a man on the other number who/that told me there were only expensive seats left.
5 I booked two tickets which/that cost 90 Euros each.
6 I paid by credit card, which is a very convenient way to pay.
7 On the day, we went to the theatre, which overlooks the River Thames in London.
8 We couldn't get into the theatre, which had been closed because of technical problems.
9 I went home with my friend, who was very disappointed.
10 Next day I phoned the theatre, who were very helpful and offered replacement tickets.

5 1 Salsa, *which means sauce in Spanish*, is a mixture of Spanish Caribbean rhythms and styles.
2 The salsa band Sonora Carrusales, *whose songs are played in salsa dance clubs everywhere*, was formed in Columbia in 1995.
3 The singer Gloria Estefan, *who was born in Cuba but now lives in the USA*, uses salsa rhythms in many of her songs.
4 The Puerto Rican American Victor Manuelle, *whose career began when he was discovered by salsa superstar Gilberto Santa*, is often thought of as a romantic salsa singer.
5 The album Travesia, *on which Manuelle improvises vocals and lyrics within a salsa tune*, was a huge success with fans.

6 1 I saw a poster *advertising* a new dance show.
3 There was an answering machine *telling* me to call another number.
5 I booked two tickets *costing* 90 euros each.
7 On the day, we went to the theatre, *overlooking* the River Thames in London.

Writing pp.84–85

2 1 to inform, to entertain
2 Two: which concert you went to, whether you would recommend it
3 facts in the first part, opinion in the second part
4 neutral

3 **Paragraph 1:** title, attention-grabbing introduction
Paragraph 2: brief description of the person/band and specific concert
Paragraph 3: what you liked
Paragraph 4: what you didn't like
Paragraph 5: recommendation; conclusion

4a B
4b A

5 Sample answer:

> ### The gig of the year
> I have to tell you about the Scissor Sisters. They give one of the best live shows of the year. They are an American band, whose style reminds you of the disco and glam-rock music of the 1970s. In 2006 they had a huge hit with 'I don't feel like dancin'.
> On stage the two members of the band you notice most are the singers Jake and Ana. What an incredible voice Jake has – a combination of opera and rock! Both he and Ana in their sexy black jackets were fantastic. As the show started Jake went straight into 'Laura' which really got the show going. The lighting and the set were amazing and you really had that disco feel.
> The only thing I wasn't really happy about was the sound. It was a bit woolly and I couldn't hear the lyrics, but once the band was into its second song nobody really cared.
> Judging from this live show they will be the best live band for years to come.

(175 words including title)

LANGUAGE SPOT: avoiding repetition

a their – good musicals
they – the audience
this – *Fame*
their – the actors
the show – *Fame*
they – the actors
ones – actors
You – the reader
their – the young actors'
they – the young actors
these – the acting and singing

It – the plot
this – the thin plot
we – the audience
them – the characters

b 1 They; **2** It; there; **3** it/to; **4** then; **5** ones

Module 6B Art and entertainment

Module 6 continues the arts theme with speaking and listening activities about different aspects of art, and Use of English texts about the Edinburgh Festival, the perfect face for comedy and actress Penelope Cruz.

To set the ball rolling ...

Ask students the difference between a *gallery* (a place showing works of art including where the art is for sale) and a *museum* (a public place showing important cultural, historical or scientific objects). In the USA, *museum* is also used for some public galleries, e.g. Metropolitan Museum of Art.

Speaking pp.86–87

1a Use the opening questions to gauge students' interest in art.

1b Do question 1 together and get students to compare and contrast the forms (*interested in* / *keen on*) and then get them to do the same for the others.

1c Remind students of alternative ways to mark stress on a word (e.g. en'joyable / enjoyable / enJOYable, etc.).

2a If time you could expand the exercise with examples of each and other people who work in the arts.

3 Follow up by eliciting other types of TV programme (e.g. sports, drama, magazine, detective series, lifestyle – e.g. cooking, decorating). Ask students which type of programme they most like watching.

4 Get students to move the odd one out to the correct group. (e.g. *viewers* in question 1 should be with TV vocabulary in question 4).

5 Reassure students that in the exam they won't be required to have any expert knowledge, but in Paper 5 they could be asked a question like this about their personal preferences.

6a Elicit the format of Paper 5 Part 2, i.e. individual long turn followed by a short response from the other candidate.

6c Tell students that the expressions may not be in the same order as they are in on the page. Play Alice's response up to *I really don't know what it is.*

6d Play the rest of Alice's response.

7 It is important that students remember this short phase of Paper 5, are prepared for the examiner's question, and listen to it carefully.

8a Both students practise an individual long turn and give a short response. Point out the task strategy.

8b/c Allow enough time for students to give each other constructive feedback.

Listening p.88

1 This is the first time students look at Paper 4 Part 1 in detail. The format is the same here as in the exam, except that there are six questions here, not eight as in the exam.

2a Students first read the task strategy.

If there is time, students could have a discussion based on the arts. They should each choose one of the following topics and prepare to speak about it by making notes. Then put them into groups for the discussion.

- Your favourite film of all time.
- The type of music you most enjoy listening to.
- A play you have enjoyed (at the theatre, on the radio, on TV).
- A novel you have read more than once.
- The painting you would most like to have hanging on your bedroom wall.

▶ **Student's Resource Book page 57**

Use of English 1 p.89

1 Establish the difference between the two types of performance before students discuss the questions in pairs/groups.

2 Start by reminding students what type of words are required in this type of exercise (structural words – prepositions, auxiliaries, pronouns, determiners, etc.). Tell the students that for some questions there is more than one possible answer. They use answers to the three questions as gist understanding.

2b Compare the example where the missing word *in* is determined by the preceding word *interested*, and question 1 where it is the word after the gap that is the biggest clue to the word required (*there*).

2c Tell students that dependent prepositions are frequently tested in the exam, but there would not be so many in one text as there are here, where the aim is to test/practise dependent prepositions.

3 Remind students of the importance of learning dependent prepositions, and find out if they have a particular method. Compare their methods with those given.

Language development 2 p.90

LOOK Go through the box with students. If they have just done Exercise 2c on page 89, they will have no difficulty remembering the adjective + preposition combinations in the text. Point out that these phrases are followed by nouns, pronouns or -*ing* forms.

1a Tell students to record the whole phrase, not just the two words. E.g., question 1 *the result of*, question 2 *feel sorry for*.

2 Students could discuss these personalised questions in pairs or small groups.

3 Highlight for students the difference between the state, expressed by *be used to*, and the action, expressed by *get used to*. You could use a simpler example to help, such as *Paul is married* (state). *Paul got married in 2001* (action).

4 Students should do this in pairs or small groups before class feedback. You could ask each group to discuss just one of the bullet points, then report back to the class.

Photocopiable activity

Photocopiable activity 6C (pp. 150–151) would work well here. Students play a version of the game 'Battleships' to practise adjective/noun + preposition combinations.

▶ **Student's Resource Book page 58**

Use of English 2 p.91

1 Possible further questions: *Do you and your friends find the same things funny? Is humour different in different countries?*

2a Elicit the advice as a means of reminding students of the strategy for this type of exercise. Before students do the task, ask if they have heard of Ricky Gervais.

Background

Ricky Gervais was born in Reading in 1961. In his early working life he was in a band, he managed a band and was a radio DJ. He started out in TV comedy with bit parts on various shows before his sudden success in *The Office*, which he co-wrote, directed and starred in. In recent years he has done stand up, written a best selling book and had small parts in Hollywood films. He was won numerous awards including Emmies, Golden Globes and BAFTAs.

---

3 Get students to look at the photo and identify the film (*Volver*) and the actress (Penelope Cruz). Give a suitable time limit to skim the text and then do the task.

Background

Penelope Cruz was born in Madrid in 1974. She initially trained as a dancer before switching to acting. She has appeared in both Spanish and Hollywood films including *Vanilla Sky*. She was nominated for an Oscar for her part in *Volver*.

4 Possible further questions: *Which actor/actress would you choose to play your life?*

Language development 3 p.92

1a Elicit examples of other awards ceremonies that students know of.

1b Point out that unlike a true Use of English text, here most of the words needed are nouns for people or occupations. Follow up by highlighting the endings used to form nouns (e.g. *-ment, -ician, -ist, -or*). Then get students to compare how the pronunciation changes is some cases (e.g. m*u*sic – mu*si*cian; presen*ta*tion – pre*sen*ter)

2b Encourage students to draw a table big enough to add other negative adjectives in future. Elicit patterns such as *im-* and *il-* adjectives, but emphasise that they are only patterns, not rules.

3b Encourage students to answer honestly! If they know each other well they could be asked to agree or disagree with what people say about themselves.

4a *Say, tell, speak, talk* are often confused. Tell students that, rather than worry about meaning, they should focus on collocation, as in the box.

4b Remind students to use the correct form of each verb.

5 Get students in pairs to tell each other what they have written. Encourage them to ask questions about each other's sentences and explain them further if necessary.

▶ **Module 6 Test: How much do you remember? TRB page 182**

▶ **Exam practice 3: Papers 2 and 4 TRB pages 183–184**

Module 6B Key

Speaking pp.86–87

1a The photo on the right shows modern art while the one on the left shows classical art. The paintings are oil paintings.

1b 1 keen on; 2 can't see the point of; 3 fascinating; 4 appeal to; 5 nothing special; 6 absolutely adore; 7 is really into

1c First syllable – boring; shocking; moving; powerful; awful; brilliant; dreadful. Second syllable – enjoyable; amusing; depressing; exciting.

2a 1 painter; 2 sculptor; b dancer; 4 TV producer; 5 reviewer

2b choreographer – arranges how dancers should move during a performance
comedian – tells jokes or make people laugh

3a soap opera – *Eastenders*; reality TV – *Celebrity Big Brother*; quiz show – *The Weakest Link*; documentary – *Panorama*; chat show – Jonathan Ross; situation comedy – *The Royle Family*; current affairs – *Question Time*

4 1 viewers – others relate to theatre; 2 final act – others relate to TV; 3 cartoon – others relate to theatre; 4 box office – others relate to TV; 5 trailer – others are film genres

6a … type of art you think is more interesting.

6b 1 Yes, she spends equal time on both parts.
2 Yes, she keeps talking for a minute, then the examiner stops her when she pauses.

6c The statue could be … .
I get the impression that … .

6d Well, I like *some modern art* but if *you ask me to choose*, I think I would *choose classical art* because *I understand it*.

7 Robert, are you interested in art?
I'm not really very keen on art. I prefer listening to music.

Listening p.88

1 1 a function – What, doing, when speaks
2 an arts topic – What, speaker, talking about
3 a place – Where, taking place
4 a feeling – How, boy, feel
5 a person – Who, talking about
6 an aspect of an exhibition – What, criticise

2a/b 1 B (*So do they give the exact dates?*)
2 C (*… until the very last page … it would probably transfer very well to stage or screen.*)
3 B (*move to the back … if I'd known how much noise there'd be … might as well put my bed on the motorway.*)
4 A (*… better to stick to the plot of the original … it just didn't hold my attention.*)

5 B (*… see him in the canteen … someone new like that.*)
6 A (*It's just the way it's been put together that I don't like.*)

Use of English 1 p.89
2a 1 True; 2 False; 3 True
2b 1 there (+ *is*)
2 which (many of which)
3 at/by/about (all possible after *surprised*)
4 for (+ *everyone*)
5 any (+ *kind*)
6 are (plural verb form after the *majority*)
7 who (non-defining clause)
8 to (bring sthg to s/one)
9 of (members of sthg)
10 in (appeared in)
11 at/by/with (all possible after *disappointed*)
12 to (get used to sthg)
2c adjectives + prepositions – 3, 11, 12
verbs + prepositions – (3), 8, 10, (11)
relative pronouns – 2, 7

Language development 2 p.90
LOOK See 2c above
1 1 of – *the result of* something
2 for – *feel sorry for someone*
3 for – *have respect for*
4 between – *no comparison between* two people/things
5 by – *be puzzled by* sthg
6 in – *get involved in* + noun
7 in – *have difficulty (in)* + -ing
8 to – *be similar to*
9 with – *be annoyed with someone*
10 of – *have no hope of* + -ing
1b 1 in – *be interested in something*
2 by/about/at – *be excited by/about something*
3 for – *be usual for someone to do something*
4 for – *have a talent for sthg*
5 from – *encouragement from*
6 for – *be famous for something*
7 of – *be capable of* + -ing
8 at – *be good at* + -ing
9 for – *be responsible for something*
10 in – *success in sthg*
11 about – *be right about something*
12 with – *a relationship with someone*

3 1 used to live
2 get used to living
3 wasn't used to filming
4 get used to hearing
5 didn't use to print
6 aren't used to watching
7 get used to people staring
8 'm not used to going

Use of English 2 p.91
2 1 extremely – adverb before adjective
2 embarrassing – adjective before noun
3 fantastically – adverb before adjective
4 employees – plural noun after noun + *of*
5 unexpected – negative adjective before noun
6 particularly – adverb before adjective
7 underestimate – verb after *should not*
8 importance – noun – *the* + noun + *of*
9 ability – noun after possessive adjective
10 similarity – noun after adjective

HELP Question 2 – -*ing*
Question 5 – both
Question 7 – prefix

3 1 recognition – noun after *for*
2 seriously – adverb after verb
3 believable – adjective before noun
4 unable – adjective after *be*
5 disappointing – adjective before noun
6 impressive – adjective before noun
7 performance – noun after possessive and adjective
8 incredible – adjective before noun
9 strength – noun before *of* + noun
10 organis(z)ations – noun after adjective

Language development 3 p.92
1a 1 Awards ceremonies; 2 To reward outstanding performances and for publicity
1b 1 entertainment; 2 musician; 3 singers; 4 director; 5 actors; 6 dramatist; 7 presenter; 8 comedians; 9 surprising; 10 performers

2a unexpected, unable, incredible
2b *un-*: untidy, unfair, unfit, unsatisfactory
in-: inexperienced, insecure
dis-: disloyal, dishonest
im-: impolite, impatient, impractical
il-: illiterate, illogical

3a 1 untidy; 2 impractical; 3 dissatisfied; 4 unsatisfactory; 5 illiterate; 6 inexperienced; 7 unfit

4a 1 The teacher ~~spoke~~ told us a horror story.
2 I can't stand it when artists ~~say~~ talk politics.
3 We all ~~talked~~ said a prayer together.
4 Excuse me, could you ~~say~~ tell me the time?
5 My brother ~~talks~~ speaks three languages.
6 ~~Tell~~ Say hello to Rosie for me.
7 Mike ~~said~~ told the police what he had seen.
8 Don't trust him. He's always ~~speaking~~ telling lies.
4b 1 speak; 2 say; 3 say; 4 talks; 5 told; 6 telling; 7 say; 8 speak; 9 tell

Teacher's Resource Book Module 6 Test: How much do you remember? p.182

1 1 C; 2 B; 3 A; 4 D; 5 B

2 1 in; 2 used; 3 of; 4 between; 5 whose

3 1 impatient; 2 descriptive; 3 friendship;
4 dissatisfaction; 5 illogical

4 1 Sarah is slowly *getting used to living on* her own.
2 I stayed in a *flat that/which belonged to* my uncle.
3 Luke *must have made* the mess in this room.
4 I *get the impression/feeling(that) Pat* can't drive.
5 Brenda is *too inexperienced to* work in this office.

Teacher's Resource Book Exam practice 3 pp.183–184

Paper 2 Writing
1 Style:
Neutral.
Content:
Say where Danny is and why a lot is expected of him (e.g. what is the sport/what type of event is it/why do people think he will do well?).
Explain what happens next and say how Danny feels about it.
You could make some reference to 'everybody's expectations' at the end of the story: does Danny do as well as everybody expected? Why (not)?

2 Style:
Semi-formal or neutral.
Content:
1 Describe the resort e.g. location, facilities.
2 Say what young people can do there.
3 Say what young people will especially like about it.

3 Style:
Formal letter.
Content:
Say why you are interested in the job.
Explain in detail the things you could do with the children, mentioning any experience you have of this sort of work and saying why you are a good candidate for the job.

Paper 4 Listening
Part 2
1 Presentation Skills
2 actress/actor
3 conference
4 (rich) uncle
5 department store
6 £2500/two thousand, five hundred pounds
7 computers/computer equipment
8 theatre/theater
9 read (from/their) notes
10 angry

Module 7 Keeping up with the fashion

Module 7 includes topics such as food and restaurants, describing clothes and changing hairstyles.

Lead-in p.93

Get students to look at the photos in pairs and briefly describe each one. Then go onto the lead-in questions. If students need help with ideas for the first question, give them prompts such as where we eat, what we eat, who we eat with, who prepares the food; what people wear, level of formality of clothes, what clothes are/aren't acceptable in different situations, where we get our clothes. In the second question, the quote means that no fashion is really new; it's just the return of an old fashion. (Geoffrey Chaucer, 1342–1400, was the greatest English writer before Shakespeare's time. His most famous work, *The Canterbury Tales*, was written in the last ten years of his life.)

Module 7A Fast food

To set the ball rolling ...

You could introduce the topic with books closed. Ask students what the expression 'Fast Food' means to them and then ask them if that is the meaning in the text here.

Reading pp.94–95

1   You could also ask if students have heard of any competitive eating events

3a Use the task strategy to remind students of good exam technique for multiple-choice questions. You could follow the procedure to do question 1 together first if you think it necessary.

3b Set a suitable time limit (10–12 minutes) for students to answer the questions.

4   You could also ask about celebrity chefs in their countries and about the use of celebrities to promote (unhealthy) food.

∙∙∙∙∙∙∙∙∙∙∙∙∙∙∙∙∙∙∙∙∙∙∙∙∙∙∙∙∙∙∙∙∙∙∙∙∙∙∙
Photocopiable activity

Photocopiable activity 7A (p. 152) could be used after the reading activity. It is a quiz on the subject of the global food and drinks market.
∙∙∙∙∙∙∙∙∙∙∙∙∙∙∙∙∙∙∙∙∙∙∙∙∙∙∙∙∙∙∙∙∙∙∙∙∙∙∙

▶ Student's Resource Book page 62

Language development 1 pp.96–97

1a With books closed, ask students how often they eat in restaurants, what type they most enjoy going to and on what occasions. Or ask them to talk briefly about the last time they went to a restaurant (who with, why, where, who paid, etc.)

Tell students not to worry about the exact meanings of the sentences in the exercise at this stage. As they do it, they could identify who the pronouns refer to and/or how waiters traditionally refer to customers – *sir* or *madam*.

1b First check students' understanding of the terminology in the table. Giving permission – you can do something; Prohibiting – you cannot do something; Obligation – no choice because of a duty to do something. When students have completed the table, elicit the form (i.e. all are followed by verbs in the infinitive). It may be necessary to highlight the fact that while *must* and *have to* both express obligation, the negative forms are quite different.

2a Do question 1 together as an example.

2b Students could go on to describe school rules or rules in a job that they do (or once did).

3a See how many different ways students can express the answer to question 2.

3b Consolidate *needn't have* with concept questions: *Did he wear a suit? Yes. Was it necessary? No.* You could add further examples, such as *I needn't have taken any money to the restaurant. Did I take it? Yes. Was it necessary? No. Why? Maybe someone else paid the bill. Did I know that before I went? No.*

4a Encourage students to think about what the two options express.

4b If students find it hard to think of food and eating rules, ask them to think of any rules they had in other areas, such as clothes, going out, use of the bathroom, tidying up.

5   The mistakes are all to do with form. All these forms express advice and recommendations.

6   Students skim the letter to get the gist. Ask *Who is writing to who?* and *Why?*

7   Give students time to think and write before comparing sentences in groups. Alternatively, this could be a homework writing activity.

▶ **Student's Resource Book page 64**

Writing pp.98–99

1 First get students to look at the photo of the cruise boat, asking them what type of boat it is, where you would find one and what people do on them. Then they discuss the questions in the book.

2 Remind students that the transactional letter/email in Paper 2 Part 1 is compulsory. It is important to understand the task fully and then to select all the information to be included.

4c When students have matched the expressions to the functions, elicit which function is needed in each of the four points to be covered in the email. E.g.: Directions – referring to questions; No time – apologising.

4d Elicit ways to finish each of the phrases, e.g. *I'm afraid there won't be enough time for a walk as the trip takes two hours.*.

4e First think about what to include in the final concluding paragraph: *We are all looking forward to meeting you next month.* Then establish how students should open the email. It is a reply, so we know the name of the person we are writing to, but it should be formal, e.g. *Dear Ms/Miss/Mrs* + name. From this, elicit a suitable closing, i.e. *Yours sincerely*.

5 The email can now be written in class or for homework. Suggest a time limit of 15 minutes.

6 Remind students to use the checklist in the Writing reference on page 196.

> **LANGUAGE SPOT:** giving directions
> **a** Prepositions of place and direction, although often considered quite basic, still cause problems for students at FCE level.

▶ **Student's Resource Book page 65**

Module 7A Key

Reading pp.94–95
3a **1** B *Unlikely as it might seem, this tiny woman …*
2 A *she found a channel for the competitiveness that had always …*
3 C *For pre-event training … trains by expanding his stomach …*
4 C *put away here means eat (40 crab cakes)*
5 B *there have been instances in Japan of people choking while speed eating*
6 D *The majority of people I spoke to regarded it as a sign of the decay of society*
7 A *her dream of buying a franchise for her own fast food outlet*
8 D *straightfaced – to say something funny without laughing*

Language development 1 pp.96–97
1a **1** customer – we = customer
2 customer – them = staff
3 waiter – you = customers
4 waiter or customer
5 waiter
6 customer
7 waiter
8 customer
9 waiter
10 customer

1b **Giving permission:**
1 You're allowed to smoke in this area.
2 You can choose any table on this side, madam.
Prohibiting:
1 We're not allowed to smoke, are we?
2 I'm afraid you can't sit there – it's reserved.
3 Children over 12 mustn't use the play area.
4 You're not supposed to use your mobile phone here.
Expressing obligation:
The speaker feels it's necessary:
1 I must try one of those desserts.
The rules or situation make it necessary:
2 I'm sorry, but you have to wear a tie to eat here.
3 I think we're supposed to leave a tip.
Expressing lack of necessity:
You don't have to give them a tip.

2a **1** must book
2 can't wear
3 's/is allowed to come
4 're/are supposed to wait
5 don't have to have
6 mustn't bring
7 aren't allowed to drink
8 can pay

3a **1** No.

2 He/She wasn't allowed to smoke/Smoking wasn't allowed/They couldn't smoke/They weren't allowed to smoke. But <u>not</u> They mustn't smoke as *must* is not used in the past.

3b **It was permitted:**
They were allowed to use the play area.
It was prohibited:
1 The children couldn't play in the restaurant.
2 I wasn't allowed to smoke.
It was necessary:
We had to pay by credit card.
It wasn't necessary:
We didn't have to book a table.
It was done but it wasn't necessary:
He needn't have dressed so smartly.

4a **1** didn't have to pay – not necessary and not done
2 were allowed to – permission not obligation
3 had to – obligation not permission
4 could – permission not obligation
5 couldn't keep – prohibited
6 had to – obligation not permission
7 have to cook – obligation
8 needn't have worried – 'not necessary but done' – not prohibition
9 didn't have to – not necessary and not done

5 **1** You ought *to* complain about that soup – it's cold.
2 You shouldn't ~~having~~ *have* a dessert if you're full up.
3 If you don't like pasta, you'd better ~~to~~ have a pizza.
4 You must ~~have~~ try that new restaurant in Castle Street.

6 **1** You have to; **2** you mustn't; **3** can; **4** You don't have to; **5** can; **6** You must; **7** You'd better

Writing pp.98–99

2 **1** Who are you writing to? The leader of a group of students coming to your school.
2 What is the purpose of the letter? To reply and to give information requested.
3 How many pieces of information should you include? four: directions, there is no time for a walk, they can get the 14:45 coach to London, and you will check about the vegetarian option.
4 What style are you going to use? – Quite formal but friendly. The group leader is important and you probably have not met her before.

3a/b The letter could have five paragraphs:
1 Response to the leader's letter
2 Directions
3 Time – no time for a walk; coach stops at pier so can catch the 14.45
4 Will check vegetarian option
5 Conclusion

4a Thank you very much for your letter. Here are the answers to your questions/queries.

4b First go straight ahead.
When you get to … .
Go round … .
Take the … turning on the …
Follow the road until … .
Keep going until …

4c **Referring to questions:**
You asked about … .
You wanted to know whether … .
Talking about possibilities:
We should manage to … .
We might be able to … .
Apologising:
I'm afraid there won't be … .
Unfortunately, I don't think … .

5 **Sample answer:**

Dear Ms Sato

Thank you very much for your recent letter. Here are the answers to your questions.

You asked about directions to the pier from the town centre. I have enclosed a simple map showing the best route.

As for getting off for a walk at Tower Island, I am afraid that, there won't be enough time. However, there will be plenty of time to get the 14.45 coach to London as it stops to pick passengers up at the pier.

You wanted to know whether the meal includes a vegetarian option. At present, I don't know but I am going to check with the cruise boat company on Monday.

If you have any other questions please do not hesitate to contact me. We all look forward to meeting you next month and hope that you will enjoy the cruise.

Yours sincerely
Aldo Addler

(143 words)

LANGUAGE SPOT: giving directions

a **1** on – outside
2 at – location point in the city
3 to – next to
4 past – beyond

> **5** on – on the right/left
> **6** across – from one side to the other
> **7** at – the crossroads is an exact point
> **8** past – the front of it
>
> **b** 1 been to; tell me the way
> 2 Where do we go
> 3 You should; find the way OK.
> 4 There's no need; you might; a bit
> 5 get there; 'll see

Module 7B How do I look?

The fashion theme continues with clothes vocabulary, attitudes to clothes, deductions from appearance, hairstyles and Milan fashion week.

To set the ball rolling ...

With books closed, students brainstorm items of clothing in groups for two minutes. Or they could talk about their favourite item of clothing, saying why they like it, where they got it, when they wear it. Alternatively, send an interestingly dressed person out of the room and then ask the other students to describe, from memory, in detail what he/she is wearing.

Speaking pp.100–101

1 Students should be familiar with the nouns but some of the adjectives (e.g. *baggy, pleated*) are likely to be new. Encourage them to deduce the meanings from the pictures.

2a It might help students to think about where as well as when people wear the items. They might be interested in the example of onomatopoeia in the word *flip-flops*

2b The phrasal verbs might need explanation if the exercise is done with the whole class. Alternatively, students could use dictionaries if working alone. Students might be familiar with 'dress-down Fridays' where office workers wear less formal clothes at the start of the weekend. Elicit the opposites of *tuck in* (untuck) and *taken in* (let out).

3a Look for examples in the classroom.

4b Students might be tempted to use an adjective from each category so point out that it would be very unusual/unnatural to use more than three or four before each noun.

5a Elicit the format of Paper 5 Part 3. If the class is not divisible by three, you could have four people in some groups (3 candidates and an examiner). Remind 'examiners' that they will need to give some feedback on the others' performance at the end.

5b 'Candidates' should give their own assessment of

how well they did before getting feedback from the 'examiners'.

6 This exercise introduces the types of question the examiner might ask. It is obviously important in this part that students listen carefully to the question and respond accordingly.

7a Students should look at question 3 again before listening to the sample answer.

7b Encourage students not just to decide who gives a better answer, but also to think about why it is better.

7c Let students discuss this in pairs or small groups before checking with the whole class.

7d Here, Julia's answer is better as it picks up on what Paul has said and expands the same point.

8a The 'examiner' should give both students a chance to answer the questions, and try to ensure that both 'candidates' get an equal chance to speak.

Listening p.102

1 This would best be done in small groups. Emphasise that students should modify the statements as in the example.

2a Remind students of the strategy for multiple matching in listening.

2b After checking answers, ask students which of the five speakers they are most similar to.

3 A *fashion victim* is someone who wears what is fashionable even if it doesn't look good on them. Ask students if they know any fashion victims. The idea of wearing second-hand clothes will come as a shock to some students!

▶ **Student's Resource Book page 67**

Language development 2 p.103

1a Point out that being modals, all the verbs are followed by the infinitive without *to*.

1b As students look at the bags, encourage them to think about what is certain and what is possible.

2 From the examples in the table, highlight the past modal form (modal + *have* + past participle) and point out that *have* here is weak and contracted in spoken English. Practise the contracted forms such as *must've* /mʌstəv/ before students do the exercise.

3 First elicit what type of word they should use after *looks/feels/seems* (an adjective). Encourage students to use both present and past modals. When they have completed the sentences, get them to compare in groups.

▶ **Student's Resource Book page 68**

Use of English 1 p.104

1a The aim here is to revise the strategy for key word transformations. Make sure that everyone is clear about why the answers are wrong. Elicit the correct answers to the two example transformations for practice.

2b Students could answer the questions about the task before checking their answers.

```
..................................................
Photocopiable activity

Photocopiable activity 7C (p. 154) would work
well here. It is a mingling activity where students
use modals of deduction to correct or respond to
other students.
..................................................
```

Use of English 2 p.105

1 You could start by asking the class if they can think of anyone that has an unusual hairstyle. The students could discuss the questions in pairs/small groups followed by class feedback.

2a Point out that the idea is to find the answers in the text, not to give their own opinions to the questions here.

2b Remind students that each answer should be correct in meaning and also in collocations with associated words. Set a time limit of about 15 minutes to do the task.

3 The discussion could also include their attitudes to beards and moustaches and other facial hair.

Language development 3 p.106

1a Point out that all the phrases in this exercise are correct in themselves, but that they aren't all correct in this context. As you check the answers, make sure students understand both phrases in each pair, by eliciting synonyms for each one (see Module 7B Key).

Background

Fashion weeks are when a number of designers come together to show their latest collections to other people in the fashion industry. They usually take place twice a year in places like Paris, New York, London, Milan, Tokyo.

1b One way to learn the phrases is by preposition. Check students know the meaning of all the phrases listed and can provide the correct preposition where needed.

2 Explain that *make statements* and *spend money* are simply different collocations, but *hope/expect* are actually different in meaning. These may need further explanation and examples:
hope = you want something to happen in the future but you don't know if it will – *When I buy a lottery ticket, I hope to win.*
expect = you think something will happen because it should – *When I work for a company, I expect to get paid.*

3 Ultimately the choice between *make* and *do* is down to collocation but students might notice that expressions with *do* emphasise an activity or process whereas expressions with *make* emphasise the creation or production of something new.

4 As you check the exercise, discuss the difference between the verbs and check that students know all forms of the verbs.

5 The words needed are all in the preceding exercises.

Background

Royal Ascot is a four-day horse racing festival which takes place in June each year in Ascot, near Windsor. Members of the Royal Family always go and it is a big social event with a strict dress code. Women have to wear dresses and hats – the hats are famously lavish and outrageous – and men have to wear morning suits – a jacket with long 'tails' at the back and striped trousers.

6 Possible further questions to practise the language: How do you make a good impression in an interview?
What do you expect to do in the next class?
What do you enjoy doing from time to time?

▶ **Module 7 Test: How much do you remember? TRB page 185**

Module 7B Key

Speaking pp.100–101

1a Picture 1: a stripy jumper, baggy trousers, flat pumps
Picture 2: trainers and tracksuit
Picture 3:a grey pleated skirt, a white silk blouse, high heels
Picture 4: green cords, a fleece, a plain leather belt
Picture 5: wedges, a strappy dress
Picture 6: ankle boots

2a Examples: bow tie – with a dinner jacket; flip-flops – on the beach, at a pool; a parka – on a scooter; a fur coat – posing; slippers – at home; sandals – in summer; a suit – at work; pyjamas – in bed; a vest top – in summer

2b dress down – some offices on a Friday, for an informal party; dress up – a special occasion; get changed – change what you're wearing; try on something – put an item of clothing on to check it fits properly; tuck something (e.g. shirt) in – to look smarter; hang something up – on a peg or on a clothes hanger; get a bigger size – when your clothes are too small; get something taken in – have someone make something smaller if it was too big when bought or after losing weight.

3a Examples: roll-neck sweater; denim jacket/jeans; suede jacket/boots; bootleg jeans; cashmere scarf/sweater/coat; cotton dress/T-shirt; moleskin (thick cotton with soft surface) trousers; chunky sweater; three-quarter length skirt/boots

3b The first syllable is usually the one with most stress.

4a opinion – old-fashioned
size/shape – fitted, short-sleeved, tight
colour – navy
pattern – patterned, checked,
origin – Italian
material – linen, viscose, woollen

6 1 talk about likes or dislikes
2 describe an experience
3 give personal information
4 give an opinion
5 make a comparison
6 make a prediction

7b Paul's answer is better as he expands his ideas and gives examples.

7c Paul used 2. It gives him time to think about what to say, but avoids a long hesitation, which the examiner could interpret as searching for language, rather than ideas.
1 This answer is very negative and defeatist. There is no attempt at keeping communication going.

3 This answer is obviously too short and cuts off the conversation.

7d Julia was agreeing.
She uses *Apart from that ...*
To add her opinion, she could have used *And there's another thing ...* or *Not only that ... .* She could not have used *Actually ...* as that would introduce a difference of opinion rather than an additional point.

Listening p.102

2a 1 A (*at work I tend to wear ... quite stylish clothes ... clothes that are businesslike. I don't feel right in casual clothes*)
2 F (*... it's always sports stuff. ... What matters is feeling relaxed*)
3 E (*At the moment, either very long or very short skirts are cool ... I wouldn't dream of wearing anything frumpy ... I try to adapt my school uniform*)
4 C (*I'll wear anything ...*)
5 B (*I do tend to spend quite a lot on my clothes ... they don't drop to pieces.*)

Language development 2 p.103

1a 1 Marlie's in her pyjamas. She ~~can~~ **must** be going to bed.
2 It ~~mustn't~~ **can't** be his jacket – it's too small.
3 That ~~might~~ **must** be Kate. I recognise that voice.
4 I think that's John's case, so he ~~couldn't~~ **might** be here.
5 She's decided not to buy those shoes. She ~~could~~ **may not/might not** have enough money.
6 Mike ~~must~~ **can't** work in a clothes shop – he knows nothing about fashion!

1b Suggested answers:
1 A It must belong to a woman. She might be rich because she has a Visa card. She must like to look nice, because she's got a mirror, lipstick and perfume in her bag.
2 C It could belong to someone on holiday or a working tour because there is a map in the rucksack.
3 B It could belong to either a man or a woman because there's nothing like make-up or aftershave. I think he/she works in a high-powered job because of the computer and calculator.

2 1 can't have left
2 may/might/could have been stolen
3 must have cost
4 may/might/could have been; may/might/could have bought
5 can't have been
6 must have had

Use of English 1 p.104

1a 1 The candidate has changed the keyword *been* to *be* and therefore incorrectly changed the tense. Correct answer: *must have been pleased*
2 The candidate has written more than five words. Correct answer: *wish I could go to*

2a 1 it can't be Kate
2 must be tired
3 haven't eaten for
4 must have just been on
5 too unfit to
6 may have been in the
7 as long as you
8 can't have left

2b 1 1, 2, 4, 6, 8
2 Present: 1, 2. Past: 4, 6, 8
3 3 present perfect simple
5 *too/enough, un-* prefix
7 conditional with *as long as*

Use of English 2 p.105

2a 1 to make statements, to shock, to copy icons
2 1960s – Beatles style, 1970s – skinhead and dreadlocks. Recently – copying fashion icons

2b 1 C – make statements
2 A – wear hair a certain way
3 D – give the impression that
4 B – hope people will
5 B – expected + to – others would need *were* (were required/supposed)
6 D – show commitment to something
7 C – claim to do something
8 A – be in fashion
9 B – in recent years
10 A – borrow from
11 C – spend time/money money on
12 D – not uncommon for

2c 8 (in fashion), 9 (in recent years)

Language development 3 p.106

1a 1 at all times = always (at the moment = now, currently)
2 in danger of = at risk (in favour of = supporting)
3 (go) from bad to worse = deteriorate (from time to time = occasionally)
4 at first = initially (at least = as a minimum)
5 by mistake = accidentally (by the way = to change the subject …)
6 to my surprise = surprisingly (to my advantage = good for me)
7 by that time = by then (by heart = remember something perfectly)
8 in a bad mood = unhappy (in a loud voice = loudly)
9 From then on = subsequently (from time to time = occasionally)

10 without fail = always (without notice = not told in advance)

1b 1 (in/at) the beginning
2 (in) conclusion
3 (from) time to time
4 (on) purpose

1c 1 in the end; 2 in fashion; 3 out of date; 4 on purpose; 5 for a change; 6 in luck

2 1 make; 2 hope; 3 spend

3a 1 do; 2 make; 3 make; 4 do; 5 do; 6 make; 7 make; 8 do; 9 make; 10 do; 11 make; 12 make

3b 1 an Armani suit; 2 a lot of money on it; 3 in cash; 4 trying it on; 5 it would be comfortable; 6 feel so good; 7 to show my friends

4 1 rise – rise [I], raise [T]
2 became
3 earned – earn money from work, win money in a competition
4 damaged – damage something, injure someone
5 resign – resign = quit a job, retire = stop work for ever.
6 healed – heal wounds, cure an illness

5 1 retired; 2 spend; 3 expect; 4 made; 5 do; 6 bought; 7 make; 8 made

Teacher's Resource Book Module 7 Test: How much do you remember? p.185

1 1 C; 2 B; 3 A; 4 D; 5 A

2 1 for; 2 on; 3 if/whether; 4 all; 5 my

3 1 worldwide; 2 unfashionable/old-fashioned; 3 comparison; 4 healthily; 5 living

4 1 Gill *can't have left (yet)* because her computer is still on.
2 I agree with you *to a certain extent/to an extent*, but you have forgotten one thing.
3 Jack *wasn't allowed to buy* a drink at the club because he wasn't a member.
4 Karen *needn't have gone to* work as there was nothing to do.
5 You *are not/aren't supposed to eat* in here.

Module 8 The important things in life

Module 8 includes topics such as love, relationships, family, living alone or with others, hobbies and free time.

Lead-in p.107

Get students to look at the photos in pairs and briefly describe each one. Then they should go on to discuss the lead-in questions, followed by class feedback. The quote by Thoreau means that if you are alone you are independent and can make all your own decisions; you don't have to compromise with a companion.

Background

The American essayist, poet, and philosopher Henry David Thoreau (1817–1862) lived by the doctrines of Transcendentalism as recorded in his masterwork, *Walden* (1854). He was a vigorous advocate of civil liberties, as evidenced in the essay *Civil Disobedience* (1849). He once spent a night in jail for refusing to pay his taxes, which he had done in protest at the American Government's support of slavery and its war on Mexico.

Module 8A Relationships

To set the ball rolling ...

Put students into pairs or groups to brainstorm different types of relationship, e.g. father–son, teacher–student, husband–wife.

Photocopiable activity

Photocopiable activity 8A (p. 155) could be used as an introduction to the reading text, or after Exercise 5 on CB page 108. It practises prepositional phrases describing stages in a romantic relationship.

Reading pp.108–109

1a Point out that the places listed are examples, and students might think of other places where people meet. You could also ask if any students want to tell the class where and how they met their partner.

2 Get students to give you a signal when they have finished, such as putting their pen down, so you can get an idea how long it is taking them.

3 Give students a time limit of 10 minutes to match the sentences then a few minutes to compare answers.

4 1 The story of Wendy and Dennis is true.

2 A *soul mate* is someone you are naturally close to, as you share the same emotions and interests and you understand each other.

▶ **Student's Resource Book page 72**

Language development 1 pp.110–111

1a If they need prompting, get them to think about the problems of going out with someone from another country such as: language barriers, cultural differences, religion, family, and acceptance.

1b You could get students to guess the answers first, then read and check.

1c Point out that all the reported sentences on the right come from the text. The students need to work out what was actually said at the time. You may want to do the first one or two with the class to get them started.

1d The aim here is to show students that we don't always change tenses in reported speech. First point out that in 1–8, there is the usual change of tense for reported speech, then ask them to discuss the question. If they find it hard, prompt with clues, e.g. *Was she happy when she was asked? Is she happy now? What has changed? – Nothing*

1e This highlights the idea of reported speech being 'one tense back'.

1f Students need to be aware of changes to time expressions and some verbs, as well as tenses. Explain that these changes do depend on context though, e.g. *I'll do it this afternoon,* reported a few minutes later, would be *He said he would do it this afternoon.* Reported the next day, it would be *He said he would do it yesterday afternoon.*

2 Tell students that they will also need to change pronouns. You could do the first one or two with them.

3a This exercise provides freer, more personalised practice. Give students a little preparation time, then get them to work in pairs. They should try to ask each other one or two questions too.

3b This would work well in groups of four. Students should report what their partner said, e.g. *She told me her favourite place is the beach,* and also any questions they asked, e.g. *I asked her when she had first gone there.*

4a Demonstrate the effect of just reporting the exact words: *I said ... and he said ... so I said ... then he said ... .* Explain that the exact words are not usually important, so we can use reporting verbs to summarise and add variety. Check meaning and pronunciation of the verbs after they have completed the sentences.

1b You may want to do this with the class, so that they can clearly see how each of the verbs fits into the table.

4c Get students to do this in pairs, using a dictionary when necessary. When students have completed the table, elicit the negative construction for each verb, e.g. verb +(object) + *not* + *to*; verb + *not* + -*ing*.

4d The aim here is to show that the structure verb (+ object) + *that* + clause is common, but not possible for all verbs.

5 Transformations from direct to reported speech are common in Paper 3 Part 4. Encourage students to look at the table in 4b for help, and remind them to think about pronoun changes.

6 Give the class a little time to prepare the sentences before they compare them in groups. You could get them started by giving some examples about yourself.

7 Point out that here the verbs are being used to report general statements about the present and so the present simple is used. After you have checked the sentences, students could discuss them, saying whether they agree with each one and giving their personal opinion.

• •
Photocopiable activity
Photocopiable activity 8B (pp. 156–157) would work well here. It uses quotes to practise reported speech and reporting verbs.
• •

▶ **Student's Resource Book pages 73–74, exercises 1–4**

Writing pp.112–113

1 Get students to do this in pairs or small groups, followed by class discussion.

2 As you go through students' answers, advise students that they should only choose the discursive composition in the exam if they are sure they have something to say about both sides of the argument.

3a Elicit why the composition should have two points for both sides – it ensures the writing is balanced, and gives students the opportunity to link their ideas coherently within the word limit.

3b This is a standard format for a discursive composition of this type. Tell students that each point should be backed up with a reason and an example.

4a/b For pairs A, C and D, style is the important issue. For pair B, it is more a question of which is a more 'open' and interesting introduction to the composition.

4c This could be done in pairs or with the whole class.

5 Give students 30 minutes to write the composition.

┌──┐
LANGUAGE SPOT: linking expressions
This focuses on other linking expressions which would be useful in discursive compositions and are tested in Paper 3.
└──┘

▶ **Student's Resource Book page 75**

┌──┐
Module 8A Key

Reading pp.108–109
1b **1** They met on the tube (the London Underground) by chance. Perhaps they bumped into each other.
2 *Meant to be* means destined or fated to happen.

3a **1** H (*the long queue* refers to getting a taxi. And *It was a decision* refers back to *she changed her mind*)
2 G (*Dennis had noticed Wendy* links to *gave me a little nod* and *trying not to make it too obvious* links to *not staring at her*)
3 C (*Seeing this* links to *the businessman's head … resting on her arm*; *It woke him up* refers to giving the man's briefcase a kick)
4 B (*the scrap of paper* refers to the note Dennis pushed into her hand; *She hadn't gone far* follows stepping onto the platform)
5 D (*it never occurred to me to refuse* refers back to his invite for a coffee which is then contrasted with the fact that there was nowhere open)
6 E (*Fortunately, Wendy saw the funny side of this* refers to *giving her the number of his ex-girlfriend*; *they started going out together* is followed by them getting on well and then Dennis proposing)
7 A (*'So … my Mister Right'* refers to *'I had fallen in love with him.'*; *Fate must have been on my side* refers to the chance meeting on the train.)

HELP **1** G; **2** C; **3** B; **4** D

5a go out **with** someone – to date, to be a couple
get on **with** someone – have a good relationship (could be with friends, parents, teacher, neighbour, etc.)
fall in love **with** someone – start to love
└──┘

5b 1 packed; 2 dropped off (to sleep); 3 got to (her) feet; 4 scribble; 5 flustered; 6 dash

Language development 1 pp.110–111

1b 1 He approached her in the National Art Museum.
2 Yes, very.

1c 1 I don't talk to strange men; 2 I am just trying to be friendly; 3 I have seen the painting before; 4 I have been looking at you; 5 Leave me alone; 6 Will you / Would you like to join me; 7 Do you like the ... ; 8 ... is the ...; 9 Do you regret; 10 am the ...

1d Because what is reported is still true in the present.

1e past perfect

1f
today	that day
tomorrow	the next day/the following day
yesterday	the day before/the previous day
last week	the week before/the previous week
next month	the following month
this	that
here	there
come	go
bring	take

2 1 what I was; 2 I was; 3 that was; 4 to come/go out; 5 I'd/I had nearly; 6 had; 7 'd/had been to; 8 it was; 9 to pick me/if he could pick me; 10 'd/would be; 11 had to be (*must* becomes *had to*)

4a 1 accused; 2 persuaded; 3 agreed; 4 suggested; 5 explained

4b verb + *to*: agree
verb + object + *to*: persuade
verb + *-ing*: suggest
verb (+ object) + prep + *-ing*: accuse
verb (+ object) + *that* + clause: explain

4c verb + *to*: decide, offer, refuse
verb + object + *to*: advise, remind, warn
verb + *-ing*: admit, deny, recommend
verb (+ object) + prep + *-ing*: apologise, insist
verb (+ object) + *that* + clause: decide, advise, remind, warn, admit, deny, recommend, insist

4d verb (+ object) + *that* + clause: agree [I], persuade [T], suggest [I], decide [I], advise [T], remind [T], warn [I/T], admit [I], deny [I], recommend [I], insist [I], explain [I]

5 1 advised her not to get married yet./advised her that she shouldn't get married yet.
2 admitted starting the argument./admitted that she had started the argument.
3 insisted on cooking dinner that night./insisted that he was cooking/would cook dinner that night.

4 warned her sister not to go out with Mike./warned her sister that she shouldn't go out with Mike.
5 apologised to his girlfriend for hurting her feelings.
6 suggested staying in that weekend./suggested that they (should) stay in that weekend.
7 offered to carry the bag for her mother.
8 refused to listen.

7 1 Sometimes people suggest that marriage is an old-fashioned idea.
2 Parents often persuade their children to get married.
3 Some people insist on getting married while they are still teenagers.
4 One couple admits getting married for financial reasons.
5 Some couples refuse to have a religious wedding.
6 A few women decide not to change their surname.

Writing pp.112–113

2 1 a teacher; to summarise a discussion and give an opinion.
2 both sides
3 fairly formal
4 a balanced discussion, good organisation and clear linking of ideas.

4a/b A – 1 – Paragraph 4
B – 2 – Paragraph 1
C – 2 – Paragraph 3
D – 1 – Paragraph 2

5 Sample answer:

Nowadays more people are deciding to live by themselves. Some people claim this is more enjoyable, whereas others disagree.

The main advantage of living alone is that there is nobody to tell you what to do, so you can live your life your own way. What is more, you can organise or decorate your house as you want. There is no one else to disagree with.

On the other hand it can be quite lonely for some people. Secondly, it is more expensive because you have to pay all the rent and bills yourself, so you have less money to enjoy yourself. Last but not least, it can be hard to find a nice flat for one person so you might not be able to live in the best area.

To sum up, there are strong arguments on both sides. In conclusion I believe that living alone is better for older people who have more money and like privacy, but not for young people, who need to share the costs.

LANGUAGE SPOT: linking expressions

1 In fact – reinforcing a point, perhaps with an example. *In addition* is used to add a further point.
2 In addition – adding a further point. *In other words* is used to rephrase, to say the same thing in a different way.
3 For instance – to introduce an example. *That is to say* is used to rephrase or explain a point.
4 Moreover – adding a further point.
5 Besides – adding a further point.
6 Nevertheless – introducing a contrasting point.
7 Even so – introducing a contrasting point.
8 On the other hand – introducing the opposite point of view.

Module 8B Hobbies

Module 8B continues the theme of 'The important things in life' with texts and activities on the topic of hobbies.

To set the ball rolling ...

Start by getting students in groups to think of two popular hobbies and two more unusual ones. Then compare and vote on which group has thought of the most unusual hobbies.

Speaking pp.114–115

1 First check that students know who the people in the photos are: Russell Crowe, Australian film actor; Kylie Minogue, Australian pop singer; Jodie Kidd, English model; George Forman, American boxer; Geena Davies, American actor; Clint Eastwood, American actor
Also, check that they know what the hobbies are. Then students work in groups to decide who does which hobby before checking their ideas.

2a Extend the activity by eliciting other ideas for each verb.

2b The exercise extends the vocabulary in 2a. Check the verbs of the odd ones out (*play darts, play pool*) then elicit more examples for each verb. Point out how the use of *a bit of / some* makes the language sound more natural. Find out what things people in the class collect or used to collect when younger.

3a Remind students that with all new vocabulary they need to record the word stress. Again check which verb in 2a is used with each activity. (e.g. play backgammon, go paragliding)

3b There are no fixed answers here. Students may disagree. The point is to practise the vocabulary and to talk about different aspects of a hobby.

4 Elicit the meaning of *to dabble in something* (to do it in a way that is not serious or fanatical) before the discussion.

5 Board games are any games played on a specially designed board and range from chess and draughts/checkers to snakes and ladders, Monopoly, Scrabble, the Game of Life, etc.

6a You could start this section with books closed and elicit areas that might be covered in Paper 5 Part 1. Help students with their questions by asking what they like to know about someone that they have just met. Emphasise that they should just make notes for the answers and not write full sentences.

6b This could be done in pairs or with the whole class mingling, each student moving on to a different partner after they have answered a question.

7a Before students listen, elicit what you would need to do to create a good first impression, e.g. being positive and attentive, speaking clearly and with reasonable accuracy and fluency, giving extended answers but not going on for too long, listening carefully to the examiner and the other candidate. After listening, point out that the two candidates may be asked the same questions or different questions, as in this example.

7b You could ask students to shout *Stop!* each time they hear Anna or Giorgio dealing with a word they don't know.

8a Give the assessors some guidance on things to look for, such as accuracy, fluency, expanding answers appropriately, making a good first impression.

8b You could do this after each turn if you have plenty of time available. If time is short it will probably be more efficient to do it when everybody has had their turn.

▶ **Student's Resource Book page 77**

Listening p.116

1a Give students 90 seconds to read the questions before they start listening.

1b After they have compared, listened again and checked their answers you could give them a copy of the audio script to highlight the part with the answers.

2 The discussion could be done as a roleplay with students in pairs; one telling the other about his/her hobbies and the other being Simon telling them what their hobbies say about their personality.

┌──┐
Photocopiable activity

Photocopiable activity 8C (p. 158) would work well here, or later in the unit whenever you feel a speaking activity is needed for a change of pace. It is a Paper 5 Part 3 type discussion in which students have to choose a leisure activity.
└──┘

Use of English 1 p.117

1 Students discuss the questions in pairs or small groups before brief class feedback. In Britain fishing is said to be one of the most popular participant hobbies. Football is more popular as a spectator activity but more people fish than play football.

2a Give students a minute to read the text and answer the questions.

2b Allow about 10 minutes for the task.

3 The discussion is a chance to react to the topic; it could include their experiences of fishing. It could also include other 'cruel' sports.

Language development 2 p.118

You could start with a quick competition to see who can think of the most words formed from the stem *able* (unable (adj.), ability (n.), disability (n.), ably (adv.), enable (v.), disable (v.), disabled (adj.), inability (n.)).

LOOK Check that students understand the distinction made in B between general ability (i.e. long-term) and specific ability (i.e. on one occasion). Also, in D, you could compare *I don't know how to* (lack of knowledge) with *I can't* (maybe lack of knowledge, maybe physical, maybe just temporary). Highlight the grammar of the alternative verbs: *know how +to* + infinitive, *manage + to* + infinitive, *succeed + in + -ing*.

1a For each question, get students to think about the time – past, present or future – and whether it is general or specific. Highlight some of the vocabulary in the exercise, e.g. *get away* = have a break, *over* = finished.

1b First get students to look at the sentences on their own, then discuss them with a partner.

2 Students can refer back to the box to either help them do the exercise or to check it after they have finished.

3 Students need to think about meaning and form.

┌──┐
Background

Lego, the construction toy using interlocking plastic bricks, started in Denmark in the 1940s, the name is derived from 'leg godt', the Danish for 'play well'. Such is the success of Lego that it has been estimated that on average, everyone in the world has 52 lego bricks and the company makes over 300 million little tyres a year, making them the largest tyre manufacturer in the world!
└──┘

▶ **Student's Resource Book page 78**

Language development 3 p.119

1a Start by getting students to read the texts and establish the interests of the three writers. Don't focus on the meaning of the verbs with *get* as these are dealt with in the following exercises but clear up any other vocabulary difficulties.

1b The *True/False* statements are intended as be a guide to what the phrasal verbs mean. Elicit meanings or get students to check in a dictionary.

2 This exercise introduces more phrasal verbs with *get*. Again, if the meaning is not clear, students should check in a dictionary.

3b Encourage students to expand their answers and develop them into a conversation.

Use of English 2 p.120

1 The aim here is to focus on some of the more lexical areas frequently tested in Paper 3 Part 4.

2a Identifying the type of language being tested in each case will help students towards the right answer.

2c Encourage students to add the preposition combinations, fixed phrases and phrasal verbs to their vocabulary books.

▶ **Module 8 Test: How much do you remember? TRB page 186**

▶ **Exam practice 4: Papers 2 and 4 TRB pages 187–188**

┌──┐
Module 8B Key

Speaking pp.114–115

1b Russell Crowe – knits; Kylie – plays Scrabble; Jodie Kidd – does archery (and some car racing); George Forman – keeps pigeons; Geena Davies – goes car racing; Clint Eastwood – plays jazz piano.
└──┘

2a Play monopoly; collect coins; learn how to draw; go water-skiing; do amateur dramatics; make models

2b 1 play darts; 2 play pool

3a *Photography* is stressed on the second syllable, the others are all stressed on the first.

7a 1 Anna: home town, house, job, free-time activities
Giorgio: home town, family, career, music.
2 They both create a good first impression. They are positive, they speak accurately and fluently, they extend their answers and they listen carefully.

7b colleagues (Anna) (*… the other people who work with me …*)
eclectic (Giorgio) (*… how do you say it, I like many different kinds of music.*)

Listening p.116

1 1 – B (*If you tell me he's a … you have pretty much drawn a map of his personality for me.*)
2 – A (*usually in the fresh air actually*)
3 – A (*What seems to be most popular … is to bring along board games like Scrabble and Monopoly.*)
4 – C (*The Dalai Lama … will spend ages repairing an old film projector*)
5 – C (*with his metal detector – so far he's found 300 old coins and …*)
6 – B (*These interests completely take over their lives*)
7 – C (*we are difficult to live with*)

Use of English 1 p.117

2a 1 Angling is fishing with a rod, line and bait (as opposed to with trailing lines, nets, etc.)
2 two: coarse and fly-fishing
3 More women are doing it

2b 1 a – *on a regular basis* – fixed expression of frequency
2 being – *be able*, in gerund as subject of clause
3 their – *on + possessive + own* – 3rd person plural
4 do – refer back to *catch* – present simple in first conditional
5 there – *there is/are* – plural
6 to – *manage to do sthg*
7 for
8 ever – record at any time
9 were – verb be in the past (*until recently*), plural (*98%*)
10 in – *succeed in* – dependent preposition
11 up – *take up* phrasal verb meaning start
12 are – present continous plural (*celebrities*)

2o verb forms – 2, 9, 12
verb + preposition – 6, 10, 11

Language development 2 p.118

LOOK C: For a father, being able to …
D: you manage to attract a passing fish; the environment agency has succeeded in getting …

1a 1 can – present, general
2 was able to – past, specific
3 could/have been able to – past, general ability/past up to now, general ability
4 couldn't – past, general negative
5 have managed to – present perfect, achieved something difficult
6 will be able to/can – both forms possible to talk about the future
7 managed to – past, specific and hard, surprising
8 managed to find/succeeded in finding – past, specific, difficult

2 1 won't be able to finish – future
2 manage to stay – you stay slim (present) and it must be difficult
3 succeeded in passing – very difficult
4 can't come – future, known now
5 couldn't win – past/specific
6 don't know how to play – present/we haven't learnt
7 wasn't able to stay – past/specific
8 couldn't swim – past/general

3 1 can use – present, general
2 could put together/was able to put together – past, general
3 succeeded in building/managed to build – past, specific
4 could/was able to reach – past, general
5 couldn't fly/wasn't able to fly – past, general
6 managed to get – past, specific, difficult
7 succeeded in winning – past, specific, very difficult
8 can/will be able to carry on – future, general

Language development 3 p.119

1b 1 T – get off (to) – start in a particular way
2 T – get back (into) – do something again
3 T – get on – progress
4 T – get up to – do something (especially something bad)
5 F – get over – feel better after unpleasant experience
6 T – get round – gently persuade someone (by being nice)
7 T – get together – meet socially
8 F – get off – finish and leave (work or school/college)
9 T – get down to – start doing something that needs time or energy
10 F – get by – to have enough (money/ability) but no more

2 1 A; 2 B; 3 B; 4 A; 5 A; 6 B

3a 1 get together; 2 get (you) down; 3 got away with; 4 get on/along; 5 get by; 6 getting up to; 7 get off

Use of English 2 p.120

1 1 a fixed phrase
2 a phrasal verb
3 a preposition following a noun

2a 1 phrasal verb
2 fixed phrase
3 phrasal verb
4 fixed phrase
5 phrasal verb
6 verb + preposition
7 noun + preposition
8 phrasal verb

2b 1 get away with cheating
2 in case we want to
3 got down to some
4 's/is unlikely (that) there will
5 had to be called off
6 didn't succeed in persuading
7 had trouble (in) writing
8 get the truth out of

Teacher's Resource Book Module 8 Test: How much do you remember? p. 186

1 1 B; 2 A; 3 C; 4 B; 5 D

2 1 with; 2 be; 3 other; 4 in; 5 that

3 1 impression; 2 unfortunately; 3 employers; 4 recommendation; 5 incredibly

4 1 The boy *denied breaking/having broken the window*.
2 We *might be able to do* it for you tomorrow.
3 She said that *she had to go that* afternoon.
4 I *know how to put* petrol in my car but that's about it.
5 She asked me *if I would lend her* some money.

Teacher's Resource Book Exam practice 4 pp. 187–188

Paper 2 Writing

1 Style:
Formal or neutral.
Content:
Talk about the importance of fashion and clothes in today's world.
Write in favour of the statement, perhaps talking about the aspects of character which might be reflected in clothes (e.g. shyness, liveliness, etc.).
Write against the statement, perhaps saying that many people have little choice (e.g. uniforms, social pressures, fashion, etc.).
Say whether you agree with the statement and give your reasons.

2 Style:
Neutral.
Content:
Give the name of the programme and what type of programme it is.
Say what you like about the programme.
Say why the programme will be good for people of all ages.

3 Style:
Neutral.
Content:
Describe the text message; why was it mysterious?
Say what happened as a result of the message.
Say how the mystery was resolved.

4 Style:
Informal.
Content:
Say which course you chose and why.
Mention things you do on the course and how you feel about it.
Talk about the other people on the course – have you made friends? What are they like/what do you do with them/why not?

Paper 4 Listening
Part 4 1 C; 2 B; 3 B; 4 A; 5 C; 6 A; 7 A

Module 9 The consumer society

Module 9 includes topics such as giving money to charity, complaining, shopping and supermarkets, customer relations and banking.

Lead-in p.121

With books closed, write *consume* on the board and ask what it means (to use time, energy, goods). Elicit related words and write them on the board: *consumer* (buys and uses products and services), *consumer goods* (that people buy to use in the home), *consumer society* (in which buying products and services is important), *consumerism* (the idea that buying and selling products is the most important activity for a person or society), *consumption* (the amount that is used).

Get students to look at the photos and ask how each one represents consumerism. Then discuss the lead-in questions.

Module 9A A matter of conscience?

To set the ball rolling ...

Ask students if they prefer making, spending, saving or giving away money, and why.

Reading pp.122–123

Photocopiable activity

Photocopiable activity 9A (p. 159) could be used as an introduction to the unit, to pre-teach vocabulary or as a follow-up to the reading. It is a board game in which students make or lose money at each turn.

1a You could start by getting students to brainstorm local or international charities that they know of before discussing the charities mentioned here. Draw students' attention to the use of *the* with an adjective (e.g. *the homeless, the elderly*) to refer to a group of people and elicit other examples.

Background

WWF, founded in 1961, is the world's largest independent conservation organisation operating in over 90 countries. **Oxfam**, started in 1942 as 'The Oxford Committee for Famine relief' in response to food shortages caused by the war, is a world leader in Emergency relief, promotes health and education, and campaigns for debt relief, Fair Trade and conflict resolution. **Age Concern** campaign for the fair treatment and well-being of elderly people in society. **Shelter**, a domestic UK charity, was set up in 1966 to ensure that everyone has a suitable, decent and affordable home.

2 Elicit a suitable time limit to skim the texts (2 minutes).

3a/b Look at the example together to remind students how to do the task then set a time limit of 10–15 minutes. Remind students that in questions like 3 and 4 where there are two answers they can be given in either order. Students could compare and justify their answers in pairs before you go through it with them.

4 This is best done in groups of three or four students.

5 Encourage students to use the context of the expressions in the text when matching them to the definitions.

▶ **Student's Resource Book page 82**

Language development 1 pp.124–125

Background

Warren Buffet made his money through successful long-term investment. His simple strategy has been to spot strong undervalued businesses and improve them. He famously ignored the technology companies that boomed then bust in 1990s. His investment company has produced annual growth of 20% per year since 1988. He is said to have modest tastes and still lives in the same house he bought in a suburb of his hometown of Omaha, Nebraska, in 1957.

The aims of the Bill and Melinda Gates Foundation are: reducing poverty and improving health and access to education. It funds research and medical care for sufferers of the most serious conditions in the developing world such as malaria, tuberculosis and AIDS.

1a Ask students what they know about Bill Gates and Warren Buffet before they discuss the question giving reasons.

1c/d Students should look carefully at the context. They may know these conditionals as zero, first, second and third.

2a This practises the first three structures in 1c and shows how the choice of structure is a personal one, depending on how likely the speaker thinks the *if* part is to happen. Do the first question together as an example. Compare two people who have entered a competition and believe they have a good chance of winning – *If you win a lot of money, what will you spend it on?* – with two people who have not entered a competition and are just imagining – *If you won a lot of money, what would you spend it on?*

2b Encourage students to expand their answers, giving reasons.

3 This practises the last structure in 1c (unreal past). Do the first one as an example, asking concept questions: *Did he set his alarm?* (no) *Did he oversleep?* (yes)

4a Students discuss this together before you check with the whole class. Explain that in example 1, 'at the moment' is not just 'at this precise second of speaking'. It is a present situation that was also true at the time of the past action.

4b If necessary, give two more examples about yourself: 1 *I trained to be a teacher (in the past). I am a teacher (now). So … If I hadn't trained to be a teacher (in the past), I wouldn't be a teacher (now). 2 I am your teacher (now). I marked your homework last week. So … If I weren't your teacher (now), I wouldn't have marked your homework last week.*

5 Tell students to think about the time in each part of the sentences – is it in the past or now/generally true? Do the first one with them and ask concept questions to check: *Do I earn more money?* (no) *Did I go for a job interview?* (yes).

6 Point out that these conjunctions are alternatives to *if* in certain situations. You could get students to look at the Grammar reference before or while they do the exercise.

7 This is a final practice of the different conditionals and conjunctions. Ask students to justify their answers.

▶ **Student's Resource Book page 84**

Photocopiable activity

Photocopiable activity 9B (p. 160) would work well here. It is a card game in which students ask and answer questions about real, imaginary and past situations.

Writing pp.126–127

1 First ask students what kinds of things people complain about, e.g. poor service, unreliable transport, poor quality goods, unfulfilled promises. These ideas could act as prompts when students discuss the questions.

2 Get students to answer the basic planning questions: who, what, why and how.

3 Students should find planning and paragraph organisation quite easy by this stage.

4a The opening phrase *I am writing to* + verb is always useful. Point out the different construction following each verb.

4b Elicit why the phrases in A are inappropriate (they are too informal).

4c First ask students if the phrases are in the order they would be used in a letter (they are). Let students complete as many as they think necessary for their letter.

6 Remind students of the importance of checking their work and how best to do it systematically.

LANGUAGE SPOT: spelling

a Tell students that as a general principle, if they are unsure of the spelling of a word they should avoid using it in the exam. But knowing which words they commonly misspell will help when they check their work.

b These are all common students' spelling errors. Students could check answers with each other, in a dictionary, or in the Spelling section of the Writing reference on page 208.

c You could follow this up in a later lesson with a short dictation of the words, either in isolation, in these sentences, or in different sentences.

▶ **Student's Resource Book page 85**

Module 9A Key

Reading pp.122–123

3a **1** C *I really applaud those people who actively do something for charity*

2 E *I think that some people only give money to charity simply to ease their conscience ... the same goes for those celebrities who get a lot of publicity ...*

3/4 A *I'm more unwilling though to just give money to beggars*

4/3 D *Rather than just giving change to homeless people ... I think it is much better ...*

5 D *I get really annoyed with ... I also disapprove of ...*

6 B *I do worry that some charities have become so big that they are perhaps spending too much on bureaucracy*

7 B *I can never pass anyone in the street holding a collection tin without asking myself whether or not I should give. I sometimes feel ... on the other hand ...*

8 E *I do my fair share to help the community in other ways ...*

9 A *I am always moved at how generous people are*

10 D *I actually make a point of giving to organisations that get less publicity*

11 C *when I die I can leave some of my money to a charity*

12 E *I've stopped feeling guilty and giving myself a hard time*

13 B *... isn't that what I pay my taxes for ... ?*

14 B *I read in a magazine that the average person only gives 1% of what they earn to charity*

15 C *... that's because I feel ashamed walking on past them ...*

5 **1** do my fair share
2 applaud
3 actively do something
4 beggars
5 moved
6 brings it home to you
7 make donations
8 feel ashamed

Language development 1 pp.124–125

1b **1** Yes, almost always
2 Yes
3 No, imaginary
4 No

1c/d Always true: *If someone from a charity comes ..., I almost always give... If + present + present*
Possible and likely: *If I see a street musician ..., I'll probably give them money. If + present + future*
Unlikely or imaginary: *If I had Warren Buffet's money, I'd leave it ... If + past + would*
Unreal in the past: *If I had been the old lady, I wouldn't have left my ... If + past perfect + would have*

2a **Possible answers:**
1 If you won a lot of money, what would you spend it on?

2 If a classmate asks you to lend him/her a small amount of money, what will you do?/If a classmate asked you to lend him/her a small amount of money, what would you do?

3 If a classmate asked you to lend him/her a large amount of money, what would you do?

4 What do you do if you need change for the phone?/What would you do if you needed change for the phone?

5 If you found a lot of money, what would you do?

6 What would you do if you lost a/your wallet or purse?

7 What would you say if you received a present you didn't like?/What do you say if you receive a present you don't like?

8 What will you buy if you go shopping at the weekend?/What would you buy if you went shopping at the weekend?

3 **1** If James had remembered to set his alarm, he wouldn't have overslept.
2 If he hadn't been late for work, he wouldn't have got the sack.
3 If he had been able to find another job, he wouldn't have started his own business.
4 The business wouldn't have been a great success if it hadn't been such a good idea.
5 If James hadn't worked very hard he wouldn't have become a millionaire.
6 So, he wouldn't have become very rich if he had set his alarm!

4a **1** at the moment, yesterday
2 last week, now

4b A 2
B 1

5 **1** earned (present – imaginary); wouldn't have gone (unreal in the past)
2 would be able (present – imaginary); hadn't spent (unreal in the past)
3 had invested (unreal in the past); would be (present – imaginary)
4 were (present – unlikely); would have reduced (unreal in the past)
5 would be (present – imaginary); hadn't missed (unreal in the past)
6 couldn't have bought (unreal in the past); weren't (present – imaginary)

6 **1** provided that
2 Unless
3 Even if
4 as long as

7 **1** Unless; hurry up; 'll miss/'re going to miss (possible and likely)
2 give; as long as/if/provided that; spend (always true)
3 If; hadn't lent; would have (mixed – unreal in the past/present imaginary)
4 'll come; as long as/if/provided that; pay (possible and likely)
5 If; didn't run; would have (present imaginary)
6 Even if; had asked; wouldn't have been (unreal in the past)
7 If; didn't work; wouldn't feel (present imaginary)
8 If; were/was; wouldn't have spent (mixed – present imaginary/unreal in the past)

Writing pp.126–127

1 **2** **Possible answers:**
a shopping website: overcharging; goods not delivered or delivered late; wrong, faulty or damaged goods delivered.
an airline: delays, cancellations, overbooking, lost luggage, poor service.
a hotel: overbooking, facilities missing or not working; room dirty, noisy, too hot, too cold.

2 **Who**: The Director of a lottery game company
What: Complaining about misleading advertisements
Why: see the handwritten notes on the advert
How: Formal letter of complaint

3 **1** B – introduction
2 D – first two complaints
3 C – further two complaints
4 A – conclusion

4a **1** complain + about
2 object + to
3 express + noun
4 draw your attention + to
4b **1** d; **2** b; **3** a; **4** c
4d **1** d; **2** c; **3** e; **4** b; **5** a
4e **Example answers:**
I hope that in future you will be more honest in your advertising.
If I do not get a satisfactory reply, I will have no alternative but to contact the media.
Please can you assure me that you will look into these matters.

5 **Sample answer:**

Dear Sir or Madam

I am writing to complain about the advertisement for your new game. Having just played the game, I realise that the advertisement is misleading.

My first complaint is that you say there are big cash prizes and everyone can win. In fact, there is only one big prize so the chance of winning is quite small. You also say that the game is cheap, but I think £5 for a game is expensive.

Furthermore you claim that the game is easy to play whereas it is actually quite complicated. Even worse, you say that all the money goes to charity but, to my horror, I have discovered that half the money goes on administration.

I am very disappointed. I hope that in future you will tell the truth in your advertisements. If I do not get a satisfactory reply I will report your company to the government.

Yours faithfully

Carlos Cazador

Carlos Cazador

(155 words)

LANGUAGE SPOT: spelling

b surprised, separate, recommend, unnecessary, committee, immediately, sincerely, receive, beginning, embarrassed, advertisement, writing

c **1** tried, loose
2 cassette, foreign, pronunciation
3 principal, their, accommodation, address
4 Unfortunately, medicine, effect
5 definitely, until, developed, responsible

Module 9B Spending money

Module 9B continues the theme of 'The consumer society' with the topics of shopping, money and banks.

To set the ball rolling ...

With books closed, put a line on the board with a smiley face at one end and a miserable one at the other and ask students where they would put shopping on it and why. They could draw their own line and put different types of shopping on it as you call them out, e.g. shopping for clothes, shoes, presents; shopping in traditional shops, in supermarkets, by mail order; Sunday shopping, late night shopping. Then they explain their line to a partner.

Speaking pp.128–129

1a Start by asking them to spend a minute in pairs comparing and contrasting the photos. Get them to give reasons as they match phrases to one or other store.

1b The difference between these three places can cause confusion so use concept questions to check understanding.

1c Check students know the pronunciation of *aisle* and stress in *organic* and *escalators*.

2 Start by asking the class whether *cost / price* are nouns, verbs, etc. Students could use dictionaries to check their answers.

3 Emphasise that students should recognise the phrases (e.g. *be out of stock*) and collocations (*special offer*).

4 Encourage them to include some of the vocabulary in the discussion.

5a At this stage students should just give a general answer rather than describe the photos in detail.

5b You could suggest that students think of two advantages and two disadvantages of each type of shopping.

6 Remind students that if they don't know a word they should try to explain or define it. Use the photos to elicit objects/ideas to explain, using the expressions in the box, e.g.: *It's a kind of staircase that moves.*
It's like a huge supermarket but with many different shops.
It's something you need/can use when you haven't got any cash.
It's when you buy things using the Internet.

7a/b Before students begin, elicit ways of checking the examiner's instructions and asking the examiner to repeat them. Point out the list of expressions for this in the Functions reference on page 215. Remind 'candidates' to try and keep going for the full minute, and remind 'examiners' to time 'candidates' and stop them after approximately one minute.

7c Encourage students to discuss their own and others' performance, and not to be too critical!

Listening p.130

1 Remind students of the type of task, and elicit the strategy. Do question 1 together as an example. Key words: What, advertised, television, computer, board game.

2 You could let students compare and discuss their answers, both between the first and second playing of each extract, and after the second playing of each one.

3 First check that students understand the words in italics. They are all in the listening extracts, which you could use to help with context and examples. Then students discuss the questions in groups, followed by class feedback.

▶ **Student's Resource Book page 87**

Use of English 1 p.131

1 You could introduce some useful vocabulary here, such as *shop around, wait for the sales, buy in bulk, get good value for money*.

2a Encourage students to recall as much of the strategy as possible before checking on page 33.

2c Give students a time limit for the task, e.g. 12–15 minutes. Don't discuss questions 5, 6, 7, 9, 10 in too much detail, as they are dealt with in Language development 2 on page 132.

Language development 2 p.132

LOOK With books closed, write some sentences on the board and get students to decide if they are correct or not, e.g.: *The results are good. The news are good. Most people likes shopping. Everyone likes shopping. The majority of people likes shopping. A few people likes shopping. Clothes are interesting. Politics are interesting. Some of the customers were complaining. More than one of the customers were complaining. There were many cafes. There were more than one cafe. A couple of people was waiting. Two weeks are not long to wait.* Students can then check which are right and which are wrong by referring to the box. Concord here means agreement in terms of number (i.e. plural verb form with plural subject).

1 Students refer back to the table to check their answers.

2 Tell students that they don't need to choose a tense – all the verbs are in the present simple – but they need to decide which verbs are singular and which verbs are plural. Students could have further practice by conducting a class/group survey into shopping habits/opinions and then reporting back the summary using quantity expressions such as *a large number, the majority of, hardly anyone*. It would be better if each student asked a different question.

3 Although this is a relatively basic grammar point, it can still cause difficulty for some students at FCE and is often tested. Students should use the information in the box to help them with the exercise.

4 This exercise gives further practice of empty subject *it* in questions 1 and 2, and both *it* and *there* in question 3 (*There are …/It's a good idea to …*).

▶ **Student's Resource Book page 88**

Use of English 2 p.133

1 You could give your own answers to the questions as an example. Get students to give examples in their discussion. They could also name their favourite and least favourite shops.

2 Elicit the strategy for word formation before students do the task.

3 Possible further questions: *Is it worth paying more to go shopping where the staff are knowledgeable and helpful?*

4 Set a suitable question for students to skim the text. E.g. Where do British people like to invest money?

5 Students should give reasons for their answers.

Language development 3 p.134

1 Students complete the quiz in pairs and/or with a dictionary. You could get them to do one section at a time, so that you can check answers and focus on differences in meaning within each section.

2 Discuss how this money vocabulary could be recorded and what other things students will need to note, such as prepositions, which verb to use with the word, whether it is formal or informal.

3 First make sure students understand all the statements. Students could discuss them in small groups. They should give reasons for their answers, and examples from their own experience if possible.

4a Students looked at forming adjectives in Module 2B and forming nouns in Module 5B. Here they look at forming verbs. Draw students' attention to the change in stress in the two-syllable 'no change' noun/verb: 'record (noun) /re'cord (verb).

4b Check students' pronunciation of *blood* /blʌd/, *bleed* /bliːd/, *choice* /tʃɔɪs/, *choose* /tʃuːz/, 'import (n), im'port (v).

• •
Photocopiable activity

Photocopiable activity 9C (p. 161) could be used here. It is a split crossword which practises money vocabulary and word formation.
• •

▶ **Module 9 Test: How much do you remember? TRB page 189**

Module 9B Key

Speaking pp.128–129

1a A (huge shop) – pick up a bargain, go to the check out, be spoilt for choice, get good value. B (designer shop) – pay a fortune, find a 'one-off', get personal service, get good value.

1b Supermarket – one shop selling mainly food but also, cleaning products, clothes, books, etc. Department store – one large shop, often on a number of floors, divided into separate departments each selling a different type of goods. Shopping Mall (US) Shopping centre (UK) – a group of separate independent shops in one covered building.

1c organic food/aisle/trolley – supermarket, escalators/changing rooms – department store / shopping centre

1d meat – butcher; medicine – pharmacy (prescription), chemist (over the counter); flowers – florist; newspapers – newsagent; vegetables – green grocer; stationery – stationers; shoes – shoe-shop

2 1 price (tag) / costs; 2 price; 3 cost / pricey (adj); 4 (no extra) cost; 5 (half) price

3 1 out of (stock); 2 pay (at the till); 3 (on special) offer; 4 put (me through – on the phone); 5 (just) hang on (a moment); 6 just (looking); 7 keep (s/one waiting); 8 return

Listening p.130

1 1 What advertised? television, computer, board game
2 What doing? faulty goods, money back, goods delivered
3 What doing? blaming, advice, suggestion
4 Where? bus station, shop, library
5 What complaining about? attitude of staff, accuracy of information, arrangements changed
6 Who talking to? hotel receptionist, conference organiser, secretary
7 Which sector? service successful, travel, health, entertainment.

8 What about? e-commerce disadvantages, new idea, research into success.

2 **1** C *Throw the dice and race round the board. Based on the hit TV programme*
2 B *I can't give you a cash refund unless the product is faulty in some way.*
3 B *I just wondered if you had any ideas on what I could do.*
4 A – *... mark the bus routes on it ... that uniformed man over there ... (Why don't we go to a shop ... take it next door to the library ...)*
5 B – *Had I known that there was a midday flight ... she said there was only one flight a day ...*
6 C – *... it's probably on my desk somewhere – can you have a look? (Or perhaps you could check with the organisers)*
7 A – *The idea has caught on fastest when there's something to be picked up, especially holiday documents.*
8 B – *... fortunately, it looks like a solution is at hand.*

Use of English 1 p.131
2b **1** ~~they have no effective way of collecting information~~ – they use loyalty cards to track how often you shop and what you buy.
2 ~~It is illegal to share information~~ – often this information is shared.
3 ~~not many customers have loyalty cards~~ – 85% of UK customers have a loyalty card.
4 ~~There is nothing we can do~~ – What can we do? Basically use other shops.

2c **1** one – (or another)
2 like – (*it seems like something*)
3 of – (*keep track of something*)
4 what – (what *something* is/are)
5 is – (*Information* –uncountable, *is shared* – passive)
6 have – (*majority* followed by plural verb, *have been* present perfect after *so far*)
7 are – (*a number of* followed by plural verb, *are becoming* present continuous)
8 being – (*cards* plural, *are being used* – present continuous passive)
9 have – (present perfect after just)
10 is – (*no one* singular, verb *be* before adjective *sure*)
11 there – (question future existence)
12 else – (*somewhere else* – in another shop)

Language development 2 p.132
1 **1** Everyone think*s* it's a good idea. (singular)
2 The majority of us agree~~s~~. (plural)
3 ✓
4 Neither of them know*s* what to buy. (singular)
5 These jeans ~~doesn't~~ *don't* fit. (plural)
6 ✓
7 Ten euros ~~aren't~~ *isn't* very ~~many~~ *much*. (singular)
8 ✓
9 ~~This~~ *These* scissors ~~doesn't~~ *don't* cut very well. (plural)
10 The United States ~~have~~ *has* a new President. (singular)

2 **1** sells (singular); **2** feel (plural); **3** causes (singular); **4** wants (singular); **5** seem (plural); **6** is (singular); **7** say (plural); **8** admit (plural); **9** confess (plural); **10** wants (singular)

3 **1** There are – existence, plural
2 it is – empty subject
3 there is – existence, singular
4 It is – It = the set meal
5 there are – existence, plural
6 it is – empty subject

Use of English 2 p.133
2 **1** smallest; **2** exhausted;
3 impatient; **4** extremely;
5 stressful; **6** friendliness;
7 satisfaction; **8** flight;
9 sight; **10** amazement.

4 **1** comparison – noun after preposition *in*
2 worryingly – adv refers to verb *saving*
3 retirement – noun after preposition *towards*
4 surprising – adjective before noun
5 eating – gerund of verb *to eat out*
6 dramatically – adverb after verb
7 investment – noun after adjective and before relative pronoun
8 owning – gerund after preposition *with*
9 unaffordable – negative adjective after verb *be* and adverb *simply*
10 preferred – adjective before noun

Language development 3 p.134

1 **1**

1 B; **2** B, B; **3** A; **4** B, B; **5** A; **6** B; **7** A

2

1 from – borrow something from somebody
2 to – lend something to somebody
3 to – owe something to
4 on – spend money on something
5 on – waste money on something
6 into – pay money into an account
7 into – change money into something else
8 from – make money from something
9 on – have money on you
10 to – leave money to someone

3a

1 (buy, get) the tickets, (make) a big profit, (ask for, get, receive) a discount
2 (pay, repay) a refund, (get, obtain, receive) a receipt, (get, take out, pay back) a loan

3b

1 discount; **2** profit; **3** refund; **4** interest; **5** bill; **6** salary; **7** fine; **8** loan

4b No change: dry, import, calm, name
Internal change: choose, bleed
Prefix: endanger
Suffix: criticise, strengthen, fatten, widen, lengthen

5a **1** criticise; **2** import; **3** endanger; **4** choose
5b widen; modernise; calm; strengthen

Teacher's Resource Book Module 9 Test: How much do you remember? p.189

1 **1** A; **2** C; **3** B; **4** D; **5** C

2 **1** on; **2** with; **3** has; **4** there; **5** by.

3 **1** creativity; **2** financial; **3** innovative; **4** advertising; **5** bleed

4 **1** We must avoid anything that *puts the children in danger/at risk* at school.
2 'I'll come at six unless *I hear from you* before then,' Keith said.
3 I'll cook for you *as long as you're* not a vegetarian.
4 If Judith's car *had started, she would/might have* been on time.
5 *Hardly anyone seems* to be polite these days

Module 10 Out and about

Module 10 includes topics such as travelling, holidays, public transport, a car accident and space tourism.

Lead-in p.135

With books closed, write *Out and about* on the board and ask students what they understand by it. It can mean both 'not home and busy' and 'away travelling'. Then get students to identify the means of transport in the photos and discuss the questions.

Background

The American novelist and travel writer Paul Theroux (b.1941) taught English in Malawi, Uganda, and Singapore for eight years before settling down in England and beginning a career as a writer. His novels include *The Family Arsenal* (1976), about a group of terrorists in the London slums, and *The Mosquito Coast* (1982), about an American inventor who attempts to create an ideal community in the Honduran jungle. He first achieved commercial success with a best-selling travel book, *The Great Railway Bazaar* (1975), describing his four-month train journey through Asia. Other travel books include *The Old Patagonian Express* (1979) and *The Happy Isles of Oceania* (1992).

Module 10A Travel

To set the ball rolling ...

With books closed, get students to write the word *travel* vertically on a piece of paper and then write words across it that they associate with the topic. Demonstrate on the board how to start, e.g.

    T I M E

    T R A I N S

    A

A D V E N T U R E

    E

    P L A N E

In pairs, students then explain the significance of their words, e.g. *time – you need a lot of time to really enjoy foreign travel, trains – my favourite way to travel*.

Photocopiable activity

Photocopiable activity 10A (p. 162) can be used at the start of the unit or as a follow-up after the reading text. It is a light-hearted questionnaire to discover what students consider important when travelling.

Reading pp.136–137

1 The prediction exercise is designed to reinforce the habit of predicting.

2 Tell students to read quickly, scanning for the information to get an overview of the text.

3 Elicit the task strategy. Then at this stage leave the class to do the task without further help.

4 You could also ask students, 'In what ways is travel is becoming easier or harder?'

5 The exercise looks at collocation.

▶ **Student's Resource Book page 92**

Language development 1 pp.138–139

1a With books closed, brainstorm places to stay while on holiday. Check/Pre-teach *self-catering* – when you arrange your own food and cooking, e.g. staying in an apartment rather than a hotel. Then get students to discuss the question, giving reasons for their preferences.

1b First students use the picture to identify the type of text (a holiday brochure). Explain that the answers to question 1 are in the text, whereas they will have to think of the answers to question 2 themselves.

1c Elicit the form of the passive (*be* + past participle) and why it is used. Point out that not stating who has done something has the effect of making the statements more impersonal and so more formal. Highlight the use of *by* when we want to say who has done something: *They were built ... by a team of highly skilled workers ...*

1d As you check students' answers, elicit why each tense is used. Explain that the passive is not a tense, and the rules of tense use are exactly the same as for active verb forms.

2a This exercise focuses mainly on forming the passive. Get students to work together identifying the correct tense in each case and establishing how to form that tense correctly.

2b Here, students have to think about both form and use, changing the sentences from active to passive to make them more formal. You could do the first one or two together as an example.

3 Start by writing two sentences on the board: *Fleming discovered penicillin. It is an important medicine.* Ask students to rewrite the sentences, emphasising the medicine: *Penicillin is an important medicine. It was discovered by Fleming.* Students then read the information in the box and answer the questions.

5 Point out that reports are often more formal and less personal, and consequently often contain a lot of passive forms.

> **Photocopiable activity**
>
> Photocopiable activity 10B (pp. 163–164) would work well here. Students write travel-related news stories based on notes.

▶ **Student's Resource Book page 94**

Writing pp.140–141

1 Students' experiences of group travel could be on language and educational trips as well as sports trips.

2 This exercise focuses on task completion, style and effect on the reader, which all contribute towards the general impression mark in the exam.

3a Elicit the two problems mentioned in the task, the location and the organisation. Get students to look at the examples under these two headings, and ask them what other things they could say, e.g. hotel far from ski lifts, small village – no nightlife, hotel not expecting everyone, no meals booked. Then get them to think about possible solutions for each problem, e.g. change location, arrange more lessons, etc.

3b Remind students to use all seven pieces of advice, and that some go with more than one paragraph.

3c Once students have matched their notes to the paragraphs, point out that they now have the basic structure of the report. Explain that they don't have to come up with a lot of complex ideas in the exam – just clear, well-organised points.

3d Encourage students to discuss the strengths and weaknesses of each of the three subject headings before deciding on the best.

3e Explain that the paragraph headings should be short but should say clearly what the paragraph is about.

4a Elicit what a topic sentence is – one sentence which summarises the main point.

4b Point out that the expressions in the table are useful for any report, but obviously it is important to use them correctly.

4c Do this with the whole class as a quick check.

5/6 Give students 20 minutes to write their report and 10 minutes to check it. They could check each other's reports, to see if they find it easier to spot other people's mistakes than their own. This may help them to look at their own writing more objectively.

> **LANGUAGE SPOT:** passive report structures
>
> This focuses on different ways of using passive structures to add emphasis when writing a report. Point out that *be supposed to* here means *be generally said to.*

▶ **Student's Resource Book page 95**

Module 10A Key

Reading pp.136–137

2 Toronto, New York, Miami, Los Angeles, Atlanta, New Orleans

3 1 B – *All around me New Yorkers rushed from destination to destination as …*
2 C – *only flirted with the US, just visiting the cosmopolitan cities around her edges.*
3 A – *the only city in the world where …*
4 C – *such familiar places to me through a thousand and one films and TV shows*
5 B – *a stretch limo, a famous hotel*
6 A – *but the can-do American attitude to life was in full-swing*
7 C – refers back to: *only 20% of the population in possession of a passport.*
8 D – *it'll take you a lifetime to discover your own country*

5 1C sweet tooth; 2E sharp suits; 3F tasteless neon lights; 4D clear sky; 5B trembling steps; 6A broad smiles

Language development 1 pp.138–139

1b 1 They stay cool, they are well decorated, there is a buffet breakfast, a barbecue area is being constructed.
2 You have to share facilities with others, the shops are not very close, breakfast is not included, and it could get too hot.

1c are grouped; were built; have been designed; have all been decorated; is served; is now being constructed; will soon be completed; can be found

The passive is used here because what has been done/is done is considered more important than who did it or does it.

1d 1 are grouped
2 is served
3 have been designed
4 have all been decorated
5 were built
6 is now being constructed
7 will soon be completed
8 can be found

2a 1 are situated (present simple)
2 were redecorated (past simple)
3 can be supplied (modal)
4 will be installed/will have been installed (future simple/future perfect)
5 are being built (present continuous)
6 has been given (present perfect)
7 must be checked (modal)
8 will be asked (future simple)

2b 1 Our facilities are always being improved.
2 All our flats have been modernised in the last two years.
3 Our kitchens have been equipped to the highest standards.
4 The beds will be made daily (by maids).
5 The holiday village can be found two kilometres outside the town.
6 A full programme of sports activities is offered (by the village).
7 Very few complaints were received last year.
8 Extra people may be accommodated (by guests) on the sofa beds.
9 The maximum number of people allowed in each caravan is indicated by/in our brochure.
10 Keys must be returned to reception on departure.

3 A by – to specify the agent (the one that does the action)
B 1 – person + passive verb + thing + by + agent
C thought (doesn't matter who thinks), said (doesn't matter who says)
D to cheer, to empty

4 1 it was composed by Schubert.
2 were given two tickets
3 was seen to steal/seen stealing
4 is believed the Prime Minister will call
5 's/has been promised a place
6 it was discovered by Fleming.
7 is thought to have hidden
8 'll/will be made to pay

5 Suggested answer:
The town has changed a lot in the last 30 years. *All the old factories have been pulled down and replaced with* hi-tech science parks. *It's felt to be* unfortunate that *one of the older schools was also demolished, as children will have to be sent* by bus to the next town. *It is said that a brand new school will be built* in the town in the next few years when *extra funding is provided by the Government. That will be appreciated by the newer residents in particular.*

Writing pp.140–141

2 1 two parts – analysis of problem and recommendations
2 formal and impersonal – it's for the Principal of the college and represents the recommendations of the committee
3 good organisation, clear analysis, logical recommendations

3b Paragraph 1: b, d,
Paragraph 2: a, e, g
Paragraph 3: a, e, g
Paragraph 4: c, f

3d C is the best. It is formal, short and clear, telling the reader immediately what the report is about.
A is too general, not mentioning the topic at all.
B is too informal.

3e Suggested answers:
Paragraph 1 – Background/Introduction
Paragraph 2 – Location
Paragraph 3 – Organisation
Paragraph 4 – Possible solutions/ Recommendations

4a Example answers:
Paragraph 1: … the problems students had on the recent ski trip.
Paragraph 2: … the location of the trip was unsuitable.
Paragraph 3: … mistakes in the organisation resulted in fewer lessons.
Paragraph 4: … in future the college uses another location.

4b The aim of this report is to … 3
In order to prepare this report … 7
It appears that … 8
The main problem was that … 4
Some students had to… 9
Not surprisingly, … 1
Although the advanced slopes …10
Some group leaders were … 6
All things considered, … 2
We have no hesitation in recommending … 5

4c passive
more
less

5 Sample answer:

College Ski Trip

Background

The aim of this report is to highlight the problems that occurred during the half-term ski-trip. As preparation, questionnaires were sent out to all participants.

Location

Students said that the advanced slopes were excellent but:

• There was only artifical snow lower down.
• There weren't enough beginners' slopes.

Organisation

The following points were mentioned:

• Only one-hour ski-lessons were included in the price – not the two-hour lessons they were promised.
• There were not enough beds in the cabins and some students had to sleep on the floor.
• Some group leaders were more interested in skiing than looking after the students.

Recommendations

Three recommendations were suggested:

1. Change to a location with beginners' slopes and go earlier in the year.
2. Make sure all details are clear in the contract.
3. Produce a handbook for group leaders, listing their duties.

All things considered, lessons need to be learnt for future ski-trips.

(158 words)

LANGUAGE SPOT: passive report structures

a 1 that the Principal is in favour.
  2 that about 50 students will attend.
  3 that many of the students (have) had difficulties getting a visa.
  4 that some of them (have) left early.

b 1 is supposed to be becoming easier and cheaper.
  2 are supposed to travel further on holiday these days.
  3 is supposed to broaden the mind.
  4 is supposed to reduce the number of private cars.

Module 10B Getting around

Module 10B continues the theme of 'Out and about' with the topics of travel, public transport and space tourism.

To set the ball rolling ...

With books closed, get students to think of the difference between the nouns: *travel* (uncountable, the activity of travelling, or *travels* plural, journeys for pleasure to places far away), *trip* (countable, a short journey or one that is not usually made) and *transport* (uncountable, the system or method for carrying passengers).

Speaking pp.142–143

1a Identify the forms of transport in the pictures with the whole class before students discuss the questions in groups.

1b Make sure students can justify their choices.

1c Remind students of ways of marking stress.

2a Students could use gerunds (e.g. driving) or means of transport (e.g. car, bus) to answer. If using the latter, get them to think of as many forms as possible for each as this will extend and reinforce the vocabulary.

2b The exercise looks at common vocabulary mistakes connected with transport. Compare *in time* and *on time*.

3 The discussion could be in groups, with the whole class or as a debate with two groups each presenting one side.

4a This is a review of the format of Paper 5 Part 2. Students discuss the statements in pairs before you go through them with the class.

4b First remind students of the meaning of *speculate* (to talk about possibilities) and *paraphrase* (to explain a word in another way).

4c Keep this fairly brief to avoid creating endless lists!

5a/b Divide the class into groups of three. If your class is not equally divisible by three, have one or two groups of four with an extra assessor. Give the examiners time to check the instructions and prepare the material.

5c Encourage everyone in each group to discuss the candidates' performance.

Listening p.144

1a Recap various forms of public transport if not following on immediately after the speaking. Remind students to give reasons for their answers in the discussion.

2a Remind students of the best strategy for this task type. Get them to look at the rubric and ask what type or types of transport will be discussed (different types of bikes).

3 Check some of the vocabulary (e.g. *look down on someone*, *status symbol*) before the discussion. Remind students to give reasons for their choices.

4 Students could use dictionaries to check the vocabulary before discussing the questions.

▶ **Student's Resource Book page 97**

Language development 2 p.145

1 Explain that in question 1 they need to think of the time referred to rather than the verb forms. Verb forms are focused on in question 2.

When going through the answers together, remind students that, as with conditionals, the wish contrasts with reality, so we use a positive verb form for a negative situation and vice versa, e.g. *I wish there was something…* (but there isn't); *I wish we hadn't moved here* (but we have).

We often use *wish + would* to describe situations over which we have no control and where we see no likelihood of change. If necessary give more examples, eliciting the wish each time:

He smokes – I wish he didn't smoke (but he does).

He can't give up – I wish he could give up (but he can't).

He won't give up – I wish he would give up (but I don't think he will).

I smoke – I wish I ~~would~~ could give up (but I can't).

2 Students will need to think about the time reference and a possible change/regret in each situation.

3 This exercise provides personalised practice of the grammar. Look at the first two questions and get students to think about what would fit. In question 1 *be* could be a main verb, e.g. *I wish I were rich*, or an auxiliary verb, e.g. *I wish I were lying on the beach now*, *I wish I were going to the party tonight*. Similarly, in question 2 *have* could be a main verb, e.g. *I wish I had more time*, or an auxiliary verb, e.g. *I wish I had done my homework*.

4 The aim here is to check students' understanding of the grammar in the box. First go through the examples in the box with students, pointing out how these expressions use the tense shift backwards to express hypothetical situations.

5 Remind students to think carefully about the time (present or past) and the choice of verb form (present or past).

6 Encourage students to write true sentence endings where the sentences are true for them.

> ••
> **Photocopiable activity**
>
> Photocopiable activity 10C (pp. 165–166) would work well here. It gives further practice of *wish/if only*, as students imagine what people are thinking in various leisure situations.
> ••

▶ **Student's Resource Book page 98**

Use of English 1 p.146

Begin with a quick review of Paper 3 Part 4, asking: *How many questions are there?* (eight) *How many marks per question?* (two) *How long should you spend on part 4?* (15 minutes) *How many words should you write?* (between two and five)

1 This question aims to revise some of the task strategy. Get students to discuss it in pairs first.

2a Point out that students shouldn't rush key word transformations. They should work slowly and carefully to avoid unnecessary mistakes.

2b Remind students that in the exam the eight questions test a wide range of structures and vocabulary.

Use of English 2 p.147

1 Some care should be exercised here as it is possible that some students may have been in car accidents that they would prefer not to talk about.

2a This is a review of the task strategy for Paper 3 Part 2.

2b Remind students that skimming the text will not only give them a general understanding; it will also help them identify the style, time frame and possible source of the text, all of which could help them complete the task.

2d Verb + preposition combinations are commonly tested in Paper 3 Part 2.

2e The difference between a verb + preposition combination and a phrasal verb can be narrow so allow some flexibility in students' choices. For example *think of* can be considered as either verb + preposition or as a phrasal verb.

3 Get students to re-read the text before the discussion. If they disagree with question 1, ask them to suggest what really happened.

Language development 3 p.148

1 With books closed, read out the examples in the box, missing out each preposition and eliciting it. Then get students to look at the examples before doing the exercise.

2 The exercise looks at verbs with different meanings when followed by different prepositions. As you go through the answers, check that students understand the different meanings of the verbs. (e.g. apologise to someone for something).

3 First ask students if they have ever considered a trip into space as a tourist. Then point out that some of the verbs can be followed by more than one preposition so they should think carefully which one is correct in the context. Advise that if they are unsure, to trust their instincts and go with what seems right.

4 Verbs of perception can be easily confused because two different verbs in English may translate as just one verb in the students' language. Encourage students to use dictionaries, and when you go through the answers check that they understand the differences:

look – a deliberate action; *see* – not deliberate; *watch* – a deliberate action over a period, e.g. a football match or TV programme

gaze – look at something for a long time because it is so interesting; *peer* – try to look at something but with difficulty; *stare* – look in a very fixed way for some time

hear – could be deliberate or not; *listen* – a deliberate action

▶ **Module 10 Test: How much do you remember? TRB page 190**

▶ **Exam practice 5: Papers 2 and 4 TRB pages 191–192**

Module 10B Key

Speaking pp.142–143

1b **1** the tube (the others are on water)
2 delivery van (the others have two wheels and are ridden)
3 tram (the others are air transport)
4 handlebars (on a bicycle, the others are from a car)
5 carriage (the others are parts of boats)
6 sidecar (on a motorbike, the others are cars)

1c ca'noe; 'rowing boat; 'moped; 'scooter; 'motorbike; de'livery van; 'helicopter; 'glider; 'spaceship; 'handlebars; ac'celerator; 'steering wheel; 'carriage; 'hatchback; sa'loon; 'sidecar; es'tate.

2a take a driving test – cars, vans, lorries; be forced to land – plane, glider, helicopter; get clamped – cars, trucks; two stops – underground train; take on as hand luggage – flying; stop in a lay-by – car, lorry, taxi; the late running of – trains, ferries; confirm your flight – flying; fasten your seatbelt – flying, driving; go for a cruise – boat; points on your licence – driving; disembark – boat, ferry; low on petrol – car, lorry/truck, motorbike, etc.

2b **1** get (into)/take/catch; **2** get off; **3** missed; **4** ridden; **5** docks/stops; **6** price/cost; **7** journey; **8** on time

4a **1** True
2 True – first, compare and contrast, then give an opinion or reaction.
3 False – you should deal with them together, comparing and contrasting.
4 True
5 False – it's an individual long turn!
6 True – only about 20 seconds.

4b **1** g; **2** c; **3** a; **4** f; **5** b; **6** d; **7** e

Listening p.144

2a **1** F – *I can fit in more business meetings than I used to*
2 C – *I hated being squashed in with other people*
3 B – *I was looking for something cheaper to run than a car*
4 E – *it's good to challenge people's expectations*
5 D – *you always know how long the journey is going to take*

Language development 2 p.145

1 **1** the present: 1, 3
the past: 2
the future: 4, 5
2 the present: *wish* + past; *if only* + *could*
the past: *wish* + past perfect
the future: *wish* + *would*; *if only* + *would*
3 *if only* is stronger/more emphatic

2 Suggested answers:
1 I wish/If only I hadn't dyed my hair bright red. I wish/If only I'd kept it blonde.
2 I wish/If only he didn't/wouldn't borrow my car. I wish/If only he would stop borrowing my car.
3 I wish/If only I could afford a taxi. I wish/If only I didn't have to take the bus.
4 I wish/If only I hadn't come to see this. I wish/If only I were/was watching something else.
5 I wish/If only he/she would hurry up. I wish/If only he/she didn't/wouldn't take so long in the bathroom. I wish I could get into the bathroom.

4 **1** A – ... but you should.
2 B – ... but it's too late to change the situation now.
3 B – ... someone else did.

5 **1** learnt – present time, past verb form
2 was/were – present time, past verb form
3 phoned – present time, past verb form
4 had met – past time, past perfect verb form/has met – present time (i.e. he knows her) present perfect verb form
5 had bought – past time, past perfect verb form

Use of English 1 p.146
1 **1** Leave it and come back to it when you've done the ones you can do.
2 Make sure you write something for every question. Don't leave any gaps.

2a **1** wish I'd gone – past; negative reality, positive verb form
2 'd rather you phoned – present situation, past verb form
3 were you, I'd book – unreal conditional (I'm not you)
4 wish I had told – past; negative reality, positive verb form. Note *truth* in answer opposite to *lying* in question
5 was hardly anyone/anybody at/in
6 is supposed to be
7 (high/about) time you stopped going
8 you mind not using – *mind + (not) + -ing*
2b **1** 1, 2, 4, 7, 8
2 I'd rather you = Would you mind if you didn't use = not using

Use of English 2 p.147
2a **1** after – you should read the text right through first for a general understanding
2 short – if you get stuck with one answer, you will have less time for the rest of the task and the rest of Paper 3
3 one – if you put more than one word, it will be marked as incorrect, even if one of the words is correct. If you can't decide between two possible answers, you should always choose one rather than put both.

2b **1** He had an unusual accident after he couldn't stop his car.
2 The police did not believe him.
2c **1** with – preposition after *crowded*
2 off – take something (foot) off something (the accelerator)
3 about/of – think about/of – to consider the possibility of doing something
4 to – to keep to something – to maintain, to prevent something increasing
5 through – to get through to someone – to contact by phone
6 could – past modal verb for ability
7 on – concentrate on something
8 into – to burst into tears – start crying suddenly
9 by – passive *was followed by*
10 on – contrast with *off*
11 no – negative after *however*
12 of – suspect someone of something
2d Questions 2, 3, 7, 12
2e Questions 4, 5, 8

Language development 3 p.148
1 **1** about; **2** from; **3** about; **4** to; **5** with; **6** in

2 **1** for (something); on (= served in a restaurant)
2 about (= consider); of (= invent)
3 to (= forced to accept); from (= leave a job)
4 as (= what he is); for (= why he is famous)
5 of (= didn't know); from (= received a call or letter)
6 to; for (apologise to someone for something)

3 **1** from – change from old to new
2 of/about – dream of/about (doing) something
3 about – wonder about doing something (N.B wonder *if* before yes/no choice)
4 at – aim at – target
5 for – pay money to someone for something
6 on – depend on someone/something
7 to/with – compare something to something
8 in – located in
9 to – look forward to something (phrasal verb)
10 to – object to (doing) something
11 with – crowded with
12 at – stare at something

4 **1** a – looked (deliberate); seen (not deliberate)
b – watch
2 a – stare (long fixed look)
b – peered (difficult to see)
c – gazed (interesting)
3 a – listened; (deliberate), hear (not deliberate)
b – listen (deliberate)
c – hear (deliberate)
4 a – feel; touching
b – watch
c – touch

Teacher's Resource Book Module 10 Test: How much do you remember? p.190

1 1 C; 2 D; 3 A; 4 B; 5 C

2 1 It; 2 about/high; 3 had; 4 of; 5 in

3 1 clubbing; 2 unexpected; 3 unrealistic; 4 hesitation; 5 resigned

4 1 You will *be shown some pictures by* the examiner.
2 People *asking/who ask questions make Nigel* nervous.
3 I *would rather you had told* me earlier.
4 Someone *is thought to have been* rescued.
5 If *only my girlfriend would call* me tonight.

Teacher's Resource Book Exam practice 5 pp.191–192

Paper 2 Writing

1 Style:
Formal report style with headings.
Content:
Talk about the economic situation in your country.
Say how easy it is for young people to get jobs – give examples.
Describe the career opportunities open to young people, mentioning qualifications needed, recruitment methods, competition for jobs, etc.

2 Style:
Formal.
Content:
Talk about public transport in your country.
Discuss the advantages and disadvantages of using public transport. Mention other reasons why people use public transport.
Say whether you agree with the statement and why (not).

3 Style:
Informal.
Content:
Tell your friend about the weather and give an idea of what activities you could do, and what to bring for them.
Tell your friend the sort of gift that would be appropriate, or you may prefer to say that it is not necessary to bring a gift.

4 Style:
Neutral/semi-formal.
Content:
Talk about the advantages and disadvantages of zoos in general – mention education, endangered species, conditions in which animals live, etc.
Talk about whether zoos should be in city centres, mentioning any alternatives.
Give your opinion and your reasons.

Paper 4 Listening

Part 3 1 E; 2 C; 3 B; 4 F; 5 A

Module 11 Well-being

Module 11 includes topics such as what makes people happy, the Queen Mother, relaxation, avoiding stress, diet, health and retail therapy.

To set the ball rolling ...

With books closed, ask students what they do to make themselves feel good. You could give one or two examples of your own to get them started, e.g. go for a walk, have a big cream cake ...!

Lead-in p.149

Elicit the meaning of the module title, 'Well-being' – a feeling of being healthy, happy and comfortable with life. Then get students to discuss the questions.

If you think it necessary, you could do an example of your own for the second and third questions. Choose three of the photos yourself and start explaining how they are related. Then give a brief example of what is most important to your well-being.

Module 11A Happiness

···
Photocopiable activity

Photocopiable activity 11A (p. 167) can be used at the start of the unit to introduce the topic, or as a follow-up to the reading exercise. It is a group discussion on factors in life that affect happiness.
···

Reading pp.150–151

1a Students discuss the questions in pairs. It's usually said that an optimist will describe the glass as half full, whereas a pessimist will describe it as half empty.

1b If students have already done the photocopiable activity, their answers from it would be relevant to question 1. Question 2 implies that when you know the secrets, it is possible to control happiness.

2 Give students a couple of minutes to do this, then go through it with them.

3 Pre-teach *temperament* – the emotional part of someone's character, how likely they are to be happy, angry, etc. Give students about 15 minutes to do the task. Then get them to compare which parts of the text helped them.

5a Point out that these words are all used in the text, either as nouns or adjectives.

5b Give one or two examples of your own to get students started. Let them choose which emotions they want to discuss, as they may not want to discuss unhappy experiences.

▶ **Student's Resource Book page 102**

Language development 1 pp.152–153

With books closed, put the class into groups and see which group is first to come up with a specified number of ways to relax (e.g. five to ten).

1a Give prompts if necessary to encourage ideas: How do you relax at the weekend?/at home?/with friends?/after a long day at work?

1b Ask students if they recognise the woman in the photo. If so, what do they know about her? They then read the extracts.

Background

Elizabeth Bowes-Lyon was born in 1900, the ninth of ten children. She married Prince Albert, the second son of King George V in 1923 and would have enjoyed a quiet life. However, in 1937 Albert's brother Edward, who had been king for less than a year, abdicated so Albert was unexpectedly crowned king, becoming George VI with Elizabeth becoming his queen.
In 1952 her husband died unexpectedly and her daughter Elizabeth became queen. The older Elizabeth became The Queen Mother and was later nicknamed 'The nation's favourite grandmother'. She was said to love breeding horses, watching racing and keeping corgis, a breed of small dog.

1c Begin by eliciting the function of the expressions in italics in the text extracts: Ask *What do the expressions explain?* – the reason for something. Tell students that the six expressions operate in three different ways grammatically. Then look at sentence 1 as an example, and ask *What did Mark do?* – he left his job. *Why?* – because it was stressful. When you check students' answers, make sure they understand that *as, because, since* all operate in the same way, and so do *because of, due to, owing to*. But these last three can operate in two different ways, i.e. followed by a noun or *the fact that* + subject + verb.

2a Point out that there are three possible answers for each sentence, and students should list them all.

2b Here students need to think about the form that follows each expression.

3a Go through the box with students before they do the exercise. Point out that *in order that* and *so that* operate in the same way as each other, as do *in order to*, *so as* to and *to*. Highlight the use of *in case* to describe precautions, a way of being safe from something that might happen, and how it is followed by the present simple when referring to the future (e.g. *I'll take an umbrella in case it rains.*)

3b Remind students to look at what follows the options in italics, as that tells them what fits grammatically.

4 As you go through the box, draw students' attention to *despite* (one word) and *in spite of* (three words) which are often confused.

5 This exercise practises all three types of clause: reason, purpose, contrast. Tell students that for each one they should identify the type of clause first, then think of a logical ending.

Photocopiable activity

Photocopiable activity 11B (p. 168) could be used here. It is a card game in which students use the three types of clause to make sentences about themselves from prompts.

▶ Student's Resource Book page 103

Writing pp.154–155

1 With books closed, write *polite* on the board. Ask students what it means for them and ask them to give examples of polite behaviour before going on to discuss the question in the book.

2 This question encourages students to read the task carefully and helps them focus on the attitude of the writer. Ask them to say where in the task they found the answer.

3a/b Students should be well practised in planning letters now, so you could either give them ten minutes to start planning the letter then compare what they have done, or elicit what they need to do to plan the letter and then let them do it.

4 First get students to read the letter and comment on content, organisation and style. Elicit that the content and organisation are good, but the style is too informal.

6 Encourage students to produce a checklist from memory first, then check the Writing reference on page 197–198 if necessary.

LANGUAGE SPOT: attitude phrases

This practises a number of phrases that can be used in this type of writing. As you check answers, make sure they know the meaning of the alternatives.

▶ Student's Resource Book page 105

Module 11A Key

Reading pp.150–151
2 1 Having the right genes, contentment, giving and receiving affection, mental and physical activity.
    2 Yes

3 1 D (*someone else with more than you, so trying to compete* links to *try to keep up with others* in lines 15–16; *frustration and anxiety* links to *dissatisfied* in line 17).
    2 F (*this is just a temporary state* links to *a level we always return to, whatever happens to us in life* in lines 23–24)
    3 C (*The latter* links to *their character* in line 29. This contrasts with *The former* line 29)
    4 B (*Such people* links to *happy people* in line 33; *They* also … in line 34)
    5 A (*being part of a social group* links to *tend to relate to other people* in line 39; *a community or a club* links to *sports teams, choirs, political parties* in lines 41–42.
    6 E (*To avoid this* links to *stress results in unhappiness* in line 50; *it is important to pick a sport* links to *But mental activity can be just as important* in line 51)
    7 G (*The key* links to *to recognise happiness* in lines 52–53; *learning to celebrate them* links to *One way of doing this* … in line 54)

5a 1 contented; 2 satisfied; 3 frustrated;
    4 anxious; 5 depressed; 6 stressed; 7 miserable

Language development 1 pp.152–153
1b 1 being happy
    2 kept dogs, watched horse racing, went fishing, listened to bagpipe music, gardening
1c 1 as, because, since
    2 because of, due to, owing to
    3 because of, due to, owing to

2a 1 as, because, since
    2 because of, due to, owing to
    3 because of, due to, owing to
    4 as, because, since
    5 Because of, Due to, Owing to
    6 because of, due to, owing to
2b 1 a was snowing
    b the snow/the fact that it was snowing
    c the snow/the fact that it was snowing
    2 a was raining
    b the rain/the fact that it was raining
    c it was raining

3a 1 in order to, so as to, to (+ verb)
2 in order that, so that (+ subject + verb)
3 in case (+ subject + verb)

3b 1 to (+ verb)
2 in case (precaution)
3 so that (+ subject + verb)
4 in order to (+ verb)
5 In order that (+ subject + verb)
6 in case (precaution)
7 so as to (+ verb)
8 so as not to (+ verb)

4 1 e – contrasting but not contradicting
2 c – *despite* + *-ing*
3 h – *although* + subject + verb (very active + not feeling well)
4 a – *even though* + subject + verb (not getting better + appetite returned)
5 g – *despite* + noun
6 b – *in spite of the fact that* + subject + verb
7 f – contrasting but not contradicting
8 d – *in spite of* + *-ing*

5 Example answers:
1 … I have tried many times/ways. Contrast.
2 … the noise of the cats outside. Reason.
3 … he knows where to pick me up. Purpose.
4 … the glorious spring sunshine … . Contrast.
5 … find out whether they open on Sundays. Purpose.
6 … the fact that we reminded him to take it. Contrast.

Writing pp.154–155

2 An older person (When we were young …)

3a 1 Most young people are polite.
2 Children have always been noisy.
3 I've seen old people get aggressive and impatient.
Points 1 and 2, or 1 and 3 could be grouped together.

3b Example answer:
Paragraph 1: Introduction; reason for writing
Paragraph 2: Points 1 and 2
Paragraph 3: Point 3
Paragraph 4: Conclusion

4 I am writing in response to the letter about young people's behaviour in last week's *Courier*. I have to disagree with the points the writer makes.
Firstly, it is simply not true that all young people are noisy and aggressive. In my experience, most young people are polite.
I also disagree with the generalisations about younger and older people. Children are no noisier today than they used to be. They have always had to play. And do you really think

older people are more polite? I have seen older people being aggressive and impatient in shops, for example.
In conclusion, while we should all have consideration for others, I think we should all try to be more patient and tolerant of each other. We were all young once!

5 Sample answer:

Dear Sir or Madam,

I am writing in response to the letter in today's newspaper about young people and the way they behave. Some of the points the writer makes are simply ridiculous.

Firstly, I cannot accept that young people today are noisier than in the past. Young children like to play and have always been like that.

It is also unfair to say that all young people are aggressive. Most are polite and friendly. It might be true that a few young people get aggressive at times because of the pressures they face but the same is true for older people. I have seen them lose their patience and temper in shops.

In conclusion, we should all realise that we were all children once. It is the world that has changed, not young people.

Yours faithfully,

(136 words)

LANGUAGE SPOT: attitude phrases

1 To be honest – What I really think is (As far as I know = I may be wrong but I think it's true that …)
2 Presumably – I imagine (Actually = I know this is true)
3 As a matter of fact – polite contradiction (Clearly = it is evident that; Naturally = Of course)
4 Certainly – I accept the fact that (Frankly = What I really think is; Surely = I don't know but I imagine it must be true that)
5 Generally speaking – as a generalisation (Roughly speaking = approximately; Strictly speaking = If we follow the rules exactly)
6 Admittedly – I admit this is true (In my opinion = I think; At least = As a minimum)
7 As far as I'm concerned – In my opinion (According to me = The facts as I have explained them are that)
8 Personally – in my opinion (Truly = honestly; In person = Not by letter or on the phone)

Module 11B Health and fitness

Module 11B continues the theme of 'Well-being' with the topics of health and fitness.

To set the ball rolling ...

Ask students how healthy they think their lifestyle is on a scale of 1–10. Ask them how healthy they were a few years ago, and how healthy they think they will be in ten years' time. What has changed, and what do they think will change?

> **Photocopiable activity**
>
> Photocopiable activity 11C (p. 169) is designed to be a lead-in to the unit and to pre-teach some of the vocabulary. It is a light-hearted questionnaire in which students find out how healthy they are.

Listening pp.156–157

1 Students describe their exercise habits in small groups. You could add a question asking if they take as much exercise as they would like to or think they should.

2a Check vocabulary in the quiz with the whole class before students do it in pairs.

3 The exercise gives further practice of prepositions. Establish why the preposition is needed in each case. (1 – after a comparative; 2 – after an adjective; 3 – part of a phrasal verb; 4 – after a verb.) Students may need dictionaries for some of the vocabulary (e.g. *saturated/polyunsaturated fats, itch, dehydrated*).

Background

Saturated fats come from meat and milk products and tend to be solid at room temperature. Unsaturated fats come from plants and fish and tend to be liquid at room temperature. Unsaturated fats are healthier.

4 Ask students if they consider their diet to be balanced and why.

5a It would be better not to refer to the pictures too specifically as it will influence the listening later. The diseases don't have to be the most deadly (e.g. malaria) but include those that are widespread (e.g. cholera, hepatitis, sleeping sickness, influenza, pneumonia).

Background

Approximately half of all deaths caused by infectious diseases each year can be attributed to just three diseases: tuberculosis, malaria, and AIDS. Together these diseases cause over 300 million illnesses and more than 5 million deaths each year.

5b Remind students that, before they listen, they should try and guess what type of information might be missing, based on the context. E.g. in question 2 the missing word is a noun (after *of*), the quality of which affects our health.

6 Conduct the listening as in the exam, playing it twice without pausing before students compare their answers.

8 If students need help with ideas, tell them to think of foods that are popular in different countries (e.g. for carbohydrates: pasta, rice, bread, potato, couscous, etc.).

Speaking p.158

1a First ask students what they remember about Paper 5 Parts 3 and 4.

1b Get examples of how to continue each expression (e.g. *Why don't we start by ... + -ing*).

2 Divide the class into suitable groups. The examiners need to read the rubric on page 214. If possible it would be good to record one or more of the groups doing the task now that they are more familiar with the format and the exam is getting closer, then play it back when students do the analysis at the end.

3a To ensure that all students have an opportunity to practise, you could tell students to change roles after every two questions.

3b Students should discuss their own performance and that of other members of their group. Encourage them to be constructive.

▶ **Student's Resource Book page 107**

Language development 2 p.159

1a With books closed, you could introduce the language point by writing on the board:

My problem is that I eat ...... much chocolate. It's ...... nice that I can't say 'No'. I don't have ...... will power to stop and it's costing me ...... a lot of money!

Ask students to think of the missing words (*too, so, enough, such*) and explain why. Then get them to look at the grammar box. Highlight the fact that *enough* is used before nouns and after adjectives, as confusing them is a common mistake with some students at FCE.

2 Students should do this in pairs, then refer back to the grammar boxes to check.

3 *As* and *like* are commonly confused by some students, partly because they both translate as the same word in some languages, and partly because of the number of different uses of *like*. Go through the examples in the box with students.

4 When students have completed the exercise, ask them if they would like to do something similar.

▶ **Student's Resource Book page 108**

Use of English 1 p.160

1a Get students to discuss the question in pairs first.

1b Students discuss this in pairs. As you go through it with them, elicit what has led to the mistakes in each case, and how they could have been avoided by following the instructions and checking carefully.

2a Students should be able to do this without too much help from the task strategy.

2b Use the analysis to highlight any areas that need revision.

Use of English 2 p.161

1 Ask the students to describe the person in the photo and how they are feeling and if they feel the same way about shopping.

2a Remind students that they should always read the text for a general understanding first, and tell them that these questions are to help focus their reading.

2b Set them a time limit of 8 minutes to do the exercise.

3 The discussion brings in other domestic activities/ chores that might be beneficial such as gardening, taking the dogs for a walk, vacuuming, ironing.

Language development 3 p.162

Look The topic of health is rich in idiomatic expressions and phrasal verbs. You could begin with books closed, brainstorming any words or phrases students already know. Then get them to do the task in the box.

1a First get students to read the text and answer the question: *Is George now more or less healthy than he used to be?* (more). Then you could do the first one with them as an example, so that they can see how the exercise works. Draw students' attention to the image of the human body as a piece of electrical equipment, with expressions like *run-down, recharge his batteries, still going strong*.

1b If possible, show students how the expressions are found in the dictionary and that if they look up an expression under one word, they might be directed to another word where the expression is listed. Point out that some of the expressions (e.g. *recharge your batteries*) appear in two places in the dictionary.

2a If students are unsure of any of the phrasal verbs, get them to use dictionaries.

3 This is an opportunity for personalised discussion. When students have finished, you could get them to think of more questions to ask each other, using both the idiomatic expressions and phrasal verbs on the page.

▶ **Module 11 Test: How much do you remember? TRB page 193**

Module 11B Key

Listening pp.156–157

2a Health Quiz –

3a Flu: headache, aching muscles, fever, cough, sneezing
Food poisoning: feeling sick, vomiting, diarrhoea, stomach cramps

3b arthritis – joints; migraine – head;
bronchitis – chest; tonsillitis – throat.

4 1 True; 2 False (but there are very few);
3 True; 4 False; 5 True

3 1 for (better for you); 2 to (be allergic / have an allergy to); 3 without (to go without something); 4 from (recover from something)

5b 2 noun – variable quality
3 noun – a group of people
4 number or quantity
5 adjective – describes people (positive)
6 noun – links to diet
7 noun – related to health
8 noun – type of drink
9 noun – countable food
10 noun – event

6 2 school dinners
3 prisoners
4 two thirds
5 long-living
6 mental health
7 memories
8 red wine
9 snacks
10 main meal

Speaking p.158

1a 1 F – they speak **together** for about 3 minutes.
2 T – e.g. discuss and choose
3 F – it should be an open discussion – expressing your ideas is more important than agreeing.
4 T – probably between three and six questions will be asked, between the two candidates.
5 F – you should develop your answers beyond a simple 'yes' or 'no'.
6 T – the examiner may ask you to respond to something the other candidate says.

1b 1 b; 2 c; 3 d; 4 a; 5 f; 6 e

Language development 2 p.159

1a 1 so – e.g. so difficult, so many, so fast
2 such – e.g. such bad behaviour
3 such, a – e.g. such a nice person

1b 1 noun (e.g. enough sleep); adjective (e.g. warm enough)
2 1c (e.g. too much, too expensive), 2a (e.g. very tired), 3b (e.g. enough sleep)

2 1 Jim's ~~so~~ *such* a good doctor that everybody likes him.
2 My yoga class is great; I'm always ~~too~~ *so* relaxed afterwards.
3 Paul has bought such ~~an~~ expensive fitness equipment! (uncountable)
4 The food is too spicy for me to eat ~~it~~.
5 ~~The~~ *There aren't enough* vegetables in your diet ~~aren't enough~~.
6 I'm ~~very~~ *too* tired to go jogging now.
7 John is so unfit ~~so~~ *(that)* he can't even run for a bus.
8 ~~The~~ *There isn't enough* money ~~isn't enough~~ for us to buy a drink.
9 You should be pleased with yourself for losing so *much* weight.
10 I'm not *old* enough ~~old for~~ to join that club.

3 1 like/such as – example
2 as – role/function
3 like – *sound* + *like*
4 like/such as – example
5 as if/as though – *look* + clause
6 As – *as* + clause

4 1 as; 2 like; 3 As; 4 like/such as; 5 like; 6 as

Use of English 1 p.160

1b 1 meeting my wife for **the** – article needed before *first time*
2 in case ~~of~~ the tickets are – *in case of* + noun, *in case* + subject + verb. Six words in the answer should have alerted the candidate to the mistake.
3 was ~~too~~ *so* tired (that) he – *too tired* + *to, so tired* + *that*
4 as long as we ~~will~~ arrive – *as long as* + present when referring to future time. Again, six words in the answer should have alerted the candidate to the mistake.

2a 1 I get back to you
2 put you up
3 weren't/wasn't so hot we
4 such a delicious
5 Judy whether she wanted
6 isn't enough room/space
7 n't/not like Tom to be
8 is not so/as popular as

Use of English 2 p.161

2a **1** shopping for fun
2 when it becomes an addiction
3 it gives exercise
2b **1** B
2 D – in the long term = over a long period of time
3 A – first step towards = progress
4 B – hardly = not
5 A – research shows results
6 D – is recognised as
7 B – be estimated that
8 C
9 C
10 A – people tend to do something = usually
11 D – the root of all ... = the origin/source
12 B – provided = if

Language development 3 p.162
LOOK

1a **1** middle-aged; **2** unwell; **3** didn't want to eat;
4 was very tired; **5** get back his energy; **6** was physically fit; **7** healthy; **8** fit and healthy

2a **1** put on; **2** cut down on; cut out; **3** picked up;
4 give up; **5** coming down with; get over;
6 take up
2b **1** 6; **2** 4; **3** 5; **4** 2; **5** 1; **6** 3

Teacher's Resource Book
Module 11 Test: How much do you remember? p. 193

1 **1** B; **2** D; **3** A; **4** C; **5** A

2 **1** in; **2** off; **3** as, **4** case; **5** such

3 **1** anxiety; **2** financially; **3** laughter; **4** healthier;
5 frustration

4 **1** These shoes *are not big enough* for my feet.
2 There were *such a lot of* people there that Ellen couldn't get in.
3 It looks *as if England are going* to win, they're 3–0 up.
4 Neil can't get a job *in spite of the fact* that he did well at university.
5 It *smells as if lunch is* ready.

Module 12 Getting your message across

Module 12 includes an extract from a novel, ways of connecting ideas, describing fiction, an interview with a journalist, advertising, celebrities, paparazzi and spin doctors (political advisers).

To set the ball rolling ...

With books closed, brainstorm ways in which we receive information, e.g. newspapers, magazines, TV, radio, books, post, Internet, email, phone, text messages, advertising, direct mail and speech.

Lead-in p.163

Get students to look at the photos and discuss the questions. Tell them that there are no hard and fast answers for the second question. You might want to discuss one or two of the photos with the class to give them an idea of the kind of answers required. Some examples of what students might come up with: Email: to communicate about work and with friends; Books: to inform, entertain or educate; Magazines: mainly to entertain, also sometimes to inform; Billboard advertising: to advertise and promote products; TV: to inform and entertain; Newspapers: to inform.

Module 12A Bookworm

To set the ball rolling ...

With books closed, you could put students into groups and see how many types of book they can think of in three minutes, or get them to draw two columns, headed 'fiction' and 'non-fiction', and write the genres into the correct column as you dictate them. Then they discuss the differences between the genres.

Fiction	Non-fiction
novels, horror, romance, short stories, crime/thrillers, contemporary, historical, best seller, blockbuster, science fiction, adventure, classics, children's, etc.	biography, autobiography, history, science, travel, sport, art, food and drink, health, philosophy, home and garden, etc.

Reading pp.165–166

1a Get students to expand with examples of what they have read recently or what they are reading at the moment.

1b Elicit as much as you can from the book cover and ask if anyone has read the book or seen the film.

Background

Patricia Highsmith's crime thriller *The Talented Mr Ripley* was first published in 1956. The 1999 film was directed by Anthony Minghella. Tom Ripley, a poor young man, pretends that he is a friend of Dickie Greenleaf, a spoilt millionaire playboy who has gone to Italy. Dickie's father offers Tom money to convince Dickie to come home but when the errand fails, Tom kills Dickie and assumes his privileged life.

2 When students have skimmed the article (give them a minute or two), discuss the question.

3a/b Give students 15 minutes to complete the task and then let them compare their answers, explaining where they found them in the text.

4a Put students into groups to discuss the questions. Ask anyone that has read the book or seen the film not to 'give the game away' until others have expressed their opinions. Encourage students to give reasons for their answers.

4b In the set book option of Paper 2, students may be asked a question like this. You could specify a number of advantages and disadvantages that each group should think of, or you could get some groups to think of just the advantages and others to think of just the disadvantages and then compare.

Remind students to give examples of films that they have seen which were based on books.

5a If appropriate, use the list of words to revise pronunciation of stress patterns, e.g. comparing *enthusi'astic* with *en'thusiasm*.

5b If students can't guess the meanings, get them to look up the words in a dictionary, deciding each time what the key word is.

Photocopiable activity

Photocopiable activity 12A (p. 170) could be used here. Students write a story based on a series of pictures.

▶ **Student's Resource Book pages 112–113**

Language development 1 pp.166–167

1b This revises different ways of connecting ideas covered earlier in the book. Get students to compare their answers before you go through them with the whole class.

2 Students should discuss the sentences in pairs and then use the table in 1b to check their answers.

3 When students have looked at the information in the box, elicit why it might be useful to make sentences shorter, e.g. to make your writing more interesting, to give it more impact, to reduce repetition. For each sentence, students need to identify whether both parts of the sentence occur at the same time or one occurs earlier, and whether the sentence is active or passive. Do the first one together as an example.

4 For each group of sentences, students should produce one longer sentence using the connecting devices given in brackets. Look at the example together to show how it has been constructed: the first sentence is reduced to a participle clause – *Written by a woma*n – and combined with the second using a relative pronoun – *who has lived in India for many years,* – resulting in some small changes to the third sentence – *the book tells us a lot about India.* If you think students are not too confident with this, do question 2 with them, then get them to work in pairs, and check their answers as they complete each one.

Background

The author of *Heat and Dust*, Ruth Prawer Jhabvala, was born in Germany in 1924. She emigrated to England and went to university in London. She moved to India in 1951 after marrying an Indian architect, and since then has written many novels set in India. She wrote *Heat and Dust* in 1975, and in 1983 the famous producer–director partnership of Ismail Merchant and James Ivory made it into a film with Prawer Jhabvala writing the screenplay.

Photocopiable activity

Photocopiable activity 12B (p. 171) would work well here. Students use a variety of connecting words and phrases to tell a story, working towards a specified ending.

▶ **Student's Resource Book page 113**

Writing pp.168–169

The book question in Paper 2 is an optional question for those students that have read one of the set books. If students have time to prepare for the question, it will give them an alternative choice in the exam. Naturally students should not attempt the question if they have not read any of the set books! A list of set texts is available from Cambridge ESOL (www.cambridgeesol.org/exams/fce).

1 If students have read different books get them to discuss all three questions. If they have all read the same book they should just discuss question 3.

2 Although students are writing about a set book, it is important in the exam that they establish what sort of writing is required. They will still need to follow the style and conventions of that sort of writing.

3a You could group students who have decided to do the same writing task and get them to do the preparation together. Alternatively, you could ask the whole class to focus on one of the tasks in this lesson, and set the other task in a subsequent lesson or for homework.

3b As students do this, monitor and check that they are just writing notes rather than whole sentences, and that the notes relate to the question.

4a You could work through this together with students, checking understanding where necessary, or they could do it in pairs or with dictionaries to help with meaning.

4b Limit this activity, either by specifying how long students have to think of other adjectives, or how many they should think of in each category. Once they have thought of some words, they could ask others to decide if they are positive or negative.

4c Go through these with the whole class, focusing on what type of word or clause could come next, e.g. *This is a story about* + a/the person/time/place who/when/where … . *It is set in* + time/place.

6 Remind students of the checklist to use when checking their work. They also refer to the checklist in the Writing reference on page 196.

LANGUAGE SPOT: avoiding repetition

Start by giving students an example of language with a lot of repetition in it, to show them why it is important to avoid, e.g. *Mike writes stories about a group of teenagers. The teenagers in Mike's stories live in a big city. The teenagers have a lot of problems in the city. Mike writes about the problems the teenagers have in the city and how the teenagers overcome the problems of city life.*

▶ **Student's Resource Book page 115**

Module 12A Key

Reading pp.164–165

2   It is a crime thriller.

3a/b **1** B – see highlighted text
2 A (*He had offered Dickie friendship, companionship and respect … and Dickie had replied with ingratitude and now hostility.*) (ll. 24–27)
3 D (*… receive Dickie's cheque every month and forge Dickie's signature on it.*) (ll. 36–37)
4 C (*The danger of it … only made him more enthusiastic.*) (ll. 40–42)
5 A
6 B (*… the only way to keep Dickie from seeing what must have been a very strange expression on his face.*) (ll. 63–64)
7 C

5a   Nouns: impatience, frustration, anger, disappointment, impulse, shame, failing, friendship, companionship, respect, ingratitude, hostility, irritation, attention, rudeness
Adjectives: enthusiastic, ashamed, amused

5b   **1** *It crossed Tom's mind* – he thought – the idea came into his mind suddenly for a short time.
2 *shoving him out in the cold* – rejecting/abandoning him
3 *step right into Dickie's shoes* – become Dickie – to adopt the life and position that Dickie had
4 *eating out of his hand* – having control over – getting him to do exactly as he wanted

Language development 1 pp.166–167

1a   **1** To find out more about the American way of life.
2 The humour. Not knowing anything about the USA before reading it.
3 Because they're too tired to look for a hotel.

1b   **a** in order to; **b** As; **c** before; **d** If; **e** who;
f While; **g** and; **h** because; **i** When;
j so … that; **k** However
1 who; **2** While; **3** before; **4** before; **5** so … that; **6** If …; **7** and; **8** However; **9** in order to;
10 As; **11** Because

2   **1** The part ~~what~~ **(that)** I liked best was the ending.
2 The main character is an old man who ~~he~~ has never left his home town.
3 It was ~~a~~ such a good book that I couldn't stop reading it.
4 ~~During~~ **While** the police look for the main suspect, Holmes makes other enquiries./During the police **search** …
5 It is set in a town where there are a lot of factories ~~in~~.

6 It can be helpful to see the film before ~~to~~ read*ing*/*you read* the book in English.
7 If you ~~will~~ like science fiction, you'll probably like this book.
8 It is a good story ~~despite~~ **but** the main character is not very realistic.
9 The police are called in ~~for~~ **to** investigate the theft of a painting.
10 I didn't like the ending because ~~of~~ I thought it was disappointing.

3   **1** Being – same time
2 Writing – same time
3 Having experienced – earlier
4 criticised – passive
5 having had – earlier
6 Having read – earlier
7 completely satisfied – past participle as adjective

4   **2** It is about a young English woman who goes to India with her child because she wants to find out the true story of her grandmother.
3 Her English grandparents lived in India together, but her grandmother fell in love with an Indian man.
4 Having arrived there, she starts to follow the same life path as her grandmother when she falls in love with an Indian.
5 Being set in two periods and telling two women's similar stories, it shows that lifestyles and attitudes change a lot over two generations, but love and relationships never change.

Writing pp.168–169

2   (a) a discursive composition
(b) an informal letter to a friend, containing a review

3a   **2** (a) mainly plot; (b) mainly plot and characters

4a   **Possible answers:**
Characters: lifelike P, weak N, passionate P, imaginative P, brave P, lovely P, successful P, interesting P, convincing P, funny P, clever P, attractive P, boring N, sensitive P/N
Events: lifelike P, weak N, unexpected P, predictable N, disappointing N, successful P, interesting P, convincing P, funny P, boring N, awful N
Setting (place): imaginative P, lovely P, interesting P, attractive P

5 Sample answer:

> *Dear Mohammed*
>
> *Thanks for your letter. Sorry I haven't replied before but I've been busy at work. You asked if I could think of a good book for your dad's birthday. I recommend the book that I have just read.*
>
> *It's called 'Animal Farm' and it was written by George Orwell. It is set on a farm where the animals get rid of the owner and take over, but it's really a story about communism.*
>
> *The story isn't exciting but it's clever. At first, after the revolution, the animals are equal but later the pigs become more powerful and start to change everything. By the end, the animals realise they have gone back to where they started.*
>
> *The characters are very convincing. Napoleon, the leader of the pigs, is strong and corrupt. Other animals are honest but weak. They all represent people or things in Russia in the 1920s and 30s.*
>
> *So if your father likes history and politics, I am sure he will like this book.*
>
> *Best wishes*
>
> *Fernando*

(170 words)

LANGUAGE SPOT: avoiding repetition

a   does = writes stories
he = Mike
done so = written stories
ones = stories
them = the stories
so = you have read any of the stories
them = the stories
not = you haven't read any of the stories
some = some of the stories

b   **1** so; **2** do so; **3** ones; **4** did; **5** not; **6** one;
7 some

Module 12B The media

The module continues the theme of 'Getting your message across' with topics such as journalism, advertising, paparazzi, and government special advisers.

To set the ball rolling ...

If your students are from the same country, ask them if they think you can tell what type of person reads each type of paper, or if you can say what someone is like from the paper they read. If your students are from different countries, get them to talk about newspapers in their countries with questions such as *Are there different types of newspaper? Which types are most popular? Do people buy a lot of newspapers? What type of news stories do they mostly contain?* You might need to pre-teach words such as *national, local, domestic, international, tabloid, broadsheet.*

Speaking pp.170–171

Here students practise a complete Paper 5, although they will have to rotate the role of examiner at each stage. If students know who their partner will be for the exam and they are in the class, it would obviously be sensible for them to work together. If possible, it would be useful to record some of the students at each stage and use the recording for whole class feedback.

1a Use local examples to check understanding of *tabloid* and *broadsheet*, which refer as much to editorial policy as to the size of the paper.

1b Use the pictures or a real paper.

1c If students don't read newspapers, it can be hard for them to distinguish between the three types of writer.

1d Draw students' attention to the collocations highlighted (e.g. *hit the headlines, meet a deadline, glossy magazines*).

2a Encourage students to build a lexical set of newspaper related words with word families developed as fully as possible with pronunciation and stresses marked (e.g. *edit, editor, editorial*, etc.).

3 If students say that adverts / advertisements have little influence on what they buy, ask them why advertisers spend so much money on advertising.

4a Give the 'examiners' a moment to look at the questions first.

5a/b Remind students to keep an eye on the time while their partner is speaking, and stop them after approximately 1 minute.

6b Again, students need to watch the time. They should stop after approximately 3 minutes.

7 Remind students to expand their answers, e.g. in question 2 the answer *No* is not enough; if students don't drive, they should say why, or what they do instead.

▶ **Student's Resource Book page 117**

Listening p.172

1a You could also ask 'Which is the most important part of the paper for you?' or 'Which part do you read first?'

1b Remind students of the importance of reading only the questions at first. The discussion questions here help focus students on that.

2 You could elicit the strategy before students listen.

3 Possible further questions: *Do you know any journalists? What qualities do they have?*

Use of English 1 p.173

1 This exercise should serve as a reminder of the task. Get students to discuss it in pairs, and give reasons for their answers.

2a As always, students should skim the text first. Give them no more than 30 seconds.

2b Give the students no more than 10 minutes to do the task and then some time to compare their answers.

3 Possible further question: *Should advertising be aimed at children?*

Language development 2 p.174

LOOK With books closed, you could begin by writing on the board *The board/classroom is messy.* Elicit and write on the board *Someone needs to clean it.* Then move *it* to the start of a new sentence to elicit *It needs cleaning/It needs to be cleaned.* Then students read the grammar box and complete the task.

1a Get students to check their answers together.

1b You could elicit what needs doing just from the picture, before students look at the prompt sentences. After completing the exercise, they could talk about what needs doing in the room/building where they are studying.

2a It might be necessary to check some of the vocabulary – *install, blunt, sharpen* – before students begin the exercise.

2b When students have done this exercise, ask them to think of other examples of people/places we go to in order to have something done.

2c Introduce the expression *DIY* (do-it-yourself) and ask students if they are keen on it. Then get them to discuss the points, giving reasons for their answers and saying where they have something done/who they have it done by, and explaining.

3 Give students a few minutes' preparation time before they discuss the questions in groups. The discussion could be extended by asking what other things they would like to have done for them.

▶ **Student's Resource Book page 118**

Use of English 2 p.175

1 This is a reminder of the basic strategy for Paper 3 Part 3. Get students to discuss the questions in pairs first, giving reasons for their answers.

2a

Background

Paparazzi are photographers (and writers) that follow celebrities in the hope of getting a story. The word comes from a character called Paparazzo, a photographer in Fellini's 1960 Italian film *La Dolce Vita*, which is all about celebrities, rich people and their parties.

2b Remind students that, as well as making grammatical changes, they may need to alter the word to fit the meaning of the sentence.

3a When students have skimmed the text and answered the questions, you could ask them if they are aware of the role of special advisers in their country and if they think they have too much power/influence. In the UK, they are also known as 'spin doctors' as one of their roles is to put a positive spin (a positive/favourable appearance) on to news and information.

4 If students are interested in politics, give them some questions to discuss such as
Do you think politicians should present information in the best possible light?
Do you believe what politicians in your country / other countries say?
Should journalists be free to say what they like?
Introduce ideas such as censorship, privacy, security and sensitivity.

Photocopiable activity

Photocopiable activity 12C (pp. 172–173) could be used here or at the end of the unit. It is a grammar auction revising common mistakes at FCE level.

Language development 3 p.176

1a Complete the first part together. The noun *responsibility* was needed in Word formation (B) on page 175.

1b This exercise focuses on words that exist in all four forms. It might be useful to point out to students that not all words are so varied. When students have completed the table, get them to highlight the endings that are used to form the various words.

1c Remind students that Use of English word formation texts are likely to include a number of negative prefixes. When students have completed the exercise, get them to identify patterns, e.g. *il-* before adjectives starting with *l*, *ir-* before *r*, *im-* before *p*, *un-* for adjectives ending in *-ic*, *in-* for adjectives ending in *-ate*, but point out that there are always exceptions!

1d In each sentence, students first need to identify which word is needed, then the form. Do the first sentence together as an example.

2 Here again, students should think about both the word needed and the form. Start by checking that students know the form of the words given, e.g. *use* – noun and verb, *lonely* – adjective.

3a Get students to focus on the clues that tell them what type of word is needed in each case.

▶ **Module 12 Test: How much do you remember? TRB page 194**

▶ **Exam practice 6: Papers 2 and 4 TRB pages 195–196**

Module 12B Key

Speaking pp.170–171

1c a foreign correspondent – lives in the country and reports with specialised in-depth local knowledge; crime reporter – researches and writes facts of the incident; columnist – writes regular articles, especially about a particular subject or with personal opinion, for a newspaper/magazine

1d 1 hit (the headlines); 2 press (release); 3 meet (deadline), (went to) press; 4 (regular) features, (weather) forecasts; 5 glossy (magazines), (brand) names, promote, launch, grab (attention).

2a 1 daily, circulation, readership; 2 journalism, editorial; 3 commercials, advertising

Listening p.172

2 1 C (*It was my father who talked me into doing journalism.*)
2 B (*You had to follow a senior reporter around … He would … give you feedback.*)

3 A (*They were terribly suspicious of us at first …*)
4 C (*All the journalists sympathised with his situation and didn't want to spoil things for him.*)
5 A (*… this is not as important as having bags of energy and commitment.*)
6 B (*In my day, it was all going out and meeting people to get stories. Now it's much more office based.*)
7 B (*… as long as your family commitments aren't going to be a problem, given the long and unpredictable hours …*)

Use of English 1 p.173

1a 1 True – the answer might depend on the small differences in meanings between the words.
2 False – understanding of the whole text is vital.
3 True – the correct word might depend on the collocations

2a 1 a confident, masculine, attractive, young man
2 on the right hand side
3 the man is unmasculine and bookish

2b 1 B world of
2 A create an image
3 D nearly all = most
4 C make an impact
5 B short (length)
6 A supporting role
7 C recent
8 D the shape of something
9 B thick glasses
10 D merged with
11 A nevertheless = contrast
12 C appeal to someone

Language development 2 p.174

1a 1 It needs shortening/It needs to be shortened.
2 They need to be replaced/They need replacing.

1b 1 It needs tidying up.
2 It needs cutting.
3 They need watering.
4 It needs rebuilding.
5 They need cleaning.
6 They need repainting.

1c 1 First money needs to be raised.
2 Then the advert needs to be written.
3 A script needs to be prepared and brought to life.
4 A good production company needs to be found.
5 An experienced director needs to be hired.
6 Well-known actors need to be recruited.
7 The advert needs to be shot in a studio you can afford.

2a 2 've had it stolen.
   3 I'll/let's have/get it repaired.
   4 I've had them checked/I'll have to get/have them checked.
   5 we'll/let's have/get it installed.
   6 I'll have/get them sharpened.

2b Example answers:
   1 To have your teeth checked/a tooth removed.
   2 To have your eyes tested/some glasses made.
   3 To have your clothes cleaned.
   4 To have your hair cut.
   5 To have your nails done.
   6 To have your photo taken.
   7 To have a picture framed.
   8 To have your shopping delivered.

Use of English 2 p.175

1 1 Sentence by sentence, to get the complete sense of what is both before and after the gap.
   2 Leave any you can't do and come back to them. When you have completed the text, you may have a better idea of what is needed.

2a 1 Hire a helicopter to get close to their subjects.
   2 By saying the stars don't deserve privacy, as they court publicity when it suits them.

2b 1 growth – *a* + noun + *in*
   2 glamorous – adjective + noun (*celebrities*)
   3 embarrassing –pictures that embarrass them
   4 frighteningly – *a* + adverb + adjective (*large*)
   5 unbelievable – negative adjective + noun (*lengths*)
   6 dangerously – verb (*fly*) + adverb + adjective (*close*)
   7 annoyance – possessive adjective (*his or her*) + noun
   8 privacy – noun
   9 romantic – possessive (*their*) + adjective + noun (*weddings*)
   10 extraordinary – possessive (*their*) + adjective + noun (*homes*)

3a 1 People who help politicians present news in a positive light.
   2 They believe they reduce the freedom of the press.

3b 1 worrying – *a* + adjective + noun (*increase*)
   2 responsibility – *whose* + noun
   3 attention – possessive (*the public's*) + noun
   4 reporters – *tell* + someone
   5 powerful – *become very* + adjective
   6 memorable – adjective + noun (*sentences*)
   7 variety – *a* + noun + *of*
   8 political – adjective + noun (*parties*)
   9 arguments – *listen to* + (adjective) + noun
   10 freedom – *the* + noun + *of* + *the* + noun (*press*)

Language development 3 p.176

1a Negative adjective: irresponsible
   Noun: responsibility
   Adverb: responsibly

ADJECTIVE	ADVERB	NOUN	VERB
believable	believably	belief	believe
worrying	worryingly	worry	worry
embarrassing	embarrassingly	embarrassment	embarrass
recognisable	recognisably	recognition	recognise
amazing	amazingly	amazement	amaze
decisive	decisively	decision	decide
thoughtful/ thoughtless	thoughtfully/ thoughtlessly	thought	think
legal	legally	legality/law	legalise
satisfactory	satisfactorily	satisfaction	satisfy
astonishing/ astonished	astonishingly	astonishment	astonish

1c illegal; unsatisfactorily; unromantic; disappear; inaccurate; immoral; improbable; illogical; irregular; imperfectly

1d 1 irresponsible – negative adjective
   2 embarrassment – noun
   3 illogical/thoughtless – negative adjective
   4 illegal – negative adjective
   5 amazement/astonishment – noun
   6 thoughtful – adjective
   7 decisive – adjective
   8 inaccurate – negative adjective

2 1 better relationship
   2 absolutely useless
   3 became fashionable
   4 chance of survival

3a 1 professionally – adverb to describe verb (*produced*)
   2 entertaining – adjective after *quite* to describe something
   unreadable – negative adjective – contrast after *but*.
   3 generalise – verb after *had to*
   stimulating – adjective to describe noun (*articles*)
   4 admiration – noun after *have great*
   creative – adjective after *so*
   criticise – verb after *like to*
   unreliable – adjective after *a bit*, negative after *however*
   5 intelligence – noun after *my*
   relationships – noun after *the*, plural = in general
   boring – adjective after *be*, negative as linked with *offensive*
   offensive – adjective after *find them*

Teacher's Resource Book Module 12 Test: How much do you remember? p.194

1 1 D; 2 B; 3 B; 4 C; 5 D

2 1 whether; 2 Having; 3 of; 4 so (therefore); 5 had

3 1 historical; 2 sympathise; 3 journalism; 4 insecurity; 5 improbable

4 1 The chickens *need to/have to be fed* every day.
2 These instructions *are totally illogical, aren't* they?
3 I'm *having some new curtains made* for the bedroom.
4 I bought the book *in order to* give it to Kathy for her birthday.
5 Read *the book before seeing* the film.

Teacher's Resource Book Exam practice 6 pp.195–196

Paper 2 Writing
Style:
Informal.
Content:
Tell your friend about the good points (food, swimming pool, etc.) of the hotel.
Warn your friend about the things which were not so good.

Paper 4 Listening
Part 2 1 Seabird; 2 motor racing; 3 reliability; 4 autopilot; 5 weather; 6 tiredness; 7 93/ninety-three days; 8 relax; 9 jogging; 10 Across the Ocean

Coursebook Exam Practice: Reading (Paper 1) pp.216–221

Part 1
1 C; 2 D; 3 B; 4 C; 5 D; 6 A; 7 A; 8 C

Part 2
9 E; 10 H; 11 A; 12 B; 13 D; 14 F; 15 C

Part 3
16 B (*At first, the administrative side was a real struggle …*)
17 E (*… working for myself, rather than … working for someone else.*)
18 D (*Tom mainly reinvests his money*)
19 E (*she does not splash her money around.*)
(18 and 19 – answers could be in any order)
20 B (*I got a grant and an office from Mencap, a charity …*)
21 D (*But what really keeps me going is the thought of all the cash I'm making.*)
22 E (*… my business aim. This was to write 'popular' books that would earn me a fortune.*)
(21 and 22 – answers could be in any order)
23 C (*I have decided not to go to university because I don't feel it has anything more to offer me.*)
24 B (*Everyone warned me … I took no notice of them.*)
25 C (*Work excites me more. I can work all day every day without a break and never get bored.*)
26 A (*It all began when Justin … was turned away for being too young.*)
27 E (*After she'd written her first book … a publisher … advised her to tear it up and start again.*)
(26 and 27 – answers could be in any order)
28 A (*What gets me excited is coming up with new ideas.*)
29 D (*I think it's worth giving up a few nights out …*)
30 B (*… the company I set up won an award …*)

UNIVERSITY of CAMBRIDGE
ESOL Examinations

Do not write in this box

Candidate Name
If not already printed, write name
in CAPITALS and complete the
Candidate No. grid (in pencil).

Candidate Signature

Examination Title

Centre

Supervisor:

If the candidate is ABSENT or has WITHDRAWN shade here

SAMPLE

Centre No.

Candidate No.

Examination
Details

0	0	0	0
1	1	1	1
2	2	2	2
3	3	3	3
4	4	4	4
5	5	5	5
6	6	6	6
7	7	7	7
8	8	8	8
9	9	9	9

Candidate Answer Sheet

Instructions

Use a PENCIL (B or HB).

Mark ONE letter for each
question.

For example, if you think
B is the right answer to
the question, mark your
answer sheet like this:

0   A B C D E F G H

Rub out any answer you
wish to change using an
eraser.

1	A B C D E F G H
2	A B C D E F G H
3	A B C D E F G H
4	A B C D E F G H
5	A B C D E F G H
6	A B C D E F G H
7	A B C D E F G H
8	A B C D E F G H
9	A B C D E F G H
10	A B C D E F G H
11	A B C D E F G H
12	A B C D E F G H
13	A B C D E F G H
14	A B C D E F G H
15	A B C D E F G H
16	A B C D E F G H
17	A B C D E F G H
18	A B C D E F G H
19	A B C D E F G H
20	A B C D E F G H

21	A B C D E F G H
22	A B C D E F G H
23	A B C D E F G H
24	A B C D E F G H
25	A B C D E F G H
26	A B C D E F G H
27	A B C D E F G H
28	A B C D E F G H
29	A B C D E F G H
30	A B C D E F G H
31	A B C D E F G H
32	A B C D E F G H
33	A B C D E F G H
34	A B C D E F G H
35	A B C D E F G H
36	A B C D E F G H
37	A B C D E F G H
38	A B C D E F G H
39	A B C D E F G H
40	A B C D E F G H

A-H 40 CAS

denote
Print Limited 0121 520 5100

DP594/300

© Cambridge ESOL

Do not write in this box

Candidate Name
If not already printed, write name
in CAPITALS and complete the
Candidate No. grid (in pencil).

Candidate Signature

SAMPLE

Examination Title

Centre

Supervisor:

If the candidate is ABSENT or has WITHDRAWN shade here ▭

Centre No.

Candidate No.

Examination Details

0	0	0	0
1	1	1	1
2	2	2	2
3	3	3	3
4	4	4	4
5	5	5	5
6	6	6	6
7	7	7	7
8	8	8	8
9	9	9	9

Candidate Answer Sheet

Instructions
Use a PENCIL (B or HB). Rub out any answer you wish to change using an eraser.

Part 1: Mark ONE letter for each question.

For example, if you think **B** is the right answer to the question, mark your answer sheet like this:

0 A B C D

Parts 2, 3 and **4:** Write your answer clearly in CAPITAL LETTERS.

For Parts 2 and 3 write one letter in each box. For example:

0 EXAMPLE

Part 1

1	A	B	C	D
2	A	B	C	D
3	A	B	C	D
4	A	B	C	D
5	A	B	C	D
6	A	B	C	D
7	A	B	C	D
8	A	B	C	D
9	A	B	C	D
10	A	B	C	D
11	A	B	C	D
12	A	B	C	D

Part 2

Do not write below here

13		13 1 0 u
14		14 1 0 u
15		15 1 0 u
16		16 1 0 u
17		17 1 0 u
18		18 1 0 u
19		19 1 0 u
20		20 1 0 u
21		21 1 0 u
22		22 1 0 u
23		23 1 0 u
24		24 1 0 u

Continues over →

FCE UoE

DP596/305

© Cambridge ESOL

Part 3

25																						25 1 0 u
26																						26 1 0 u
27																						27 1 0 u
28																						28 1 0 u
29																						29 1 0 u
30																						30 1 0 u
31																						31 1 0 u
32																						32 1 0 u
33																						33 1 0 u
34																						34 1 0 u

Part 4

SAMPLE

35		35 2 1 0 u
36		36 2 1 0 u
37		37 2 1 0 u
38		38 2 1 0 u
39		39 2 1 0 u
40		40 2 1 0 u
41		41 2 1 0 u
42		42 2 1 0 u

denote Print Limited 0121 520 5100

© Cambridge ESOL

UNIVERSITY of CAMBRIDGE
ESOL Examinations

Do not write in this box

Centre No.

Candidate Name
If not already printed, write name
in CAPITALS and complete the
Candidate No. grid (in pencil).

Candidate Signature

Candidate No.

SAMPLE

Examination Title

Examination
Details

Centre

Supervisor:
If the candidate is ABSENT or has WITHDRAWN shade here

Test version: A B C D E F J K L M N   Special arrangements: S H

Candidate Answer Sheet

Instructions

Use a PENCIL (B or HB).
Rub out any answer you wish to change using an eraser.

Parts 1, 3 and 4:
Mark ONE letter for each question.

For example, if you think **B** is the
right answer to the question, mark
your answer sheet like this:

0 A B C

Part 2:
Write your answer clearly in CAPITAL LETTERS.

Write one letter or number in each box.
If the answer has more than one word, leave one
box empty between words.

For example:

0 N U M B E R   1 2

Turn this sheet over to start.

FCE L   DP599/306

© Cambridge ESOL

Part 1

	A	B	C
1	A	B	C
2	A	B	C
3	A	B	C
4	A	B	C
5	A	B	C
6	A	B	C
7	A	B	C
8	A	B	C

Part 2 (Remember to write in CAPITAL LETTERS or numbers)

Do not write
below here

SAMPLE

	1 0 u
9	
10	1 0 u
11	1 0 u
12	1 0 u
13	1 0 u
14	1 0 u
15	1 0 u
16	1 0 u
17	1 0 u
18	1 0 u

Part 3

	A	B	C	D	E	F
19	A	B	C	D	E	F
20	A	B	C	D	E	F
21	A	B	C	D	E	F
22	A	B	C	D	E	F
23	A	B	C	D	E	F

Part 4

	A	B	C
24	A	B	C
25	A	B	C
26	A	B	C
27	A	B	C
28	A	B	C
29	A	B	C
30	A	B	C

denote 0121 526 5100

© Cambridge ESOL

Photocopiable activities teacher's notes

Pre-course: FCE exam quiz

> • Use at the start of the course, before Module 1A.
> **Aim:** To raise awareness of various aspects of the FCE exam and to answer some common questions.
> **Time:** 15–20 minutes
> **Activity type:** Pairwork/Groupwork. Students find out how much they know about the exam by doing a quiz.
> **Preparation:** Make one copy of the quiz (p. 125) per student.

Procedure

1 Ask students what FCE stands for. Is it: **A** First Certificate Exam or **B** First Certificate in English? (Answer – **B**.) Tell the students that they are going to do a quick quiz to learn more about the exam.

2 Give out a copy of the quiz to each student and set a time limit (5 minutes) to complete it. Students should first have a go on their own and then compare with a partner or in groups.

3 Refer students to the Exam overview on page 6 of the Coursebook and the Top 20 Questions printed on the inside front cover and get them to check their answers.

4 Discuss answers with the class and answer any other questions about the exam that the students have.

> **1** B; **2** A; **3** C (you can't pass/fail individual papers); **4** C; **5** B (both questions have equal marks); **6** A; **7** C; **8** B (in Parts 1, 2 and 4 you speak to the examiner, in Part 3 just to your partner); **9** B (in Paper 2 poor spelling and handwriting can affect the overall impression mark); **10** C; **11** T (each paper is rounded up/down to 40 marks); **12** T (the word count is a guide but if you write too little you can't answer the question, if you write too much the examiner might not read it); **13** F (*isn't* counts as two words; *is* + *not*); **14** F (as long as the examiner can recognise the word. Words spelt out loud must be correct.); **15** F (in pairs or a group of three where there is an odd number)

Follow-up

Show students where they can find the Exam reference in the Coursebook (p. 178) and explain that they can find more detailed information about the exam there.

1A Lifestyle and families

> • Use this activity after Reading (CB pp. 10–11) or as an introduction to Module 1A.
> **Aim:** To practise giving and exchanging personal information.
> **Time:** 20–25 minutes
> **Activity type:** Pairwork/Groupwork. Students play a board game answering questions about themselves and their families.
> **Exam focus:** The questions are similar to possible questions in Paper 5 Parts 1 and 4.
> **Preparation:** Make one copy of the board game (p. 126) per group of four students enlarged to A3 size if possible. One dice per group and counters of different colours (students can make their own).

Procedure

1 Divide the class into groups of four (or three) and give each group a copy of the board game and counters. Quickly demonstrate how to play the game.

2 Tell students to expand on their answers if they wish.

3 Each student starts from a different corner of the board. They take it in turns to roll the dice and move around the board. When they land on a square they read out the question (or another student reads it out to them), and answer it. The other students can ask a follow-up question. The next student then has a turn.

4 If anyone lands on a square with a question that they have already answered they move forward to the next square. In squares with a slash (e.g. *house/flat*) students should choose the most appropriate word for their situation when reading out the question.

5 As the students are discussing the answers make a note of typical/common mistakes. As there is no 'start' or 'finish' there are no winners and the game can be played for as long or short a time as is available.

Follow-up

Spend 5–10 minutes giving students feedback on their performance, both positive and negative, and correct any common mistakes noted. (You could write students' incorrect sentences on the board and, in pairs, get students to correct them.)

1B Habits

> • Use after Language development 1 (CB pp. 12–13).
> **Aim:** To practise using language to describe present and past habits.
> **Time:** 25–30 minutes
> **Activity type:** Pairwork. Students compare a house and its inhabitants in the 1930s with the same house today.
> **Preparation:** Make one copy of the pictures (pp. 127–128) for each pair of students.

Procedure

1 Elicit a few examples of how students spend time at home, e.g. *I eat dinner with my parents, then I ...*.

2 Divide the class into pairs. In each pair, give one student picture A and one picture B and tell them their picture is of a family spending time at home. Tell them not to show their pictures to each other at this stage.

3 Students describe what is happening in their picture to find out if they have pictures of the same house or different houses. Remind students that we usually use the present continuous when describing a scene in a picture, e.g. *a boy is playing*.

4 Establish that it is the same house but a different time. Picture A is in the 1930s and picture B is the same house now. Students look at both pictures to compare modern-day and 1930s lifestyles. Remind students to use the target structures *would* and *used to* by eliciting/giving a model, e.g. *Families used to be much larger. People didn't have bathrooms so they would wash in the kitchen.*

5 Compare ideas with the whole class.

Follow-up

Students discuss if changes are for the better or not. They could also discuss how their lifestyle is different from their parents' when they were the same age.

1C Collocations: adjectives and nouns

> • Use after completing Language development 3 (CB p. 22).
> **Aim:** To practise some common adjective + noun collocations from Module 2, and introduce some new ones.
> **Time:** 25–30 minutes
> **Activity type:** Groupwork. Students match adjectives to nouns and then use the collocations to complete a text.
> **Exam focus:** Collocations are tested in Paper 3 Part 1.
> **Preparation:** Copy and cut up one set of adjective cards (grey) and one set of noun cards (white) per group of 3–4 students, and one copy of the text per student (pp. 129–130).

Procedure

Part 1

1 Write the following nouns on the board and ask students if they can remember which of them collocate with *sour*: *milk, tea, look, sound, banana, grapes.*

2 Divide the class into groups of 3–4. Give each group a set of adjective cards (grey) and noun cards (white).

3 Tell students to work together to match them. Check the answers with the class before they go on to do Part 2 of the activity. Answers are the same collocations as for Part 2 of the activity, but in no particular order.

Part 2

1 Give each student a copy of the text and ask them to work individually to complete it, using the adjective + noun combinations from the first part of the activity.

2 Check answers with the class.

> 1 guided tour; 2 unique opportunity; 3 domestic life; 4 high speed; 5 slight change; 6 exact date; 7 wide gap; 8 hard work; 9 quick breakfast; 10 central heating; 11 strong influence; 12 memorable experience; 13 natural light; 14 valuable paintings; 15 final destination

Follow-up

Ask students to think of the opposites of some of the collocations, e.g. *high speed – low speed, wide gap – narrow gap, strong influence – weak influence,* etc.

2A Work

• This activity can be used after Reading (CB pp. 24–25). (See also Alternative below.)

Aim:	To practise giving and exchanging opinions and reaching a consensus. To revise and extend jobs vocabulary.
Time:	30 minutes
Activity type:	Groupwork. Students discuss a number of jobs in different categories and reach a consensus.
Exam focus:	Paper 5 Part 3
Preparation:	Make one copy of the cards (p. 131) per group of 3–4 students.

Suggested answers:
1 Some surveys suggest being a miner is the most stressful because of the physical dangers, others say that being a prison officer is.
2 Although some company directors and musicians are very highly paid, on average the answer is more likely to be a lawyer or a surgeon.
3 In the UK the answer is a judge because, in addition to formal legal training, you need many years courtroom experience as a lawyer before becoming a judge.
4, 5 and 6 are a matter of opinion.

Procedure

1 Pre-teach some of the more difficult vocabulary, e.g. *miner, surgeon, chef, midwife, traffic warden, bouncer, civil servant* and *undertaker* by putting the words on the board and getting students in groups to discuss meanings and/or refer to dictionaries. Check pronunciation of difficult words, e.g. *chef, architect, pilot*.

2 Divide the class into groups of 3–4. Explain that students should discuss each question giving reasons to support their opinions.

3 Students choose a card at random from the set and discuss the question. When/If they reach a consensus they choose another card. Set a time limit (5–10 minutes per card) and signal when time is up.

4 While students are discussing the questions check that they are supporting their opinions with reasons and encouraging turn-taking. Stop after the first round and give feedback on their use of functional language.

5 Conduct feedback with the class, correcting common mistakes. Compare answers between the groups.

Follow-up

In their groups, students think of a job in each category that beats those listed.

Alternative

Use the cards one at a time for 5-minute speaking activities at different times during the unit.

2B Experience

> • Use after Language development 1 (CB pp. 26–27) and before the Writing section.
>
> **Aim:** To practise asking and speaking about past experiences using the past simple and present perfect (simple and continuous) tenses.
>
> **Time:** 25–30 minutes
>
> **Activity type:** Students roleplay interviewing candidates for a job.
>
> **Preparation:** Make one set of rolecards (p. 132) per group of four students.

Procedure

1 Elicit the meaning of *au pair* (a young person, who lives with a family in a foreign country to look after the children, in order to learn the language). Ask what skills or qualities are needed to be an au pair.

2 Divide the class into groups of four. In each group students A and B are a couple looking for an au pair, students C and D are applicants for the job.

3 Students read rolecards and have a few minutes to prepare their questions/answers. Applicants should think about questions they could ask (hours of work/own room/time off, etc.) at the end of the interview.

4 First A interviews C, while B interviews D, giving the applicants a chance to ask questions at the end. For any information not on the card applicants should answer as themselves. Employers can invent any details of the job not given.

5 A interviews D while B interviews C.

6 The two employers discuss and choose who they prefer for the job while the applicants discuss who seems nicer to work for.

7 A and B announce who gets the job.

Follow-up

Discuss whether students like the idea of being an au pair in the UK or elsewhere.

2C Articles

> • Use after Language development 2 (CB p. 34).
>
> **Aim:** To practise use of articles *a/an*, *the* and zero article.
>
> **Time:** 25–30 minutes
>
> **Activity type:** Pairwork. Students complete a story by adding articles where necessary and then retell it to a partner.
>
> **Exam focus:** Paper 3 Part 2.
>
> **Preparation:** Prepare enough copies (pp. 133–134) so that half the students have story A, and half B, with the answer keys removed.

Procedure

Explain that some stories have a 'moral' and elicit what that means (a practical lesson about what to do or how to behave which you learn from the story). Tell the students that they are going to read and tell two stories with a moral.

Part 1

1 Divide the class in two. Give the students in one half a copy of story A and students in the other half story B.

2 Give them 5 minutes to read the story and fill in the gaps with either *a*, *the* or ø (when no article is required).

3 Get them to compare their answers in pairs or small groups explaining choices.

4 Give out the answer keys to each group and help with any problems or questions.

Part 2

1 Form the students into pairs with an A and a B in each.

2 They tell each other their story. Stronger students should retell the story from memory, paying attention to the use of articles, weaker students can read the text. Their partner has to try to guess what the moral of the story is.

3 Ask students which story they prefer and why.

3A Tourism

> • Use after Reading (CB pp. 38–39).
>
> **Aim:** To practise language associated with tourism and language used for discussion.
>
> **Time:** 30–40 minutes (+ Follow-up)
>
> **Activity type:** Whole class. Students debate the pros and cons of tourism.
>
> **Exam focus:** The organisation of ideas and much of the functional language is relevant to Paper 2 Part 2 (discursive composition).
>
> **Preparation:** Make one copy of either A or B (pp. 135–136) for each student.

Procedure

1 Ask students where they have been as tourists. Elicit a variety of destination types, e.g. cities, places of natural beauty, historic towns, coasts, mountains, developed and developing countries.

2 Ask the students if they think their visits were generally good or bad for the places they visited. Divide the class into two groups according to their answers to the question (one group = good effect, other group = bad effect).

3 Explain that the class is going to debate the motion *'Tourism should be encouraged: it is good for a country.'* One group must present the argument in favour and the other group present the argument against.

4 Write the motion on the board and give the two groups a few minutes to think of ideas to support their side of the argument. When their ideas dry up give each side their cue card and let them continue discussing it.

5 Ask each group to elect a proposer and a seconder and decide which points each will present. Ask students to try to use the 'useful language' on the cards when presenting their argument.

6 The four speakers present their arguments (A, B, A, B) with the rest of the class listening. Allow a few questions or points from the rest of the class.

7 Take a vote on those who support the motion and those who oppose it.

Follow-up

Ask students if they have heard of the motto from ecotourism *'Take nothing but photos, leave nothing but footprints'* and consider what it means. In pairs or groups, ask students to think of other dos/don'ts for good tourism and report them back to the class.

3B Adjectives and adverbs

> • Use after Language development 1 (CB pp. 40–41).
>
> **Aim:** To practise using adverbs of degree and adjectives studied in Unit 5.
>
> **Time:** 25–30 minutes
>
> **Activity type:** Groupwork. Students play a game of pelmanism, matching adjectives and adverbs to gapped sentences.
>
> **Preparation:** Make a copy of both sets of cards (pp. 137–138) per group of 4–5 students, copied onto card if possible and cut up into individual cards.

Procedure

1 Put students into groups of 4–5. Demonstrate how to play the game.

2 Place the cards face down on the table, in their two sets (grey and white). Students take it in turns to turn over a card from each set – one sentence card and one adjective/adverb card. If they match the student keeps the pair and has another turn. If they don't match the student should turn them face down again in the same place.

3 Groups can discuss whether a pair matches or not and ask for help where necessary. As the students play go round the groups monitoring the pairs of cards collected. If any are wrong explain why and return the cards to the game. Some words can be used in more than one sentence.

4 The winner is the student with the most pairs.

1 surprisingly/remarkably; **2** hardly; **3** bleak; **4** lively; **5** well; **6** hard; **7** friendly; **8** fast; **9** rather/pretty; **10** extremely; **11** practically; **12** absolutely; **13** a bit; **14** pretty/rather/quite; **15** quite a; **16** actually; **17** as well; **18** seriously; **19** remarkably/surprisingly; **20** rather/pretty

3C *-ing* forms and infinitives

- Use after Language development 2 (CB p. 48).

Aim:	To practise using words/phrases that need to be followed by verbs in either the infinitive (with or without *to*) or *-ing* form.
Time:	20–25 minutes
Activity type:	Groupwork. A game, combining A cards and B cards to make correct sentences.
Exam focus:	Paper 3 Parts 1 and 4.
Preparation:	Make one copy of both sets of cards (pp. 139–140) for each group of four students.

Procedure

1 Explain that the items on the A cards are followed either by the *-ing* form or the infinitive (with or without *to*). In some cases both are possible.

2 Tell the students that, in the game, they will need to combine A and B cards, making a logical sentence, either positive or negative, in any tense. Demonstrate with two cards, e.g.

(*think of* + *learn* = *I'm thinking of learning Spanish next year.*)

3 Shuffle the A cards and deal out three to each player, and place the remaining cards face down on the table. Turn the top card over and place it next to the pile. Do the same with the B cards.

4 Students take turns to combine an A card or a B card in their hand to make a sentence, placing the cards on the table in front of them as they do so. After making a sentence they replace the two cards by taking one from each of the face-down piles.

5 If students cannot make a sentence, they can use their turn to change one of their cards, taking either the face-up card or the next face-down card from the corresponding pile. The card they put down goes on the face-up pile. Players should always have six cards (three from each set) in their hand.

6 Other players in the group accept or contest sentences. As students play, monitor their use of the structures, if necessary checking by asking students to repeat the pairs in front of them, returning the cards to the pile if they are not correct.

7 The student with the most pairs is the winner.

4A Raising money

- Use after Reading (CB pp. 52–53).

Aim:	To practise giving and exchanging opinions and reaching a consensus.
Time:	20–30 minutes
Activity type:	Groupwork. Students discuss possible ways of raising money for a club that they belong to and reach a consensus on the best way of raising the money.
Exam focus:	Paper 5 Part 3. Paper 5 Part 4 in the Follow-up activity.
Preparation:	Make one copy of the activity (p. 141) per group of 3–4 students (or one per pair if you use the Variation.)

Procedure

1 Check that students are familiar with the concept of a *charity*. Ask students to name some charities that they have heard of and how charities raise money. Tell them that in some countries individuals often raise money for charities and elicit possible ways of doing so.

2 Pre-teach: *bungee jump, busking, raffle.*

3 Divide the class into groups of 3–4 students and explain that for this activity they are all members of a club or society that needs to buy some new equipment.

4 Give each group a copy of the activity and tell them that they must work together to decide on the best method to raise some money.

5 Model the activity using *run a marathon* as an example, using the language in the speech bubbles and referring to the four prompt questions.

6 Give students a time limit (10 minutes) to discuss and agree on the best method.

7 Different groups should report back to the class and explain their choice.

Variation

Doing the activity in larger groups will encourage more discussion, but for more authentic exam-type practice do the activity in pairs.

Follow-up

Ask students if any of them have ever done anything like this before for charity. Ask if they ever give money to buskers, beggars or street collectors and why/why not.

4B Narrative tenses

> • Use after Language development 1 (CB pp. 54–55) and before the Writing section.
>
> **Aim:** To practise narrative tenses.
> **Time:** 20–25 minutes
> **Activity type:** Groupwork. Students work out a scenario from clues and devise a story.
> **Exam focus:** In Paper 2 Part 2 (narrative composition/short story) narrative tenses are particularly relevant.
> **Preparation:** Make one copy of the picture (p. 142) per group of 2–4 students.

Procedure

1 Find out if students read detective stories or watch such programmes on TV. Tell students that for this activity, they will be detectives.

2 Set the scene. It is 9 May, a man called Peter disappeared a few days ago and they are looking for him. In his flat they find various items which are clues to what has happened.

3 Divide the class into groups of 2–4 and give each group a copy of the picture.

4 Students have 5–10 minutes to discuss what the picture tells them about Peter and the time before he disappeared. Elicit an example, e.g. the coke bottle – *He had been drinking coke/He had drunk a bottle of coke* or *He was writing/had been writing a letter.*

5 Compare ideas with the whole class, paying attention to use of tenses.

6 Students have 5 minutes to put the clues together to make a story to say what happened.

7 The class compare their different stories.

Suggestions for items:
He was/had been writing a letter. He had been to/visited Moscow. He had been smoking/He had smoked nearly a whole packet … . He had been eating a pizza/He hadn't finished his pizza. He had been sent a letter by someone called Natasha, etc.

Possible solution:
Peter had been going out with a Russian girl called Natasha and had been to Moscow to visit her and had a great holiday. After he had left she wrote to him to say it was all over, so he booked another flight and went back to see her … .

4C Confusing adjectives

> • This is an extension to Language development 3 (CB p. 64).
>
> **Aim:** To extend work on comparing and contrasting commonly confused adjectives.
> **Time:** 30–45 minutes. Note that this activity is in two parts, which can be done on separate occasions.
> **Activity type:** Part 1: whole class. Students mingle, teaching each other the difference between confusing adjectives.
> Part 2: groupwork. A board game asking and answering questions using the adjectives.
> **Exam focus:** Paper 3 Part 1
> **Preparation:** Part 1: one set of the vocabulary cards (p. 143) per class, cut up; dictionaries.
> Part 2: one copy of the board game (p. 144), enlarged to A3 if possible, per group of 4–5 students; dice and counters.

Procedure

Part 1 (10–15 minutes)

1 Distribute the Part 1 vocabulary cards. If there are more students than cards, some can share.

2 Students check the difference between the words in a dictionary and think of or look up examples to explain the meanings.

3 Students mingle and, each time they meet another student, they ask them to explain the difference between the words on their card (without showing it to them). Students help/teach each other where necessary.

Part 2 (15–25 minutes)

1 Divide the class into groups of 4–5 students and give each group a copy of the board game.

2 Students take it in turns to roll dice and move around the board.

3 At each square they read the question and decide who in the group to ask, choosing the correct word from the alternatives each time.

4 Monitor the whole class, noting errors for feedback at the end.

5A The human body

- Use as an introduction to Module 5A and Reading (CB pp. 66–67).

Aim:	To generate interest in the topic of the human body and to pre-teach some important vocabulary for the Reading section in Module 5A. To practise giving and exchanging opinions.
Time:	20–25 minutes
Activity type:	Individual and pairwork. Students complete a general knowledge quiz on the subject of the human body and compare answers.
Preparation:	Make one copy of the quiz (p. 145) per student.

Procedure

1 Tell the class that they are going to do a general knowledge quiz on the subject of the human body. Ask the students how much they know about the subject and if they study/studied biology at school.

2 If there are any doctors or medical students in the class sit them together.

3 Give each student a copy of the quiz and a time limit of 5–6 minutes to complete the quiz.

4 Students then compare their answers in pairs.

5 Check the answers with the whole class.

> **1** C; **2** A; **3** B (in an adult, and the male brain is slightly heavier than the female!); **4** B (it's in the centre but the left side is bigger so it leans that way); **5** B (in a reasonably fit young adult); **6** C; **7** A (the study of mental illness is psychiatry); **8** C; **9** B (DNA stands for 'deoxyribonucleic acid'); **10** A (the liver is about 1.5 kgs); **11** B; **12** C (in Europe)

Follow-up

Ask students what surprised them most in the quiz.

5B The future

- Use after Language development 1 (CB pp. 68–69).

Aim:	To practise using a variety of future forms.
Time:	20–25 minutes
Activity type:	Pairwork. Students complete a timeline of their future and discuss it with a partner.
Preparation:	Make one copy of the activity (p. 146) per student.

Procedure

1 Ask students how they feel about the future. Do they worry about it? Or do they enjoy making plans?

2 Draw a rough copy of the path (see activity) on the board and explain that it is a map of the future. Demonstrate with your own examples, e.g. *I'm visiting some friends this week.*

3 Using the exam as an example, demonstrate/elicit how many different tenses might be possible for talking about a future event.

- *The exam takes place every (March).*
- *I am taking the exam in (March).*
- *My mum thinks I will pass!*
- *I am going to study hard before the exam.*
- *We will be taking the exam in mid (March).*
- *I will have taken the exam by the summer.*

4 Give each student a copy of the activity.

5 Students mark points on the path and label them according to their plans, hopes and predictions. Point out that, if students need to, they can use the verbs in the box for ideas.

6 Students should think about which tense they will use to talk about each point but should not write out the sentences in full. They tick the boxes in the table as they think of an example for each tense.

7 After a suitable time limit (7–8 minutes) the students form pairs and explain their diagram to their partner. Their partner can ask follow-up questions about their plans if they wish.

5C Forming nouns

> • Use after Language development 3 (CB p. 78).
>
> **Aim:** To consolidate and extend forming nouns from verbs.
>
> **Time:** 15–20 minutes
>
> **Activity type:** Groupwork. Students play a game of dominoes, joining suffixes to verbs to make nouns.
>
> **Exam focus:** Paper 3 Part 3
>
> **Preparation:** Make one copy of the dominoes (p. 147) per group of 4–5 students, cut up into individual dominoes.

Procedure

1 Review the concept of forming nouns from verbs by adding a suffix. Use the following verbs and elicit the nouns: *develop-ment, accept-ance, discuss-ion.*

2 Divide the class into groups of 4–5, giving each group a set of dominoes. Demonstrate how the final -*e* that is dropped is shown in brackets, e.g. *combin(e)* + *-ation = combination.*

3 One student deals four dominoes to each player, the rest of the dominoes remain face down on the desk in a pile.

4 Students take turns to place a domino, building a chain, (using either end). As they place each domino they should say the word they have formed.

5 After placing a domino students take another from the pile. If they are unable to place a domino to make a word, they take one from the pile and the next student has a turn.

6 As the students are playing, monitor that they have placed the dominoes correctly (especially with the difficult -*ance* and -*ence* endings).

7 The winner is the first to get rid of all their dominoes.

Follow-up

Point out how pronunciation changes in some words as the noun is formed, either in sounds, e.g. *please* /iː/ *pleasure* /e/) or stress, e.g. *prefer – preference, hesitate – hesitation* and ask students to find other examples.

6A Ambition

> • Use at the start of Module 6A before Reading (CB pp. 80–81).
>
> **Aim:** To raise interest in the topic of ambition.
>
> **Time:** 20–25 minutes
>
> **Activity type:** Individual and whole class. Students complete a questionnaire to see how ambitious they are.
>
> **Preparation:** Make one copy of the questionnaire (p. 148) per student.

Procedure

1 Write the word *goal* on the board and ask students what they think of. Elicit its meaning of *ambition* as well as *football*. Elicit other words of similar meaning (*target, aims, dream*). Elicit the adjective of *ambition* (*ambitious*).

2 Pre-teach the following words/phrases: *community, put off, to mix with someone.*

3 Give each student a copy of the questionnaire. Students have 5 minutes to answer the questions working individually.

4 Explain the scoring system – odd questions: 2 points for *yes* and 1 point for *maybe*, even questions: 2 points for *no* and 1 for *maybe*.

5 Check totals: the higher the score the more ambitious the person is. 12 is the average. Compare scores within the class and see who is the most/least ambitious person in the class.

6 Elicit different types of ambition (work, money, family, spiritual, health, etc.)

Follow-up

Students ask a partner what their ambitions are and report back to the class.

6B The arts (relative clauses)

• Use after Language development 1 (CB pp. 82–83).	
Aim:	To practise relative clauses and arts vocabulary.
Time:	15–20 minutes
Activity type:	Groupwork. Students play a game defining words for their team members to guess.
Exam focus:	Paper 3 Part 2
Preparation:	Make one copy of the cards (p. 149) per group of 4–5 students and cut them up.

Procedure

1 Ask if students are interested in the arts (music, dance, theatre, etc.). Ask how often they go to performances and if they have ever performed in public.

2 Divide the class into groups of 4–5 students. Give each group a set of cards and get them to sort them into words they know and words they don't. Get students to explain the words they know to the class. Teach the meaning of any that no one knows.

3 Each group collects up all their cards and shuffles them well.

4 Students play a game defining the words on the cards, using phrases such as *a person who … / a place where … / a thing which …* Demonstrate with a couple of cards. Give each group a copy of the useful language in speech bubbles at the foot of the photocopiable page.

5 The first player in the team takes a card from the pile and without showing it to their team, defines the word. When the team guess it, the player puts it down on the table and defines the next word. If the player can't define the word or the team can't guess it the player puts it to the bottom of the pile and continues.

6 After every minute or so shout 'Change!' and the player passes the pile to the next person in the team who has a go at defining words.

7 After 5–10 minutes stop the game. The winning team is the one with the most cards on the table.

6C Adjectives and nouns + preposition

• Use after Language development 2 (CB p. 90).	
Aim:	To practise dependent prepositions with adjectives and nouns from Module 6B.
Time:	20–25 minutes
Activity type:	Pairwork. Students play a version of the game 'battleships'.
Exam focus:	Paper 3 Parts 1 and 2
Preparation:	Make one copy of worksheets A and B (pp. 150–151) for each pair of students.

Procedure

1 Tell students that they are going to play a version of a game called 'battleships' and ask if anyone knows how to play it.

2 Divide the class into pairs and give each student a worksheet for Student A or B, telling them not to show each other their worksheets.

3 Each student has a shaded complete side (on the left) and an unshaded, incomplete side (on the right).

4 Demonstrate how, on the shaded side, students pick six squares for their partner to find. They select three blocks of two squares together (vertically or horizontally) and mark them. These are the areas the partner will be looking for.

5 When they are ready to begin Student A chooses a word on the unshaded side and adds the preposition, putting it into a sentence, e.g. *I have a good relationship with my brother*. If the preposition is correct and the square is a selected one B says 'hit' and A writes in the preposition and marks it with an *X*. If it is not a selected one B says 'miss' and A can write in the answer. If the preposition is incorrect B says 'wrong' but does not say if the square is a hit or miss. It is then B's turn.

6 Students take it in turn to hunt for the hidden squares. If more than one preposition is possible students only need give one.

7 The game is over when one player has identified which six squares their partner selected.

7A Global food and drink

> • Use before Reading (CB pp. 94–95).
>
> | | |
> |---|---|
> | **Aim:** | To practise giving and exchanging opinions and to generate interest in the reading topic. |
> | **Time:** | 20–25 minutes |
> | **Activity type:** | Pairwork/Groupwork. Students complete a quiz on the subject of global food/drink. |
> | **Exam focus:** | Paper 5 Part 3 |
> | **Preparation:** | Make one copy of the quiz (p. 152) per student. |

Procedure

1 Ask students to work in pairs to name five global food/drink companies, e.g. McDonald's, KFC (Kentucky Fried Chicken), Coca-Cola, Starbucks, Mars, Nestlé, Cadburys, Ferrero, etc.

2 Put students into pairs or groups of three. Tell them that it is a competition to see which pair is the most knowledgeable about the global food market. They are not expected to know the answers but will have to guess them. Show them the speech bubbles containing useful language for discussion.

3 Give each pair/group a copy of the questionnaire and a suitable time limit (10 minutes) to discuss the questions.

4 Check answers with the whole class. Find out which pair is the winner. Ask which answers surprised them most.

> **1** C; **2** C; **3** B (in the 'Happy Meals'); **4** C (in 10,800 outlets); **5** D (but 34% of sales are in North America); **6** A; **7** B (with sales of $2 billion a year); **8** A; **9** B (8.7kg/person/year, then – USA, France and Italy); **10** D (3.6kg/person/year, then – UK, Turkey and Egypt)

Follow-up

Ask students to think of three positive and three negative aspects of globalisation and then discuss them with the whole class.

7B Cultural guide

> • Use after Language development 1 (CB pp. 96–97).
>
> | | |
> |---|---|
> | **Aim:** | To practise expressions of permission, necessity, advice and recommendation. |
> | **Time:** | 15–20 minutes |
> | **Activity type:** | Pairwork. Students complete a cultural guide. |
> | **Exam focus:** | Paper 3 Part 4 |
> | **Preparation:** | Make one copy of the activity (p. 153) per student. |

Procedure

1 Ask students when they give flowers, e.g. birthdays, anniversaries, to people in hospital and if there are any 'rules' that they follow.

2 On the board put the table:

You	should(n't)/ought to are(n't) supposed to are(n't) allowed to must(n't)/have to	give	an even number. an odd number. white flowers. a single flower.

Get students to make sentences that show various ways of saying the same thing, e.g. *In some countries you are supposed to give an odd number/you aren't supposed to give an even number*.

3 Pre-teach: *earlobe, escalators, edible, sole*.

4 Divide the class into pairs and give each student a copy of the activity. Students work together to make 12 sentences that they think are true. Check answers with the whole class.

> **1** not supposed to, red (red is only used for names of the dead)
> **2** aren't supposed to, teacher's (use the title 'Teacher')
> **3** must, before (the bath is for soaking/relaxing)
> **4** shouldn't, earlobe (it is a rude gesture)
> **5** mustn't, your left (the left hand is unclean)
> **6** mustn't, coin (it shows disrespect to the king whose head is on the coins)
> **7** are supposed to, on the right
> **8** must, to an older person (it shows respect)
> **9** ought to, lift
> **10** shouldn't, gifts
> **11** mustn't, the soles of your feet (it shows disrespect)
> **12** are supposed to, hands

Follow-up

Students write more sentences for their own country and share them with the class.

7C Modals of deduction

• Use after Language development 2
(CB p. 103).

Aim:	To practise using modals of deduction (past and present).
Time:	15–20 minutes
Activity type:	Whole class mingle. Students respond to or correct remarks made by other students.
Exam focus:	Paper 3 Part 4
Preparation:	Prepare one copy of the activity (p. 154) per class, cut up into individual cards. Prepare two sets if there are more than 16 students.

Procedure

1 Write a sentence on the board, containing a factual mistake such as: *I'm 20 years old, I was born in 1980* (where the age and date don't add up) and ask students what is wrong with it.

2 Elicit possible corrections: *You can't be 20/ You must be ??, if you were born in 1980.* or: *You can't have been born in 1980/you must have been born in 19??.*

3 Give each student a card. They read it and decide on the answer or spot what is wrong with it. At this stage if students don't know what the correction should be they could check with the teacher.

4 Students stand up and mingle, telling people the information on their card.

5 Each student they meet listens and responds or 'corrects' it. If they don't know what the correction should be they can ask the other student to explain. If students can give the correct response they score a point, before moving on to speak to another student.

6 The winner could be the first one to win a set number of points or the one with the most points after a set time.

Notes: (some examples)
• Penguins live in the Antarctic not the Arctic.
• Brazilians speak Portuguese.
• The first moon landing was in 1969.
• The Euro was introduced in 2002.
• In Japan people drive on the left.
• The Berlin Wall came down in 1989.
• People didn't watch TV in the 1920s.
• There are no snakes in New Zealand.

8A Relationships (prepositions)

• Use as an introduction to Module 8A before Reading (CB pp. 108–109).

Aim:	To activate students' knowledge of phrases that refer to relationships (most of which are used in the unit).
Time:	15–20 minutes
Activity type:	Individual and pairwork. Students complete expressions about relationships by adding missing prepositions and then order them.
Exam focus:	Paper 3 Part 1
Preparation:	Make one copy of the activity (p. 155) per student. Dictionaries would be useful.

Procedure

1 Ask students to define *relationship*. Establish that there are many different types of relationships (parent/child, family, teacher/student, client/server, etc.) and that this activity is about boyfriend/girlfriend relationships.

2 Give each student a copy of the activity and a suitable time limit (5 minutes) to work individually to complete the gaps. Point out that, in some, no preposition is required.

3 Students compare their answers with a partner.

4 Give students the answers, checking meaning.

5 In pairs, students discuss a logical order for them. Point out that there is no correct answer, it's a matter of opinion and that some expressions are very similar. Compare answers with the whole class.

---

be attracted *to* someone; fall *in* love (with someone); to split *up* (with someone); to get engaged *to* someone; to go *out* (with someone); to propose *to* someone; to finish *with* someone; to separate *from* someone; to be *in* love *with* someone; to chat someone *up*; to fancy ø someone; to get *on* well (with someone); to ask someone *out*; to get married *to* someone; to catch ø someone's eye; to fall *out* (with someone); to take someone *out*; to have a crush *on* someone; to flirt *with* someone; to move *in* (with someone)

8B Reported speech

> • Use after Language development 1 (CB pp. 110–111).
>
> | | |
> |---|---|
> | **Aim:** | To practise reporting what someone said and use reporting verbs. |
> | **Time:** | 20–25 minutes |
> | **Activity type:** | Pairwork. Students put quotes into reported speech and guess who said them. |
> | **Exam focus:** | Paper 3 Part 4 |
> | **Preparation:** | Make one copy of A and B (p. 156–157) for each pair of students. |

Procedure

1 Put the quote 'I want to live because there are a few things I want to do' on the board. Ask students if they know who said it before he died (Aneurin Bevan, politician, died 1960).

2 Divide students into pairs and give each student either copy A or B.

3 Students have a few minutes to think about how they will put the quotes into reported speech. Before they start, point out the example on their sheets.

4 Write some of the reporting verbs from Module 8A on the board, e.g. *warn, advise, promise, suggest* and remind students to try to use them in the activity.

5 Students take it in turn to ask. If their partner doesn't know the answer they can guess from the choices at the bottom of their sheet.

Follow-up

In pairs, students think of their own favourite quotes from films or books to ask the rest of the class.

8C Leisure activities

> • Use after Listening (CB p. 116).
>
> | | |
> |---|---|
> | **Aim:** | To discuss leisure interests and to practise giving and exchanging opinions and reaching a consensus. |
> | **Time:** | 25–30 minutes |
> | **Activity type:** | Groupwork. Students choose a leisure activity to do together. |
> | **Exam focus:** | Paper 5 part 3 |
> | **Preparation:** | Make one copy of the activity (p. 158) per group of 3–4 students. |

Procedure

1 Ask students how they usually spend their weekends. What influences their choice (hobbies/interests, money, time available, friends)?

2 Introduce the activity – students work in a group to choose a way to spend a weekend together doing something special (maybe before one goes off to study/join the army/get married, etc.).

3 Divide students into groups, mixing students up from usual partners if possible, and give each group a copy of the activity.

4 Remind students that they will need to discuss, suggest, agree, disagree, and reach a consensus. Elicit some functional language they could use and if necessary refer them to the Functions reference (CB p. 215).

5 Students have 10 minutes to discuss and choose a trip.

6 Groups feed back to class on which trip they chose and why.

Follow-up

Find out if any of the students have ever done any of the activities given and if they enjoyed them.

9A Money

• Use either at the start of Module 9 to activate the vocabulary or as a review after Reading (CB pp. 122–123).

Aim: To practise vocabulary around the topic of money and to generate interest in the topic of the unit.

Time: 25–35 minutes

Activity type: Groupwork. Students play a board game where they gain or lose money each turn.

Exam focus: Paper 3 Part 1

Preparation: Make one copy of the game (p. 159) per group of 3–4 students (enlarged to A3 if possible). One dice per group and counters of different colours.

Procedure

1 Students brainstorm first ways to gain money, e.g. *earn, win, inherit* then ways to lose money, e.g. *spend, pay, go bust*, then adjectives that describe having or not having money, e.g. *well off, wealthy, broke, bankrupt*. Build up three lists of the words on the board.

2 Divide the class into groups of 3–4. Each group has a copy of the game.

3 Students place counters on square 1. One player in each group is also chosen to be the banker.

4 For a quicker game use dice, for a longer game use a coin, moving one square for heads and three for tails.

5 Each player starts with £1,000. At each turn players throw the dice and move around the board. The banker keeps a running total of how much they have and if they invest in a business or shares.

6 While students are playing, monitor and help with vocabulary. Continue until everyone has finished.

7 At the finish, anyone who started a business (in square 5 or 7) who hasn't lost it (21) or sold it (22) has double what they put in. Anyone who invested in the stock market (square 6) has double what they invested.

8 The winner is the one with the most money!

Follow-up

Discuss whether students are savers or spenders, cautious or risk-taking with their money.

9B Conditionals

• Use after Language development 1 (CB pp. 124–125).

Aim: To practise making conditional sentences and recognising which is required in a given situation.

Time: 20–40 minutes (or see Variations below).

Activity type: Groupwork. Students make, ask and answer questions on real and hypothetical issues.

Exam focus: Paper 3 Part 4

Preparation: Make one copy of the activity (p. 160) per group of 3–4 students. Cut up into individual cards.

Procedure

1 Write on the board: *If you (stop be) a teacher, what you (do)?* Ask students to make questions from it and elicit three conditional forms are possible (*If you stop/ stopped/had stopped being a teacher, what will you do/ would you do/would you have done?*). Demonstrate how time expressions (*next year, last year*) would affect your choice of conditional.

2 Divide the class into groups of 3–4 students.

3 Shuffle the cards and place face down on the table.

4 Students take it in turns to take a card from the pile and make a question in an appropriate form and choose which of the people in the group they would like to answer it. Demonstrate with one of the cards. Point out that the conditional form they choose depends on either how likely they see the event or which time phrase they choose.

5 Students ask each other the questions and discuss answers, refusing to answer if they don't think the question is formed correctly.

6 Monitor closely and check that students are forming the questions correctly.

Follow-up

Discuss any interesting or amusing answers given.

Variations

1 For a quicker game select fewer cards.

2 Use the cards a few at a time as 5-minute fillers over the next few lessons.

9C Money vocabulary

> • Use after Language development 3 (CB p. 134).
> **Aim:** To revise money vocabulary from Module 9 and practise word formation.
> **Time:** 15–20 minutes
> **Activity type:** Pairwork. Students work together to complete a crossword.
> **Exam focus:** Paper 3 Part 3
> **Preparation:** Make one copy of crosswords A and B (p. 161) for each pair of students.

Procedure

1 Give students the word *tax* and get them to think of all the words formed from it (*taxes, taxable, untaxable, taxation*).

2 Explain that they will work together to complete a crossword which contains nouns and adjectives related to money. They will have to form clues using the roots of the words, so they will need to think what type of word it is and what the root is.

3 Demonstrate with examples 'It's the noun of the verb *to tax*' (= *taxation*) or 'It's the adjective of the noun *price*' (= *priceless*).

4 Divide the class into pairs and give students in each pair either Part A or Part B of the crossword.

5 Students check the form and meaning of the words on their half of the crossword.

6 Students take it in turns to ask for clues, e.g. *What's 3 across?* with their partner giving a word formation clue: *It's the noun of … .* or *It's the (negative) adjective of… .*

7 When they have finished students check answers by showing each other their completed crosswords, which should be identical.

10A Travel

> • Use at the start of Module 10A before Reading (CB pp. 136–137).
> **Aim:** To pre-teach some vocabulary and generate interest in the topic of travel.
> **Time:** 20–30 minutes
> **Activity type:** Individual, then whole class. Students complete a travel survey and find a travelling companion.
> **Preparation:** Make one copy of the questionnaire (p. 162) per student.

Procedure

1 In pairs, students have a minute to tell a partner about their most recent holiday.

2 Discuss the difference between going on holiday and travelling. Explain the purpose of the activity: to find the most suitable travelling partner in the class.

3 Pre-teach difficult vocabulary, e.g. *exotic, basics, souvenirs, racy novel*.

4 Students spend 5 minutes choosing their answers individually.

5 Students mingle and ask questions in order to find out who in the class has the most similar answers to them.

6 Students select a travelling companion with similar likes and interests to themselves.

Follow-up

Companions plan a trip together and report their plans back to the class.

10B Passives

> • Use after Language development 1 (CB pp. 138–139).
>
> | | |
> |---|---|
> | **Aim:** | To review passive structures. |
> | **Time:** | 15–20 minutes |
> | **Activity type:** | Groupwork. Students prepare extracts of travel news. |
> | **Exam focus:** | Paper 3 Part 4 |
> | **Preparation:** | Make one copy of the activity (pp. 163–164) and cut up into individual cards. |

Procedure

1 Ask students what type of news might be included in a section of 'Travel News', e.g. strikes, delays, new ideas/companies, special offers.

2 Tell students that the class is going to prepare a travel news feature.

3 Divide the class into six groups (fewer with a small class). Give each group one card.

4 Each group uses the information on the card to write the news story, adding more information if they wish. Remind students to use passive structures where they would be more appropriate.

5 Groups take it in turn to read out their stories to the class.

6 Give feedback on their use (or not) of passive structures and give alternative ways of expressing points if necessary.

Variation

In Procedure, step 3, the six stories could be neatly written out and compiled into a class newspaper.

10C Wishes and regrets

> • Use after Language development 2 (CB p. 145).
>
> | | |
> |---|---|
> | **Aim:** | To practise making sentences with *wish* and *if only, it's about time* and *I'd rather.* |
> | **Time:** | 20–30 minutes (or see Variation below) |
> | **Activity type:** | Groupwork. Students use picture cues to imagine what wishes people are making in different leisure situations. |
> | **Exam focus:** | Paper 3 Part 4 |
> | **Preparation:** | Make one copy of the activity (pp. 165–166) per group of three students and cut the cards up. |

Procedure

1 Introduce the activity by asking students about the leisure facilities in their town. What does it need? What needs improving? What was better in the past?

2 Write on the board *I wish, If only, It's about time* and *I'd rather*. Get students to use them to express their ideas, e.g. *I wish/It's about time we had a sports centre.*

3 Divide the class into groups of three and give each group a set of cards face down on the table.

4 One student should take a card from the top of the pile and place it face up on the table. Each student should, in turn, think of at least one wish/regret per card. For every correct sentence, accepted by the others in the group, a student scores 1 point.

5 Remind students to use the structures on the board. Wishes could be about the speaker/thinker, other people in the picture or the situation as a whole. Wishes could be about the present or the past.

6 Demonstrate activity with one of the cards, e.g. the first card: *I wish he would let me in/If only I hadn't worn trainers.*

7 Set a time limit (10 minutes). The winner in each group is the student with the highest score.

Variation

Use cards a few at a time as 5-minute fillers over the next few lessons.

11A Happiness

• Use at the start of Module 11A, before Reading (CB pp. 150–151).

Aim:	To generate interest in the topic of happiness. To practise discussing and trying to reach a consensus.
Time:	15–20 minutes
Activity type:	Pairwork. Students rank factors that create happiness.
Exam focus:	Paper 5 Part 3 (collaborative task)
Preparation:	Make one copy of the activity (p. 167) for each pair of students.

Procedure

1 Ask students if they feel happy today or not. At this stage try to focus students on superficial things, e.g. *It's raining, It's Friday,* etc. Tell them that in this activity you want them to think about true happiness and contentment.

2 Divide the class into pairs and give each pair a copy of the activity.

3 Check quickly for any unknown vocabulary. If you feel it's necessary, refer students to the Functions reference on (CB p. 215).

4 Set a time limit of 5–10 minutes. (**Note:** in the exam they would have about 3 minutes).

5 Students work together to decide which points are more or less important and agree on the three which are the most important.

6 Hold class feedback to compare opinions.

Follow-up

Discuss which of the points in the list are easier or harder to obtain.

11B Clauses of reason, purpose and contrast

• Use after Language development 1 (CB pp. 152–153).

Aim:	To practise using linking words to make clauses of reason, purpose and contrast.
Time:	20–25 minutes (+ Follow-up)
Activity type:	Groupwork. Students make sentences from prompts to win points.
Preparation:	Make one copy of the activity (p. 168) per group of 3–4 students and cut up into individual cards.

Procedure

1 Divide the class into groups of 3–4 students. Each group has a pile of linking word cards (grey) and topic cards (white).

2 Explain that the object of the activity is for students to make sentences using the linking words and the topic words, e.g. *although* + *music*: *Although I like classical music, I don't often go to concerts.*

3 Students shuffle the linking words (grey) and place in a pile face down, then do the same with the topic cards (white).

4 Students take one card from each pile and use them to make a true sentence about themselves. They can use the word on the topic card or any related to the topic. If students are stuck they can change one of the two cards by putting it to the bottom of the pile and taking the next one from the top.

5 Other students in the group listen and judge if the sentence is grammatically correct or not (referring any disputes to the teacher).

6 If correct, the student keeps the cards and gains a point. If incorrect, the cards go back to the bottom of the pile. At the end the student with the most cards/points is the winner.

7 Teacher gives feedback on students' performance, eliciting more examples of any clause types that are causing problems.

Follow-up

Students choose three linking words from the grey cards and write three sentences about themselves, two of which are true and one false. They then read them out to their group, who guess which one is false.

11C Health

> • Use at the start of Module 11 before Listening (CB p. 156–157).
>
> **Aim:** To introduce the unit topic of health and to pre-teach some vocabulary.
>
> **Time:** 20–30 minutes
>
> **Activity type:** Individual and pairwork. Students do a light-hearted questionnaire to find out how healthy they are.
>
> **Preparation:** Make one copy of the questionnaire (p. 169) per student, with the answer key removed.

Procedure

1 In pairs students discuss who they think is the healthiest person in the class and why, or they tell a partner about the healthiest person they know.

2 Give each student a copy of the questionnaire and 5–10 minutes to complete it.

3 Give students the key. Students check their answers and work out their score. (Question 6: note that although too much sunshine can be harmful, a little sunshine is better for you than none at all.)

4 Dictate the analysis below.

5 Find out who is the healthiest in the class (the person/people with the highest score).

6 In pairs, students compare the answers they gave.

Analysis:

0–10 I am surprised that you made it this far! The clock is ticking. You need to make some drastic changes to your life and quickly.

11–20 Not too bad, but you still have a long way to go. There are signs of hope for you so don't give up.

21–30 You are doing well but don't get complacent, you can still do a lot more. With a bit of effort you could soon make the top group.

31–40 Are you an athlete? Or just a liar? You seem to be doing almost everything right, perhaps you should relax and let your hair down a bit.

Follow-up

In groups students think of other factors or tips for a healthy life.

12A Stories

> • Use after Reading (CB pp. 164–165).
>
> **Aim:** To revise storytelling and to look at how extracts can be taken from a story.
>
> **Time:** 25–30 minutes
>
> **Activity type:** Groupwork. Students put together a story from picture prompts and write an extract.
>
> **Preparation:** Make six copies of the picture story (p. 170) and cut up (fewer if the class is too small for six groups of 2–3 students).

Procedure

1 Ask students if they enjoy reading fiction, how many novels they read a year and how it compares to watching movies.

2 Divide the class into six groups, (or groups of 2–3 students in classes of fewer than 12 students).

3 Give each group a set of cut-up pictures and 5 minutes to put them in order, discussing what is happening in each picture, and summarising the whole story.

4 With the whole class elicit a group version of the story, establishing names for the characters, time and locations.

5 Collect one set of pictures, shuffle and give one to each group, pointing out that they now each have an extract from the story.

6 Each group has 10 minutes, working together, to write their extract. Encourage them to think about what has happened previously and about each character's feelings and motivation. Monitor, helping with tenses and encouraging them to use richer vocabulary.

7 Students read out their extracts in order. Alternatively collect them in and give students a copy to read.

Story: possible Synopsis

The young woman got married and had a baby, but her husband had to go away to fight in a war. She received a letter saying he was dead, so she decided to emigrate to another country to start a new life. After some time she met someone and remarried. Then, one day her first husband appeared at the door – he had not been killed, but had been a prisoner of war, and when he was released he came to look for her.

Follow-up

Ask students if they think it would make a good movie and, if so, who they would cast in the various roles.

12B Conjunctions and connectors

• Use after Language development 1 (CB pp. 166–167).	
Aim:	To practise using connecting words and participle clauses while telling a story.
Time:	20–25 minutes
Activity type:	Groupwork. Students play a game, taking turns to tell parts of the same story, but working towards different endings.
Exam focus:	Paper 2 Part 2, Paper 3 Parts 2 and 4
Preparation:	Make one copy of the activity (p. 171) per group of 3–4, cut up into the four cards.

Procedure

1 Divide the class into groups of 3–4 and give each student a card.

2 Explain the object of the game: to finish a joint story with the words on their card. Students tell the same story taking it in turns to tell a part.

3 Select one student to begin the story. Turns then rotate around the group.

4 At each turn students must follow on logically from what came before but try to turn the story in the direction of their ending by introducing characters, objects or incidents as necessary.

5 Each turn, a student must try to use one of the structures listed on the card which is then ticked off. Each student can use each structure once only.

6 Other students can challenge if they think the link is not logical or the use of the structure is incorrect. If they cannot think of a sentence using one of the target structures, they can make up another sentence, just to continue the story.

7 When someone has ticked off five structures from their card they can finish the story (with the ending on their card) and win the game.

8 As students are playing, monitor by helping with use of target structures and noting errors to correct at the end of the activity.

12C Media mistakes

• Use after Language development 3 (CB p. 176).	
Aim:	To practise word-building and focus on common student errors.
Time:	25–30 minutes
Activity type:	Pairwork and whole class. Students gamble for points on whether sentences are correct or not.
Exam focus:	Paper 3 Parts 1 and 3
Preparation:	Make one copy of each page (pp. 172–173) per pair of students.

Procedure

1 Write on the board: *I don't know how Sarah was yesterday but she looked happily.* Ask students, in pairs, to decide if it is correct or not. If incorrect, they should say why and be able to correct it.

2 Explain the object of the game; to win as many points as possible by gambling on whether sentences are correct or incorrect.

3 Give each pair of students a copy of the worksheet (Common mistakes) and 10–15 minutes to look at the sentences and decide if each one is correct and if they are sure. Students can risk 1, 2, 5 or 10 points for each sentence depending on how sure they are.

4 Hand out cut-up game cards, students put *correct* and *incorrect* cards on the desk in front of them. Check answers one by one. For every question each pair puts 1, 2, 5 or 10 points on either the *correct* or *incorrect* card in front of them.

5 For each sentence select a pair to say why they made their choice and to correct the sentence if necessary. If a pair is wrong they lose the number of points they have put down, if they are right then they win that number.

6 Pairs write down their own points adding + or – to their score each time, e.g. they might write *+5* or *10* in the points column, depending how much they risked and if they are correct or not.

7 At the end students add up the total. Any pairs with more than 60 pass, the pair with the highest score wins.

> **1** ✗ (*as* a journalist); **2** ✓; **3** ✗ (*now/at the moment I'm working*); **4** ✓; **5** ✗ (*it* was boring/I was *bored*); **6** ✗ (*one another/each other*); **7** ✓; **8** ✗ (*illegal*); **9** ✗ (*such an* interesting story); **10** ✓; **11** ✓; **12** ✗ (that had *robbed* a bank); **13** ✗ (a bit *depressing*); **14** ✗ (on a *two-year* contract); **15** ✗ (an *inconvenient* time)

How much do you know about the FCE exam?

Answer the following questions by choosing the correct answer A, B or C.

1 How many papers are there in the exam?
A 4
B 5
C 6

2 What's the pass mark?
A about 60%
B about 65%
C about 70%

3 Do you need to pass all the papers?
A Yes, of course!
B No, passing most of them is enough.
C No, it's the total mark that is important.

4 In Paper 1 (Reading) which part is the most important?
A Part 1, because the questions are worth more marks.
B Part 3, because there are more questions.
C All three parts are equally important and have the same number of marks.

5 In Paper 2 (Writing) do you have to answer all the questions?
A Yes, so write quickly.
B You must answer question 1 and one other from Part 2.
C You can answer any two questions.

6 In Paper 3 (Use of English) do you lose marks if the answer is wrong?
A No, so take a chance if you don't know, you might be lucky.
B Yes, so only write an answer if you are really sure.
C Sometimes, it depends on how the examiner is feeling.

7 In Paper 4 (Listening) how many times do you hear each part?
A Only once, so listen carefully.
B Twice (or more if you ask the examiner nicely).
C You will hear each part twice before going on to the next part.

8 In Paper 5 (Speaking) do you speak to the examiner or your partner?
A You only discuss things with your partner.
B Sometimes to the examiner and sometimes to your partner.
C You say everything to the examiner.

9 Is correct spelling essential?
A Yes – all words must be spelt correctly in all papers.
B It's essential in Papers 2 and 3.
C No – everyone knows English spelling is difficult!

10 Which of the following can you take into the exam: a dictionary, a bottle of water, a lucky rabbit's foot?
A all of them
B none of them
C just the water and lucky rabbit's foot

Decide if the following statements are _True_ (T) or _False_ (F).

11 All papers are worth the same number of marks.
True ☐   False ☐

12 In Paper 2 Part 2 (Writing) you should write between 120–180 words.
True ☐   False ☐

13 Contractions count as one word in Paper 3 (Use of English).
True ☐   False ☐

14 Spelling must always be correct in Paper 4 (Listening).
True ☐   False ☐

15 You can take Paper 5 (Speaking) on your own if you are shy.
True ☐   False ☐

125

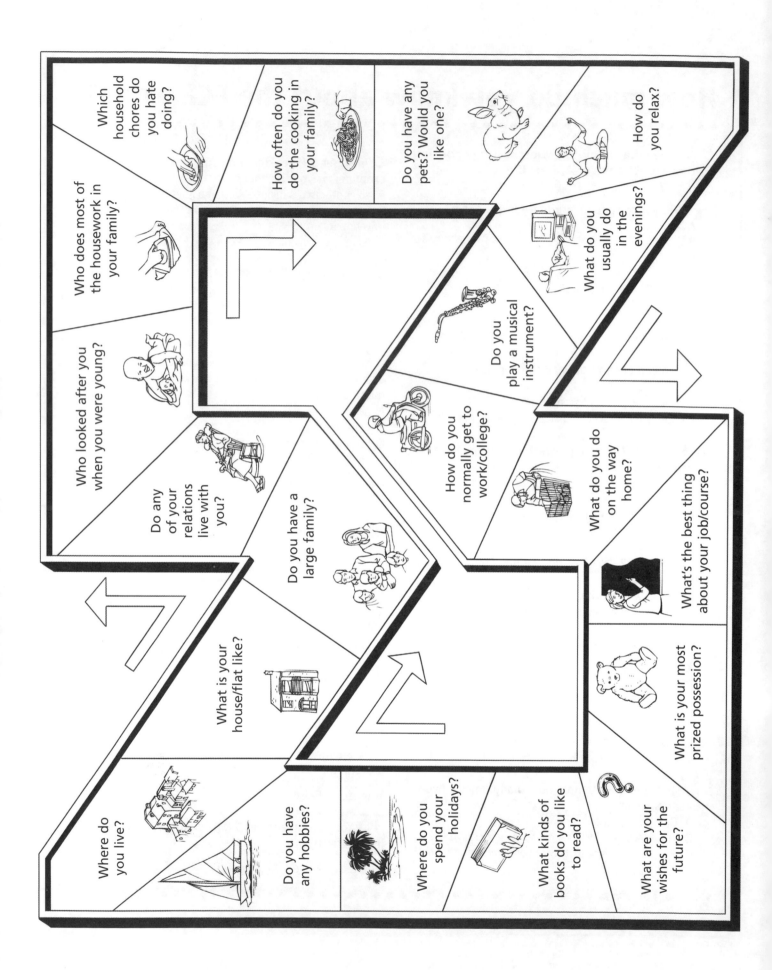

Which household chores do you hate doing?

How often do you do the cooking in your family?

Do you have any pets? Would you like one?

How do you relax?

Who does most of the housework in your family?

What do you usually do in the evenings?

Do you play a musical instrument?

Who looked after you when you were young?

How do you normally get to work/college?

What do you do on the way home?

Do any of your relations live with you?

Do you have a large family?

What's the best thing about your job/course?

What is your house/flat like?

What is your most prized possession?

Where do you live?

Do you have any hobbies?

Where do you spend your holidays?

What kinds of books do you like to read?

What are your wishes for the future?

Picture A

Picture B

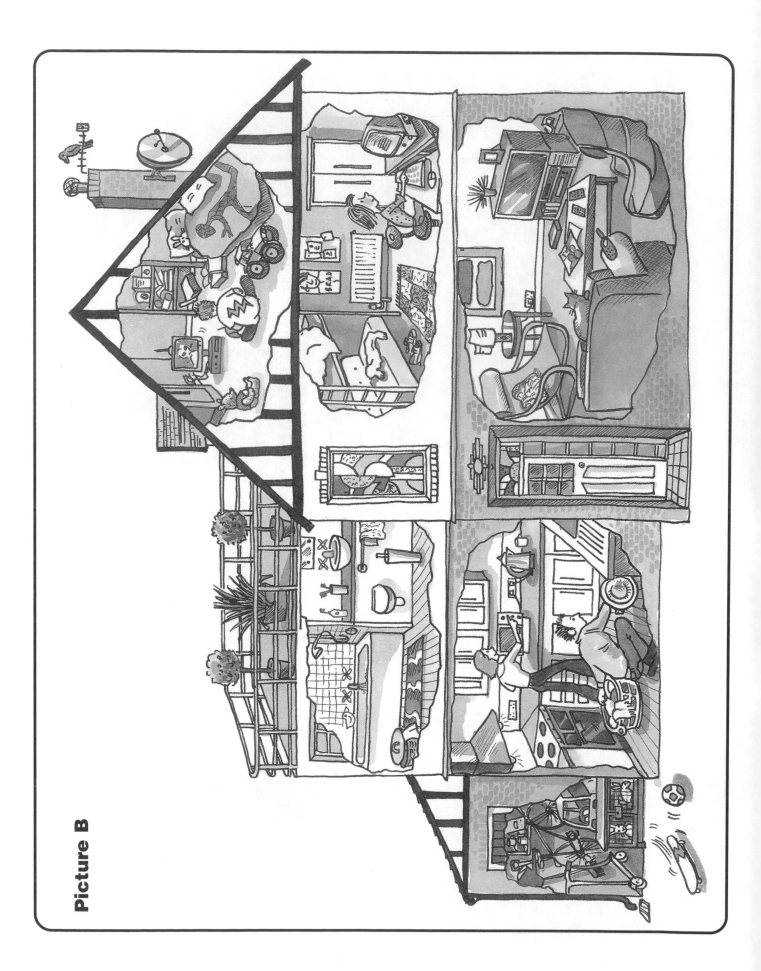

Part 1

unique	final	quick
high	memorable	valuable
strong	natural	domestic
wide	central	exact
hard	guided	slight

opportunity	destination	breakfast
speed	experience	paintings
influence	light	life
gap	heating	date
work	tour	change

Part 2

Complete the text with the correct collocation.

Streatham Palace

Come for a day out at Streatham Palace. Join our knowledgeable staff on a **(1)**................. of this magnificent home. There is nothing else like this in London so this is a **(2)**................. to learn about **(3)**................. in the eighteenth century before the modern era of electricity and **(4)**................. communication. There has only been a **(5)**................. to the appearance of the house since it was built sometime between 1760 and 1780, the **(6)**................. is not known.

See the **(7)**................. in lifestyles between the rich house owner and the life of the staff. Staff at the time were used to **(8)**................. ; they worked twelve hours a day, six days a week. Actors in period costume play the parts of the people who lived there, telling you about their lifestyles.

After a **(9)**................. in the kitchen, the staff would start work. One of the first jobs was making up the fires in every room each morning. (These were the days before **(10)**................. !).

In the main part of the house you can see the **(11)**................. of French design, shown in the choice of furniture and fabrics. Visit the fantastic dining room where an invitation to dinner would have been a truly **(12)**................. . In the living room the large windows fill the room with **(13)**................. . The house contains many **(14)**................. by famous British artists of the time.

In the main bedroom see the huge bed that was made in 1825 as a present for an Indian Prince but never reached its **(15)**................. .

The tour continues to the area where the staff lived in the attic and finishes in our tearoom and gift shop.

This is a chance to make history come alive!

1 Which of these jobs do you think is the most stressful?

- fire fighter
- prison officer
- football referee
- miner
- actor
- soldier

2 Which of these jobs is the best paid? Which one should be the best paid?

- company director
- surgeon
- lawyer
- politician
- accountant
- musician

3 Which of these jobs requires the longest training?

- judge
- dentist
- vet
- ballet dancer
- architect
- chef

4 Which of these jobs would you find the most satisfying?

- midwife
- teacher
- farmer
- pilot
- photographer
- builder

5 Which of these jobs do you think is the easiest to do?

- librarian
- fashion model
- DJ
- traffic warden
- lifeguard
- bouncer

6 Which of these jobs do you think is the most useful for society?

- lorry driver
- dustman
- civil servant
- undertaker
- shop assistant
- TV/radio newsreader

Employer A

You and **B** are a couple. You have three children (8, 5 and 18 months). You have had two au pairs before.

You want an au pair who:

- **is artistic/musical**
  study?   what?   how long?

- **is experienced at looking after children**
  experienced?   how long?   who?   when?

- **speaks good English**
  study?   how long?

- **has lived/worked abroad**
  yes/no?   where/when?

- **can cook for a large family**
  experience of cooking?
  how long?   how often?

Employer B

You and **A** are a couple. You have three children (8, 5 and 18 months). You have had two au pairs before.

You want an au pair who:

- **is into sports**
  which sports?   how long?
  played cricket/hockey?   been skiing?

- **is fit/energetic**
  exercise?   played games with kids?

- **is a good driver**
  drive?   how long?
  any accidents?   driven on the left?

- **is good with pets**
  experience?
  what animals looked after?
  experience of fish or snakes?

- **is good with computers**
  studied computing?
  used Internet for homework?

Applicant C

In the future you want to be a dancer or an actor.
Now, you want to be an au pair in the UK because you need to learn English.

You:

- **can cook quite well**
- **can drive**
- **hate computers**
(For everything else answer as is true for you.)

You want to work for a family that:

- **has had an au pair before**
  yes/no?   how many?   how long?   when?

- **knows the local area well**
  lived there – how long?

Applicant D

In the future you want to run your own business.
Now, you want to be an au pair in the UK because you need to learn English.

You:

- **are a great cook**
- **passed your driving test recently**
- **don't like animals**
(For everything else answer as is true for you.)

You want to work for a family that:

- **knows about your country and traditions**
  visited?   when?

- **has lots of holidays (and trips to places)**
  how many this year?

Story A

Complete the gaps with *a/an, the* or *ø* (if no article is required).

The Girl and the Wolf

One afternoon .... wolf waited in .... dark forest for .... girl to come by. He was very hungry because it had been .... long time since he had eaten anything. Finally, ... little girl did come along .... path and she was carrying .... basket of food.

.... girl was happy, ... weather was good, ... sun was shining and .... birds were singing. She loved .... nature and being with .... animals. 'What .... beautiful day!' she thought. She was happy that it was .... holiday and that she wasn't at .... school.

.... wolf asked her if she was going to visit her grandmother and she said that she was. So .... wolf asked her where her grandmother lived and .... little girl told him. Then he ran off. When .... little girl opened .... door of .... Granny's house she saw that there was somebody in .... bed listening to .... radio, wearing .... nightcap and nightdress. When she was no nearer than ten metres from .... bed she saw that it was not her grandmother but .... wolf, because everybody knows that .... wolf in .... nightcap looks nothing like your granny. So she took .... gun from her basket and shot .... wolf dead.

Moral: It is not so easy to fool .... little girls nowadays as it used to be.

Key (story A):

One afternoon *a* wolf waited in *a* dark forest for *a* girl to come by. He was very hungry because it had been *a* long time since he had eaten anything. Finally, *a* little girl did come along *the* path and she was carrying *a* basket of food.

The girl was happy, *the* weather was good, *the* sun was shining and *the* birds were singing. She loved *x* nature and being with *x* animals. 'What *a* beautiful day!' she thought. She was happy that it was *a* holiday and that she wasn't at *x* school.

The wolf asked her if she was going to visit her grandmother and she said that she was. So *the* wolf asked her where her grandmother lived and *the* little girl told him. Then he ran off.

When *the* little girl opened *the* door of *x* Granny's house she saw that there was somebody in *x* bed listening to *the* radio, wearing *a* nightcap and nightdress. When she was no nearer than ten metres from *the* bed she saw that it was not her grandmother but *the* wolf, because everybody knows that *a* wolf in *a* nightcap looks nothing like your granny. So she took *a* gun from her basket and shot *the* wolf dead.

Moral: It is not so easy to fool x little girls nowadays as it used to be.

Story B

Complete the gaps with *a/an, the* or *ø* (if no article is required).

The Girl and the Shoe

There was once .... poor young girl who was very unhappy. She had to spend all .... day cleaning .... house. She had two big ugly sisters who were unkind to her.

One day all .... girls were invited to .... party. .... beautiful young girl couldn't go because her big ugly sisters said she had to stay at .... home and do some housework. Anyway, although she loved .... music and dancing, she didn't have anything to wear.

Suddenly .... fairy godmother appeared. 'What .... pity!' said .... fairy godmother, 'Let me help you.' and gave her everything she needed: .... clothes, shoes and .... golden carriage. .... girl went to .... party and had .... great time. She met .... rich young man and danced with him all .... night.

At .... midnight she had to leave and was in such .... hurry that she left one of her shoes behind. .... young man kept it and spent .... next few days looking for .... girl who had lost it. Finally, he came to her house and asked her to try it on. .... shoe fitted perfectly. He asked her to marry him. She refused and said that first she wanted to go to .... university and get .... job, then when .... time was right she would consider getting married.

Moral: *These days .... marriage is less important than .... career.*

Key (story B):

There was once ***a*** poor young girl who was very unhappy. She had to spend all ***x*** day cleaning ***the*** house. She had two big ugly sisters who were unkind to her.

One day all ***the*** girls were invited to ***a*** party. ***The*** beautiful young girl couldn't go because her big ugly sisters said she had to stay at ***x*** home and do some housework. Anyway, although she loved ***x*** music and dancing, she didn't have anything to wear.

Suddenly ***a*** fairy godmother appeared. 'What ***a*** pity!' said ***the*** fairy godmother, 'Let me help you.' and gave her everything she needed: ***x*** clothes, shoes and ***a*** golden carriage. ***The*** girl went to ***the*** party and had ***a*** great time. She met ***a*** rich young man and danced with him all ***x*** night.

At ***x*** midnight she had to leave and was in such ***a*** hurry that she left one of her shoes behind. ***The*** young man kept it and spent ***the*** next few days looking for ***the*** girl who had lost it. Finally, he came to her house and asked her to try it on. ***The*** shoe fitted perfectly. He asked her to marry him. She refused and said that first she wanted to go to ***x*** university and get ***a*** job, then when ***the*** time was right she would consider getting married.

Moral: *These days **x** marriage is less important than **a** career.*

Group A – For

'Tourism should be encouraged: it is good for a country.'

- Creates work – many jobs are needed in tourist industry.
- Good for local economy – tourists spend money and for the country it brings in foreign exchange.
- Educational – people learn about other places, languages, etc.
- Helps to preserve and protect monuments, traditions and cultures – that's what tourists like to see.
- Transport is improved – tourists need better roads, trains, etc.
- Cultural exchange – visitors and tourists learn about each other's cultures.

Useful language – presenting

Sequencing:

Firstly, … .

Secondly, … .

Finally, … .

Expressing opinions:

I think/believe that … .

In my opinion … .

It seems to me that … .

Concluding:

To sum up … .

In conclusion … .

Useful language – discussing

Responding:

I understand what you are saying, but … .

But don't you think …?

Suggesting:

What about …?

Don't forget that … .

Group B – Against

'Tourism should be encouraged: it is good for a country.'

- Increases local prices – tourists will pay more than locals, so prices go up.
- Tourists use valuable resources – water, land, food, etc. go to tourists not locals.
- Creates pollution, disturbs wildlife.
- Destroys local culture – everywhere becomes the same.
- Jobs are seasonal and low-skilled – shop, restaurant and hotel work.
- Tourists don't respect places and people they visit – tourists can be rude and offend against local religions and customs.

Useful language – presenting

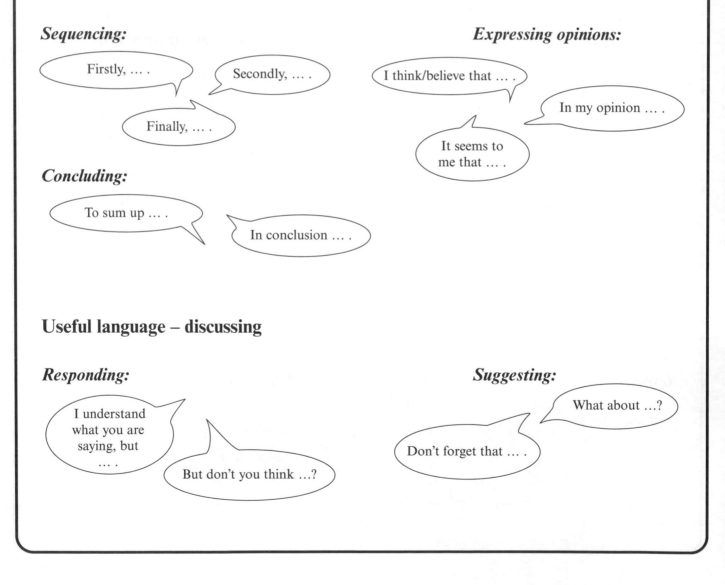

Sequencing:

Firstly, … .

Secondly, … .

Finally, … .

Expressing opinions:

I think/believe that … .

In my opinion … .

It seems to me that … .

Concluding:

To sum up … .

In conclusion … .

Useful language – discussing

Responding:

I understand what you are saying, but … .

But don't you think …?

Suggesting:

What about …?

Don't forget that … .

Set A: sentence cards

1 I had thought it would be really difficult to find, but it was .... easy.	11 It is .... impossible to find a parking space in the town centre, but occasionally you are lucky.
2 The tour had .... started when it started to rain.	12 We were .... starving when we got home as we hadn't eaten all day.
3 The situation is difficult and the future of the island looks	13 The castle is worth visiting, but the climb up to it is .... tough.
4 The town centre is very .... on a Saturday evening when all the bars and clubs are busy.	14 Why don't you come in autumn? The weather is usually .... good then.
5 The food is good so it's .... worth visiting this restaurant.	15 Famous residents include Fleming, who is .... well-known writer.
6 They try really .... to attract more tourists each year.	16 I tried sailing, which was .... very easy after the first few minutes.
7 We received a .... welcome from the smiling staff when we arrived at the hotel.	17 The CD was faulty and the case was damaged ....
8 Plans for the future need to be made now as the population is rising	18 If you don't improve safety someone could be .... injured.
9 Unfortunately, it is .... far from the city centre.	19 I was amazed – booking the holiday on line was .... simple and only took a few minutes.
10 The restaurant at the top of the mountain is .... expensive, so few people can afford it.	20 The service in the restaurant was .... slow and when the food did come it was cold.

Set B: adjective/adverb cards

surprisingly	pretty
hardly	quite a
bleak	as well
well	seriously
hard	remarkably
friendly	lively
quite	fast
extremely	absolutely
practically	actually
a bit	rather

Set A

think of	eager	keen on	regret
agree	enjoy	let	remember
apologise for	finish	look forward to	stop
can't help	hard	make	teach
decision	have trouble	opportunity	try
dream of	interested in	refuse	unable

Set B

wear	make	go	learn
watch	build	take	get
play	study	write	buy
feel	work	clean	spend
live	read	tidy up	predict
change	walk	turn down	ignore

Your club/society wants to raise money to buy some new equipment. Look at the options below and decide what the best method to raise the money would be. Discuss them and agree on the best way. For each method think about:

- how much money you would need to start with
- how long it would take
- how easy it would be for you
- how successful it would be.

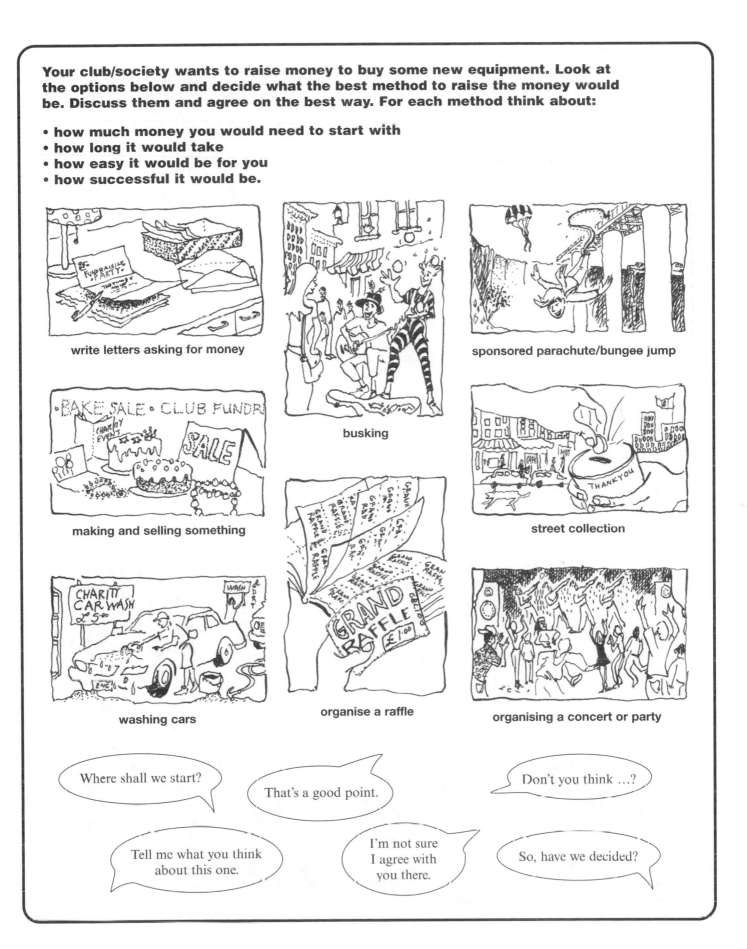

write letters asking for money

busking

sponsored parachute/bungee jump

making and selling something

street collection

washing cars

organise a raffle

organising a concert or party

Where shall we start?

That's a good point.

Don't you think …?

Tell me what you think about this one.

I'm not sure I agree with you there.

So, have we decided?

Missing person

It's 9 May and Peter Brown is missing. Where is he? Why? What happened? Look at his room – what can you say about him before he disappeared?

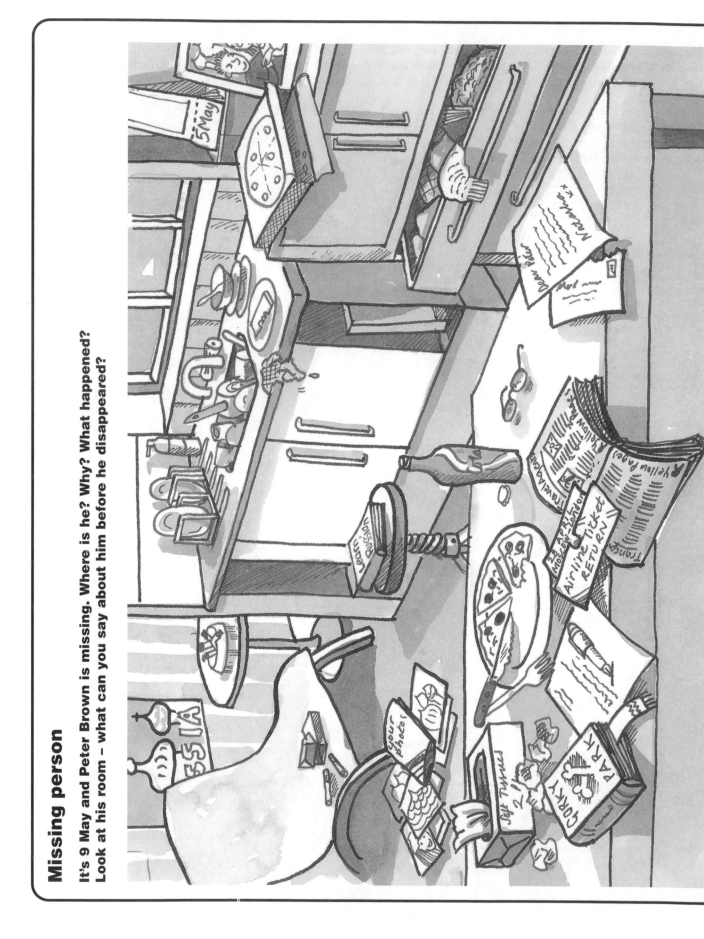

Part 1

alone – with no one else (physical) **lonely** – unhappy, missing friends (a feeling)	**shy** – not confident speaking to unknown people **nervous** – worried/frightened about something that may happen
imaginative – creative, with a good imagination **imaginary** – not real, fictitious **fantastic** – very good	**slim** – opposite of fat (positive) **thin** – opposite of fat (negative)
childish – behaviour like a child (negative) **childlike** – appearance, quality	**priceless** – worth a lot of money **worthless** worth nothing **invaluable** – very useful, essential
economic – trade and industry **economical** – good value, using money/time well	**terrific** – very good **terrifying** – very frightening **terrible** – very bad
similar – almost the same (before noun) **alike** – the same (not before noun) **familiar** – easy to recognise, known	**convenient** – not causing problems **useful** – helping you get what you want
classic – well known, typical, influential **classical** – traditional	**high** – distance from ground **tall** – for people, and narrow things **long** – horizontal measure
foreign – from another country **strange** – unusual, different	**old-fashioned** – not modern, not usual any more **out of date** – no longer useful/correct
fun – enjoyable **funny** – amusing, makes you laugh	**injured** – hurt physically by accident **wounded** – hurt with a weapon (in a fight/war)

Part 2

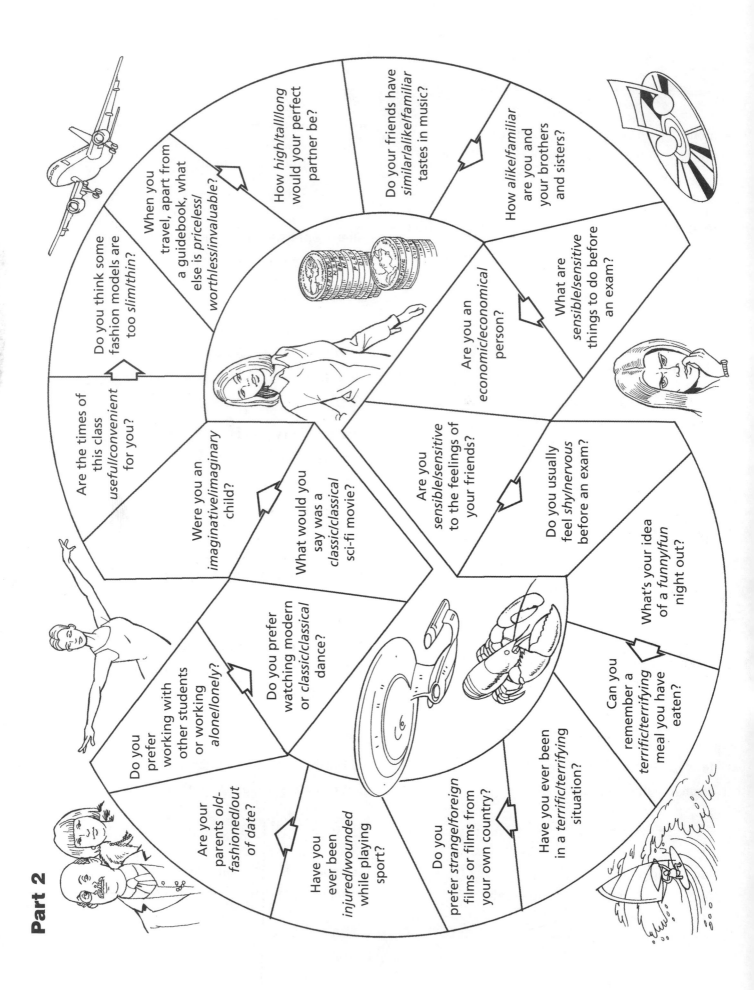

How high/tall/long would your perfect partner be?

Do your friends have similar/alike/familiar tastes in music?

How alike/familiar are you and your brothers and sisters?

When you travel, apart from a guidebook, what else is priceless/worthless/invaluable?

Do you think some fashion models are too slim/thin?

What are sensible/sensitive things to do before an exam?

Are you an economic/economical person?

Are the times of this class useful/convenient for you?

Were you an imaginative/imaginary child?

What would you say was a classic/classical sci-fi movie?

Are you sensible/sensitive to the feelings of your friends?

Do you usually feel shy/nervous before an exam?

Do you prefer working with other students or working alone/lonely?

Do you prefer watching modern or classic/classical dance?

What's your idea of a funny/fun night out?

Are your parents old-fashioned/out of date?

Have you ever been injured/wounded while playing sport?

Do you prefer strange/foreign films or films from your own country?

Have you ever been in a terrific/terrifying situation?

Can you remember a terrific/terrifying meal you have eaten?

PHOTOCOPIABLE

The **human body** quiz

How much do you know about the human body? Can you answer these questions by choosing A, B or C?

If you're not sure, have a guess!

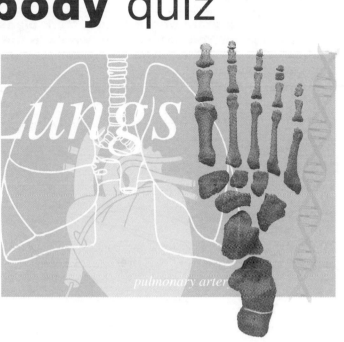

1 How many bones are there in the human body?
A 68
B 149
C 213

2 How much blood does an average adult have?
A 5 litres
B 6.5 litres
C 8 litres

3 How heavy is your brain?
A 0.6 kg
B 1.4 kg
C 3.2 kg

4 Is your heart
A on the left?
B in the centre?
C on the right?

5 What is a typical heartbeat for someone resting?
A 40–60 beats a minute
B 60–80 beats a minute
C 80–100 beats a minute

6 The study of how characteristics are passed from one generation to another is called
A genealogy.
B jeanetics.
C genetics.

7 Psychology is the study of
A mental processes.
B mental illness.
C mental intelligence.

8 Information in your body is stored in genes. How many are there in each cell of your body?
A 10,000
B 25,000
C 50,000

9 Genes are made up of a chemical called
A ADN.
B DNA.
C NAD.

10 The largest organ in your body is
A the liver.
B the heart.
C the lungs.

11 How many muscles are there in the human body?
A about 300
B about 600
C about 900

12 How much does a new-born baby weigh on average?
A 2.4 kgs
B 2.9 kgs
C 3.4 kgs

Your future

Look at this diagram of the future. Mark plans or predictions about <u>your</u> future on the diagram. You can use the words in the box or your own ideas.

go	meet	get	buy	change school/job
give up	find	become	take up	start work/a business
travel	move house	get married	have a baby	retire

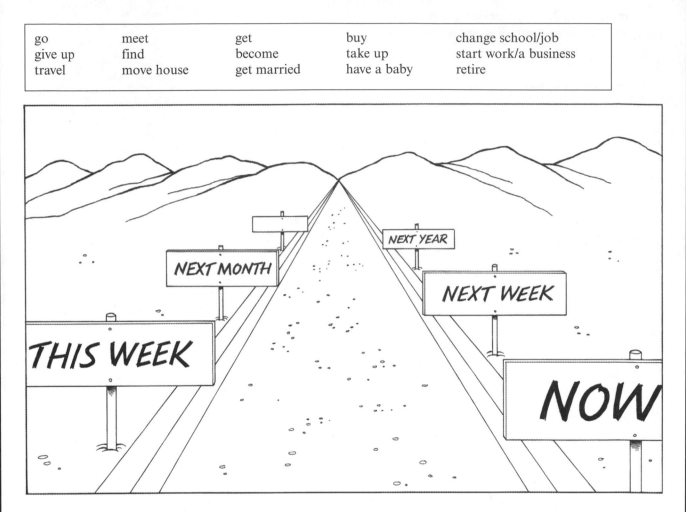

Think about which tense you will use to talk about each point that you have marked on the diagram. Tick (✔) the *Can you use it?* column in the table each time you use one of the forms.

Form	Example	Can you use it?
Present simple	The exam takes place every … .	
Present continuous	I am taking the exam in … .	
Will/Shall	I hope I will pass!	
Going to	I'm going to study hard.	
Future continuous	We will be taking the exam at that time.	
Future perfect	We will have taken the exam by… .	

ure	excite	ion	encourage
ment	combin(e)	ment	exist
ation	perform	ence	surviv(e)
ance	correspond	al	assist
ence	fail	ance	contribut(e)
ure	hesitat(e)	ion	embarrass
ion	approv(e)	ment	press
al	achieve	ure	organis(e)
ment	appear	ation	protect
ance	clos(e)	ion	attend
ure	refus(e)	ance	propos(e)
al	confirm	al	prefer
ation	depend	ence	imagin(e)
ence	restrict	ation	pleas(e)

HOW AMBITIOUS ARE YOU?

Answer the following questions by choosing *Yes*, *No* or *Maybe* each time.

1 Do you want to be an important person in your community?
Yes ☐   Maybe ☐   No ☐

2 Do you tend to be lazy?
Yes ☐   Maybe ☐   No ☐

3 Do you compare your ability and performance with that of other people?
Yes ☐   Maybe ☐   No ☐

4 Do you set your targets low in order to avoid disappointments?
Yes ☐   Maybe ☐   No ☐

'One day, Mr Blond, all this will be mine …'

5 Do you try to do things immediately rather than put them off until later?
Yes ☐   Maybe ☐   No ☐

6 Are you satisfied with your current achievements?
Yes ☐   Maybe ☐   No ☐

7 When you play a game is it important that you do well?
Yes ☐   Maybe ☐   No ☐

8 Would you prefer to laze on a beach rather than work/study?
Yes ☐   Maybe ☐   No ☐

9 Do you prefer to mix with ambitious and successful people?
Yes ☐   Maybe ☐   No ☐

10 Do you sometimes have days when you haven't done a thing?
Yes ☐   Maybe ☐   No ☐

11 Are you embarrassed if you are caught being lazy?
Yes ☐   Maybe ☐   No ☐

12 On an escalator, do you let it carry you along rather than walking up it yourself?
Yes ☐   Maybe ☐   No ☐

audience	standing ovation	director
choreographer	curtain	interval
rehearsals	stalls	first night
stage	review	front row
conductor	role	composer
ballet	costume	performance
box office	orchestra	programme
encore	critic	principal dancer
actors	spotlight	backstage
a play	concert	theatregoer

It's a place where … .

They're people who … .

It's a thing which … .

It's a time when … .

He/She's a person who … .

It's an occasion when …

Student A

similar *to*	congratulations *on*	full *of*	annoyed	relationship	famous ....
tired *of*	attitude *to/towards*	respect *for*	excited	capable	comparison ....
enthusiastic *about*	interested *in*	solution *to*	relevant	advantage	fed up ....
responsible *for*	no hope *of*	difference *between/in*	unusual	invitation	proud ....
right *about* something/*for* someone	linked *to*	satisfied *with*	result (n.)	included	suitable ....
involved *in* something/*with* someone	suspicious *of/about*	ready *for*	worried	keen	jealous ....

at   of   in   for   with   on   about   to   between

Student B

annoyed *with* someone/ *about* something	relationship *with/between*	famous *for*	similar	congratulations	full ....
excited *about/at*	capable *of*	comparison *with/to*	tired	attitude	respect ....
relevant *to*	advantage *of*	fed up *with*	enthusiastic	interested	solution ....
unusual *for*	invitation *to* something/ *for* someone	proud *of*	responsible	no hope	difference ....
result (n.) *of*	included *in*	suitable *for*	right	linked	satisfied ....
worried *about*	keen *on*	jealous *of*	involved	suspicious	ready ....

towards   of   in   for   with   on   about   to   between

The global food and drink quiz

Can you answer these questions by choosing A, B, C or D? If you're not sure, have a guess!

1 How many branches of McDonald's are there in the world?

A 5,000
B 15,000
C 30,000
D 50,000

2 How many countries does McDonald's operate in?

A 48
B 99
C 121
D 187

3 McDonald's is the world's largest distributor of what?

A orange juice
B toys
C spoons
D forks

4 How many people work for KFC worldwide?

A 50,000
B 100,000
C 300,000
D 500,000

5 How many countries is Coca-Cola sold in?

A 140–160
B 160–180
C 180–200
D more than 200

6 How long does it take the Coca-Cola corporation to sell 1 billion (1,000,000,000) cokes?

A 2 days
B 6 days
C 10 days
D 14 days

7 What is the best selling confectionery brand in the world?

A Kit Kat
B M&M's
C Snickers
D Hershey Bar

8 Brazil is the world's largest producer of coffee. Which country is the second largest?

A Vietnam
B Kenya
C Guatemala
D Colombia

9 Which country drinks more coffee per person than any other?

A USA
B Switzerland
C Italy
D France

10 Which country drinks more tea per person than any other?

A Egypt
B UK
C Turkey
D Ireland

I'm not sure.

Personally, I think/reckon it's … .

I think it could/might be … .

Which one shall we go for?

CULTURAL DOS AND DON'TS

Work together to make 12 statements that you believe to be true.

1 In Korea you are (*supposed to / not supposed to / not allowed to*) write someone's name in (*pink / green / red.*)

2 In China you (*mustn't / aren't allowed to / aren't supposed to*) use your (*teacher's / partner's / neighbour's*) name when talking to him or her.

3 In Japan you (*don't need to / are allowed to / must*) wash (*before / while / after*) you have a bath.

4 In Greece you (*shouldn't / ought to / are allowed to*) touch your (*earlobe / nose / chin*) while you are talking to someone.

5 In Muslim countries you (*don't have to / mustn't / don't need to*) pass or receive things with (*your left / your right / both*) hand(s).

6 In Thailand you (*mustn't / ought to / have to*) put your foot on a (*cigarette / coin / apple*) if you drop it and it is rolling away.

7 In the UK you (*don't have to / are supposed to / aren't allowed to*) stand (*on the left / on the right / at the bottom*) on escalators on the Underground.

8 In Japan and Korea you (*must / mustn't / shouldn't*) use both hands when giving something (*valuable / to an older person / edible.*)

9 In Spain you (*aren't supposed to / ought to / are allowed to*) say 'hello' to everyone when you enter a (*bar / lift / bus.*)

10 In Arabic countries you (*must / shouldn't / don't need to*) open (*gifts / letters / umbrellas*) in front of the person who gives them to you.

11 In Buddhist countries you (*can't / mustn't / don't need to*) point (*the soles of your feet / a finger / an umbrella*) at people or religious images.

12 In Germany you (*are supposed to / aren't supposed to / oughtn't to*) keep your (*hands / knife and fork / phone*) on or above the table during a meal.

I've got a great photo of my grandad standing on the ice with lots of penguins. It was taken on a trip to the Arctic.

I remember going to Berlin about ten years ago and seeing the famous wall and wondering how much longer it would last.

My friend Jorge speaks Spanish as he comes from South America, but I can't remember if he's from Brazil or Colombia.

My brother is working in Italy now. I can't remember where exactly, but it is a town with a famous leaning tower.

My house used to be a railway station on a line that disappeared in the 1950s. It was built about 200 years ago.

I've been driving for years and have never had an accident. I think I was 15 when I passed my test.

My father got his first mobile phone in the 1970s. It was expensive, but very useful.

The first time I used some Euro banknotes in 2000 I thought that they were ugly, but now I quite like them.

My favourite painting by the artist Monet is his picture of the airport at Giverny.

Yesterday I was reading about the type of television programmes people watched in the 1920s – they were very different from now.

My cousin recently returned from a holiday in South Africa. He told me all about the strange animals he saw there, such as kangaroos.

My favourite picture of my friend Lucy is one of her sitting with a surfboard on a beach in Switzerland.

I think my parents got married in 1971, but I'm not sure. I know it was on the same day that people first landed on the moon.

I usually go on holiday with my friend John who arranges everything. This year I think we are going skiing in Holland.

My friend had a car accident in Asia. I can't remember if it was Japan or Korea, but it was a place where people drive on the left.

My friend in New Zealand is always having problems. Recently she was bitten by a snake when she was hill walking.

Relationships

Add the missing prepositions: *in, out, to, from, up, on, with,* or *ø*
(if no preposition is required) to the expressions below.

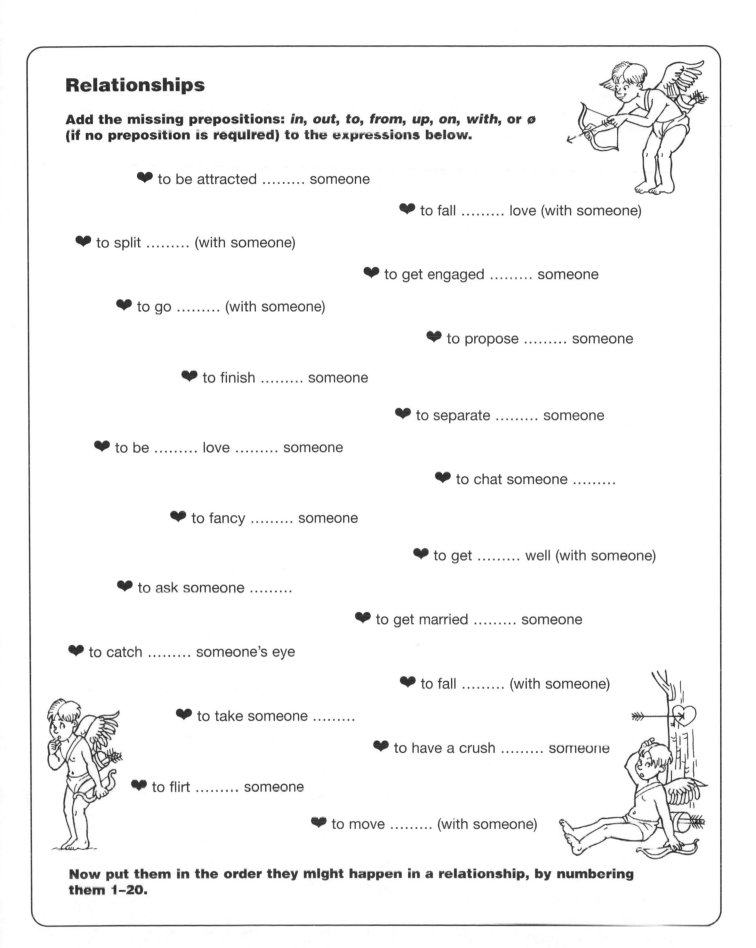

❤ to be attracted .... someone

❤ to fall .... love (with someone)

❤ to split .... (with someone)

❤ to get engaged .... someone

❤ to go .... (with someone)

❤ to propose .... someone

❤ to finish .... someone

❤ to separate .... someone

❤ to be .... love .... someone

❤ to chat someone ....

❤ to fancy .... someone

❤ to get .... well (with someone)

❤ to ask someone ....

❤ to get married .... someone

❤ to catch .... someone's eye

❤ to fall .... (with someone)

❤ to take someone ....

❤ to have a crush .... someone

❤ to flirt .... someone

❤ to move .... (with someone)

Now put them in the order they might happen in a relationship, by numbering them 1–20.

Student A

Put these last words from famous people into reported speech and report them to your partner. Don't say who said them, use 'Who ...?' so your partner can guess. Use reporting verbs (said, told, asked, explained, etc.).

EXAMPLE: Lawrence Oates, explorer
"I am just going outside and may be some time."
Who said that he was just going outside and may be some time?

I am about to – or I am going to – die; either expression is correct.
Dominique Bouhours – French Grammarian

Am I dying, or is my birthday?
Nancy Astor (to her family sitting round her bed)

I have had a hell of a lot of fun and enjoyed every minute of it.
Errol Flynn – actor

I don't have the passion anymore, and so remember it is better to burn out than fade away.
Kurt Cobain – singer in Nirvana

I have not told half of what I saw.
Marco Polo – traveller

Tomorrow I shall no longer be here.
Nostradamus – fortune teller (to his assistant)

I have never felt better.
Douglas Fairbanks Senior – Actor (to his doctor)

My wallpaper and I are fighting a battle to the death. One or other of us has to go.
Oscar Wilde – writer

I'm going away tonight.
James Brown – singer

Listen to your partner's quotes and choose from the following answers.

1 Elvis Presley – singer, at his last press conference
2 Viscount Palmerston – Prime minister
3 Edmund Gwenn – actor
4 Thomas de Mahay – Marquis de Favras, when given his death sentence
5 Lou Costello – actor/comedian
6 Louis XIV – king
7 Anton Chekhov – writer
8 H G Wells – writer
9 Salvador Dali – Painter

Student B

Put these last words from famous people into reported speech and report them to your partner. Don't say who said them, use 'Who ...?' so your partner can guess. Use reporting verbs (said, told, asked, explained, etc.).

EXAMPLE: Lawrence Oates, explorer

"I am just going outside and may be some time."
Who said that he was just going outside and may be some time?

I see that you have made three spelling mistakes.

Thomas de Mahay – French aristocrat (to a court official while reading his death sentence)

Where is my clock?

Salvador Dali – Painter

Go away. I am all right.

H G Wells – writer (to his doctor)

Die, doctor? That is the last thing I shall do.

Viscount Palmerston – Prime minister

I'm dying. It's been a long time since I've had champagne.

Anton Chekhov – writer

I hope I haven't bored you.

Elvis Presley – singer (to journalists)

That was the best ice-cream soda I ever tasted.

Lou Costello – actor/comedian

Yes, but not as tough as doing comedy.

Edmund Gwenn – actor (to a friend who asked if dying was tough)

Why do you weep? Did you think I was immortal?

Louis XIV – king

Listen to your partner's quotes and choose from the following answers.

1 Errol Flynn – actor
2 Oscar Wilde – writer
3 Dominique Bouhours – French Grammarian
4 Nostradamus – fortune teller
5 Douglas Fairbanks Senior – Actor
6 Nancy Astor – MP
7 James Brown – singer
8 Marco Polo – traveller
9 Kurt Cobain – singer in Nirvana

A weekend away

You and your friends have decided to spend a weekend together doing something interesting. Look at the activities in the pictures and choose the one that would be most interesting for you, as a group.

A meditation course

A golfing trip

A trip to a grand prix race

Working on a conservation project

A trip to a health farm/beauty spa

A music festival

Camping in a local forest

Horse-riding in the mountains

PHOTOCOPIABLE

14 Buy and sell shares in a quick trade. Make £700.

13 You are caught speeding. Pay a fine of £200.

12 You are careful with your money. Save £400.

11 Splash out on a new DVD player. Spend £500.

10 Get into debt. Pay £200 in interest.

15 Interest rates go up. Earn an extra £300.

23 Finish How much are you worth? Shares £x2 Business £x2

9 See a bargain in the sales. Spend £200.

16 You are extravagant with your money – use £400 of savings.

22 Your business, if you have one, (5,7) is valued at £30,000. Sell it!

8 Get a new job and a pay rise. Save £500.

17 Lend a friend £200 – never see him again! Lose £200.

21 Your business, if you have one, (5,7) goes bust, bankrupting you. Lose everything!

7 Invest in a friend's new business. Put in 25% of what you have.

18 At work your company does well. Get a bonus of £1,200.

19 Lose money on a gamble investing in property. Lose £4,000.

20 The stock market crashes. Lose £3,000.

6 Invest half your money in the stock market. Put in 50% of what you have.

1 Start You have £1,000 in the bank.

2 Win £5,000 on the lottery.

3 You get a grant of £2,000 to spend on your house.

4 Inherit £6,000 from your aunt.

5 Start a business. Put in all your money.

What you (do), if you (go) into the red last/next month?

If you (win) a lot of money, what you (do) with it?

If you (start) a business one day, what it (be)?

What you (say), if I (ask) you to lend me some money yesterday/tomorrow?

What you (do), if you (find) some money in the street?

When/If a shop assistant (give) you too much change, what you (do)?

What you (do), when this course (finish)?

If you (not do) this course, what you (do) now?

If you (not start) this course, what you (do) now?

What you (do), if you (cannot) do the homework this week?

If I (have) a party at the weekend, you (come)?

If you (visit) anywhere in the world, where you (go)?

If you (change) one law, what it (be)?

If you (feel) ill this/tomorrow morning, what you (do)?

If you (watch) TV tonight, what you (watch)?

If/When you (make) your favourite meal, what you (cook)?

If you (go) to a party, what you usually (wear)?

If/When you (have) a cold, what you (do)?

Where you (go), if you (have) another holiday this/last year?

What you (say), if I (say) I love you?

If/When you (get) a headache, what you (do)?

Student A

Crossword grid (Student A) with the following filled letters:

- 1 Across: WEALTHY
- 2 Down: TAXABLE
- 5 Across (row with AX): ...
- 7 Across: UNINSURED
- 6 Down: UNPROFITABLE
- 9 Across: REDUCTION
- 11 Down: FORTUNATE
- 12 Down: RECEIPT
- 13 Across / 14 Down: INSURANCE
- 16 Across: EARNINGS
- 17 Across: LOAN
- 19 Across: ALLOWANCE

Student B

Crossword grid (Student B) with the following filled letters:

- 3 Across: WITHDRAWAL
- 4 Down: AFFORDABLE
- 5 Across: INEXPENSIVE
- 7 Down: UNECONOMICAL
- 8 Across: VALUATION
- 10 Down: FINANCIAL
- 13 Across: DISCOUNTED
- 15 Down: WINNINGS
- 18 Across: INHERITANCE
- 20 Across: EXPENSE
- 21 Across: INVESTMENT

Find the perfect (travelling) partner.

Look at the sentences below and choose the answers that are most true for you.

1 When I am on holiday I prefer

A to stay at home and relax. ☐
B to stay in my country. ☐
C to visit a country I know. ☐
D to visit a new country. ☐

2 For holiday accommodation I prefer

A camping. ☐
B youth hostels. ☐
C cheap hotels. ☐
D luxury hotels. ☐

3 I prefer to go on holiday

A on my own. ☐
B with one close friend. ☐
C with a big group of friends. ☐
D with my parents. ☐

4 For the arrangements, I prefer to

A do it all myself in advance. ☐
B let a travel agent do it all. ☐
C make them as I go along. ☐
D just see what happens. ☐

5 My ideal holiday would be

A a safari. ☐
B a tropical beach holiday. ☐
C in an interesting city. ☐
D in the mountains. ☐

6 I like to take

A just a few basics. ☐
B a small backpack. ☐
C a suitcase. ☐
D as much as possible. ☐

7 On holiday, what I like to see most is

A exotic animals. ☐
B famous works of art. ☐
C fantastic sunsets. ☐
D good-looking locals. ☐

8 When I travel I usually read

A a local phrase book. ☐
B a guidebook. ☐
C a racy novel. ☐
D a timetable. ☐

9 The thing I enjoy most on holiday is

A doing nothing. ☐
B visiting museums. ☐
C physical exercise. ☐
D learning about local customs. ☐

10 I think travel should be about

A history and culture. ☐
B food and drink. ☐
C falling in love. ☐
D looking for adventure. ☐

11 My photos are mainly of

A me. ☐
B historical buildings. ☐
C local people. ☐
D wild parties. ☐

12 I like to bring back

A lots of photos. ☐
B a few souvenirs. ☐
C traditional local crafts. ☐
D a new partner. ☐

PHOTOCOPIABLE

Record Climb

Keiko Fujita, a 65-year-old Japanese woman, has climbed Everest by the North Face — the oldest person to do so. A team of local climbers helped her.

Everest facts

- Highest mountain in the world.
- First successful climb to the top was in 1953 by Tenzing and Hillary.
- Situated on the border of Nepal and Tibet.
- People consider the North Face to be the hardest route to the top.

New Car Rental Company

Some people have started a new Internet-based car rental company. They call it Simple Cars. You can find them at www.simplecars.com.

Simple Cars facts

- You must reserve and pay for cars online.
- You can collect a car from 22 airports around Europe.
- They charge customers per hour.
- People say they are the cheapest rental cars in Europe.

Record Balloon Flight

Diane May has flown a balloon solo non-stop around the world — the first woman to do so.

Flight facts

- A team of experts helped her.
- The wind blew her off course twice.
- A storm almost forced her to crash.
- She equipped her balloon with the latest technology.
- Her friends expect her to try to break another record next year.

New Hotel

A company has announced that they are going to build a new hotel in Cairo next to the pyramids. A famous architect is going to design it and a local company will build it. Tour groups will use it, mainly.

Pyramid facts

- Someone built them 4,500 years ago.

- The government has protected them for many years.

- We think that conservation groups are opposing the plans.

Discount Card

Some organisations in London have launched a 'Tourist discount card'. They will also give cardholders a chance to book things more easily.

Card facts

- Hotels and train stations sell the card.

- You can use it to get up to 25% discount at many places.

- It costs £100.

- Many hotels, travel companies and restaurants in London accept it.

- We think it is the first discount card just for tourists.

Holiday Company in Trouble

Zoom Holidays has announced big discounts on their holidays after losing many customers. They have reduced some prices by 30–40%. They will give a free flight to all customers that book this month.

Company facts

- Two men started the company five years ago.

- The company employs 1,700 people.

- Analysts do not expect the company to survive.

Happiness

Here are some things that might offer 'the secret of true happiness'.

Talk to each other about how important each one is and then choose the <u>three</u> that are most important.

✸ Excellent health and fitness

✸ Being in a stable relationship with a loving partner

✸ Having an interesting and worthwhile job

✸ Material wealth and a high standard of living

✸ Being good-looking and having a great figure

✸ A wide circle of supportive friends and family

✸ Being content spiritually

✸ Achieving promotion and/or respect at work

owing to	due to	because of
since	as	so as to
so that	in order to	in spite of
even though	despite	to
whereas	in case	although

money	clothes	friends
happiness	music	parents
work/job	holidays	children
food/drink	lifestyle	school
health	family	weekends

How healthy are you?

For each question choose the best answer for you.

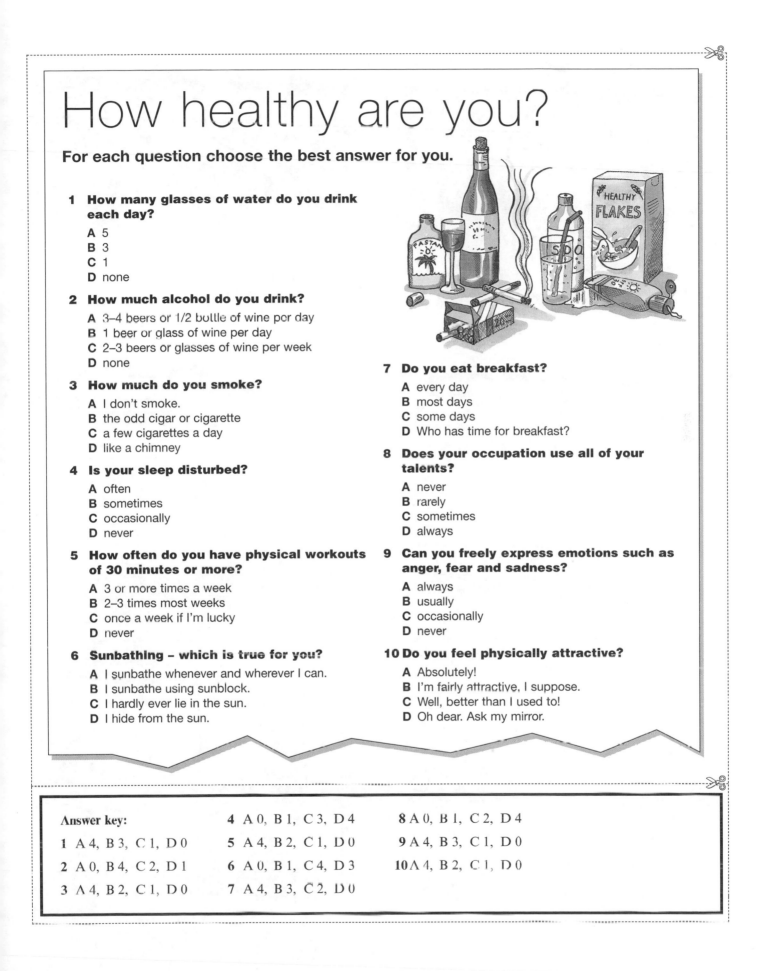

1 How many glasses of water do you drink each day?

A 5
B 3
C 1
D none

2 How much alcohol do you drink?

A 3–4 beers or 1/2 bottle of wine per day
B 1 beer or glass of wine per day
C 2–3 beers or glasses of wine per week
D none

3 How much do you smoke?

A I don't smoke.
B the odd cigar or cigarette
C a few cigarettes a day
D like a chimney

4 Is your sleep disturbed?

A often
B sometimes
C occasionally
D never

5 How often do you have physical workouts of 30 minutes or more?

A 3 or more times a week
B 2–3 times most weeks
C once a week if I'm lucky
D never

6 Sunbathing – which is true for you?

A I sunbathe whenever and wherever I can.
B I sunbathe using sunblock.
C I hardly ever lie in the sun.
D I hide from the sun.

7 Do you eat breakfast?

A every day
B most days
C some days
D Who has time for breakfast?

8 Does your occupation use all of your talents?

A never
B rarely
C sometimes
D always

9 Can you freely express emotions such as anger, fear and sadness?

A always
B usually
C occasionally
D never

10 Do you feel physically attractive?

A Absolutely!
B I'm fairly attractive, I suppose.
C Well, better than I used to!
D Oh dear. Ask my mirror.

Answer key:

1 A 4, B 3, C 1, D 0	4 A 0, B 1, C 3, D 4	8 A 0, B 1, C 2, D 4
2 A 0, B 4, C 2, D 1	5 A 4, B 2, C 1, D 0	9 A 4, B 3, C 1, D 0
3 A 4, B 2, C 1, D 0	6 A 0, B 1, C 4, D 3	10 A 4, B 2, C 1, D 0
	7 A 4, B 3, C 2, D 0	

A

'And that's why he never went to the city again.'

	✔
Conjunction + clause (*when/while …*)	☐
Conjunction + *-ing* (*after/before -ing …*)	☐
Modifier (*… so/such a … that …*)	☐
Clause of purpose (*… to/in order to …*)	☐
Clause of reason (*as/since …*)	☐

Participle clauses:

Present (*-ing … he/she/they …*)	☐
(*Not -ing … he/she/they …*)	☐
Perfect (*Having + past participle … he/she/they …*)	☐

B

'And she never mentioned the incident from that day onwards.'

	✔
Conjunction + clause (*when/while …*)	☐
Conjunction + *-ing* (*after/before -ing …*)	☐
Modifier (*… so/such a … that …*)	☐
Clause of purpose (*… to/in order to …*)	☐
Clause of reason (*as/since …*)	☐

Participle clauses:

Present (*-ing … he/she/they …*)	☐
(*Not -ing … he/she/they …*)	☐
Perfect (*Having + past participle … he/she/they …*)	☐

C

'It was almost midnight by the time they had cleared up all the mess.'

	✔
Conjunction + clause (*when/while …*)	☐
Conjunction + *-ing* (*after/before -ing …*)	☐
Modifier (*… so/such a … that …*)	☐
Clause of purpose (*… to/in order to …*)	☐
Clause of reason (*as/since …*)	☐

Participle clauses:

Present (*-ing … he/she/they …*)	☐
(*Not -ing … he/she/they …*)	☐
Perfect (*Having + past participle … he/she/they …*)	☐

D

'When she got home she realised it had been in her bag all along.'

	✔
Conjunction + clause (*when/while …*)	☐
Conjunction + *-ing* (*after/before -ing …*)	☐
Modifier (*… so/such a … that …*)	☐
Clause of purpose (*… to/in order to …*)	☐
Clause of reason (*as/since …*)	☐

Participle clauses:

Present (*-ing … he/she/they …*)	☐
(*Not -ing … he/she/they …*)	☐
Perfect (*Having + past participle … he/she/they …*)	☐

Common mistakes

1 First decide if the following sentences are *correct* or *incorrect*. Put a tick (✔) or a cross (✖) in the first column.

2 Then decide how many points you want to risk on each sentence – 1, 2, 5 or 10 – and write this in the second column. The more sure you are, the more you should risk. You have 20 points to start with.

3 Check your answers with the rest of the class. If you are right, you win the number of points you risked. If you are wrong, you lose them. The team with the most points at the end are the winners!

20

		✓ OR ✖	POINTS
1	When I left university I worked like a journalist for a local paper for a few years.		
2	He has hardly worked since becoming a freelance journalist.		
3	I used to work on radio but actually I'm working for a TV company.		
4	There was a very low attendance at yesterday's news conference.		
5	I tried to read the article but I couldn't finish it because I was really boring.		
6	My sisters and I usually give each others books for Christmas.		
7	She's a good journalist because she writes well.		
8	Journalists must be careful that they don't do anything unlegal.		
9	It was a so interesting story that I read it twice.		
10	The problem with some reports is that they are inaccurate.		
11	She had lots of frightening experiences when she was a war correspondent.		
12	The front-page story was about a gang that had stolen a bank.		
13	I didn't read the story about the economy; it looked a bit depressed.		
14	They employed the reporter on a two years contract.		
15	I don't watch the TV news as it is always on at an unconvenient time.		
		TOTAL	

Game cards

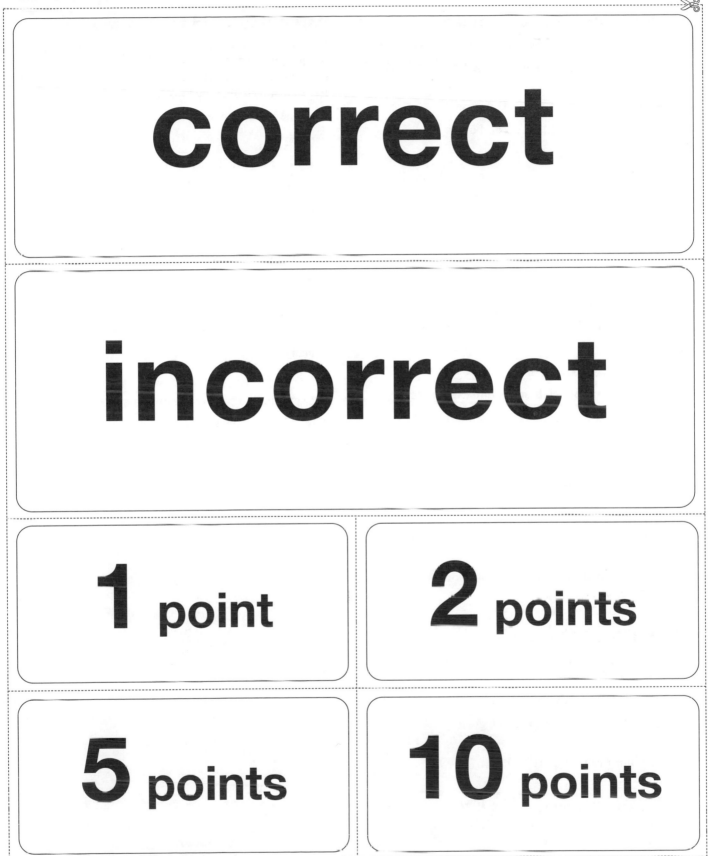

correct

incorrect

1 point

2 points

5 points

10 points

Module 1 Test: How much do you remember?

Part 1 Multiple-choice cloze

Choose which answer A, B, C or D best fits each space.

1 I prefer theatre to cinema because I like .... performances.

   A alive   B direct   C live   D personal

2 Sam and Linda both .... to be quite well off.

   A believe   B seem   C see   D think

3 New Year is one of the most .... celebrated festivals in the world.

   A fully   B widely   C largely   D completely

4 We didn't know he was a police officer as he was in .... clothes.

   A plain   B simple   C uniform   D secret

5 I'm not lazy but I hate doing .... chores.

   A house   B housework   C household   D housewife

Part 2 Open cloze

Think of the word which best fits into each space.

1 Clare didn't .... to like cheese but now she loves it.

2 Pete looks .... his brother but his personality is very different.

3 As a child, my brother loved fishing; he .... do it for hours.

4 Can you tell the difference .... British and American English?

5 .... anyone living in that house now or did they all move out?

Part 3 Word formation

Use the word given in capitals at the end of each sentence to form a word that fits in the space.

1 The village has only 250 ....   INHABIT

2 I like Maggie because she has a great ....   PERSON

3 Ten countries took part in the .... competition.   NATION

4 Mike lives on the .... of the town.   SKIRT

5 The problem with Jack is that he is very ....   TALK

Part 4 Key word transformations

Complete the second sentence so that it has a similar meaning to the first sentence, using the word given. Do not change the word given. You must use between two and five words, including the word given.

1 He never remembered to lock the back door.

   always

   He .... the back door.

2 John's cooking is much better than Jane's.

   nearly

   Jane's cooking .... as John's.

3 Would you like me to collect you at 8.00p.m.?

   up

   Shall .... at 8.00p.m.?

4 He has a few more books than I do.

   many

   I don't have .... he does.

5 Every time I try to speak my boss interrupts me.

   is

   My boss .... when I speak.

Module 2 Test: How much do you remember?

Part 1 Multiple-choice cloze

Choose which answer A, B, C or D best fits each space.

1 Sorry I'm late. I was .... in traffic for two hours.

   A standing   **B** stopping   **C** sitting   **D** starting

2 It's important to do your homework if you want to keep .... the class.

   A on with   **B** up with   **C** up to   **D** down on

3 In his latest film, Lacey plays a .... who likes living dangerously.

   A role   **B** part   **C** character   **D** protagonist

4 Our postman .... our mail at about 8.00 a.m.

   A delivers   **B** gives   **C** sends   **D** gets

5 Nigel's only got a part-time .... but he's looking for a full-time one.

   A career   **B** work   **C** profession   **D** job

Part 2 Open cloze

Think of the word which best fits into each space.

1 I look forward to .... from you soon.

2 Carol likes studying science, and so .... Eve.

3 How long .... this been going on?

4 Can you play .... guitar or any other instrument?

5 It was .... days later that Norma found her glasses.

Part 3 Word formation

Use the word given in capitals at the end of each sentence to form a word that fits in the space.

1 It was .... of Mark to leave the children on their own.   RESPONSIBILITY

2 Linda can't drive a normal car because of her ....   ABLE

3 It's horrible! It's the .... kitchen I have ever seen.   DIRT

4 The company are .... about when I go on holiday.   FLEX

5 Florence was given the job on the .... of her qualifications.   STRONG

Part 4 Key word transformations

Complete the second sentence so that it has a similar meaning to the first sentence, using the word given. Do not change the word given. You must use between two and five words, including the word given.

1 Paul took up tennis three years ago.

   playing

   Paul .... three years.

2 Susan started to like jazz when she was a teenager.

   has

   Susan .... she was a teenager.

3 There's very little to do at the weekends.

   hardly

   There .... at the weekends.

4 Nina's looking for a job that suits her better.

   more

   Nina's looking for a .... job.

5 I can attend an interview at any time.

   available

   I .... an interview at any time.

Exam practice 1: Writing and Listening

Paper 2 Part 2

Write your answer in **120–180** words in an appropriate style.

This is part of a letter you received from an English pen friend.

> *In your last letter, you said you were going on a picnic in the country with some friends Where did you go? What was the food like? I'd love to know whether you enjoyed yourselves.*

Write your **letter**, answering your friend's questions and giving relevant details. Do not write any addresses.

Paper 4 Part 4

You will hear an interview with Anita Perry and her son Darren, who is training to be a clown in the circus. For questions **1–7**, choose the best answer (**A**, **B** or **C**).

1   Anita suggests that Darren's fascination with clowns
   A started when he learned not to be frightened of them.
   B was understandable given his family history.
   C came as something of a surprise to her.

2   Darren's family first considered circus work after
   A his father lost his job.
   B his brothers had completed university.
   C his mother had failed to find work locally.

3   When Darren said the family could join a circus, at first his father
   A doubted if they had the right skills.
   B said they couldn't afford a caravan.
   C didn't think it was a serious suggestion.

4   How did Darren feel when his father wrote off to various circuses?
   A unsure how easy it would be to find work
   B worried about whether they'd like the work
   C confident that they would all be offered work

5   What problem did Anita have during the family's first period with a circus?
   A It was hard not having a holiday.
   B It was difficult living in a small space.
   C It was tough being away for a whole year.

6   What does Darren say about life in the circus?
   A He loves performing in front of the public.
   B He wishes he could go to normal school lessons.
   C He's learning useful skills by watching the experts.

7   How does Anita feel now about their decision to join the circus?
   A She sometimes wonders if it was a mistake.
   B She's pleased that they took the risk.
   C She's got used to the discomforts.

Module 3 Test: How much do you remember?

Part 1 Multiple-choice cloze

Choose which answer A, B, C or D best fits each space.

1 It's .... a long way; I think we should go by car.

   A fairly   B pretty   C very   D rather

2 That new exhibition of Mexican art is very ....

   A wonderful   B marvellous   C impressive
   D incredible

3 Only one of these cars was ever made so it's totally
   ....

   A unique   B rare   C unusual   D strange

4 The critics love Newman's art but he hasn't had much
   .... success.

   A economic   B economical   C commercial

   D businesslike

5 We were just going out when there was a sudden
   heavy ....

   A rain   B downpour   C drizzle   D hail

Part 2 Open cloze

Think of the word which best fits into each space.

1 The capital is about two hours .... by train.

2 How do you .... coming round for a meal
   this weekend?

3 I haven't decided .... to go for my holiday this
   year.

4 Tom wants to be a vet because he's very interested
   .... animals.

5 I began .... read this book last week.

Part 3 Word formation

Use the word given in capitals at the end of each sentence
to form a word that fits in the space.

1 The survival of many animals is
   .... by humans.   THREAT

2 There are some .... between the
   two animals.   SIMILAR

3 Can the difference in the results be
   explained .... ?   SCIENCE

4 Terry's probably the .... person
   I know.   FRIEND

5 .... is good for the economy but
   bad for wildlife.   TOUR

Part 4 Key word transformations

Complete the second sentence so that it has a similar
meaning to the first sentence, using the word given. Do
not change the word given. You must use between two and
five words, including the word given.

1 I smoked until my 26th birthday.

   stopped

   I .... 26.

2 Did you pay that bill, do you know?

   remember

   Do .... that bill?

3 Dan doesn't live very far from his office.

   fairly

   Dan's office .... his house.

4 Five years ago very few tourists went to the city.

   any

   There .... the city five
   years ago.

5 The children had wanted to go to the zoo for ages.

   forward

   They had been .... the zoo
   for ages.

Module 4 Test: How much do you remember?

Part 1 Multiple-choice cloze

Choose which answer A, B, C or D best fits each space.

1 It was .... of Steve to arrive late.

   A normal B usual C typical D general

2 Liz .... a company selling sports equipment on the Internet.

   A set off B set up C set out D set on

3 When I took up sailing, I loved it from the word ....

   A go B start C begin D do

4 If you've never tried windsurfing, you should .... it a go.

   A get B give C have D try

5 Greg has .... for the yoga course that starts next week.

   A written up B taken up C drawn up D signed up

Part 2 Open cloze

Think of the word which best fits into each space.

1 Let's start .... talking about why it went wrong.

2 Kevin couldn't find his watch, so .... the end he bought a new one.

3 We .... been waiting 30 minutes when the bus finally came.

4 I don't get .... opportunity to speak French nowadays.

5 Sorry .... interrupt, but can I ask a question?

Part 3 Word formation

Use the word given in capitals at the end of each sentence to form a word that fits in the space.

1 There is nothing we can do; doctors say the illness is ....   TREAT

2 It would be more .... to take a taxi than to walk home.   SENSE

3 I don't want to sit next to Jack; he's so ....   BORE

4 I found the tourist office very .... about the city.   INFORM

5 I couldn't live without my personal organiser; it's ....   VALUE

Part 4 Key word transformations

Complete the second sentence so that it has a similar meaning to the first sentence, using the word given. Do not change the word given. You must use between two and five words, including the word given.

1 The course was cancelled because there weren't many people.

   lack

   The course was cancelled because .... people.

2 That day Nick started work at 6.00a.m.

   been

   Nick .... 6.00a.m that day.

3 Ann watched TV from 8.00a.m to 10.00p.m.

   at

   Ann .... 9.00p.m.

4 He left, then later I arrived at his house.

   time

   He .... I arrived at his house.

5 She left university, then got married immediately.

   soon

   She got married .... left university.

Exam practice 2: Writing

Paper 2 Part 1

1 You are planning to do an evening class with a friend who has sent you a letter and a leaflet advertising a music school. Read the letter and the leaflet together with your friend's notes. Then write to the school asking for the information which your friend has suggested, adding any relevant questions of your own.

I think this is the type of course we're looking for. Could you write to the school to get more details? I've made some notes and maybe you can think of any other questions we need to ask.

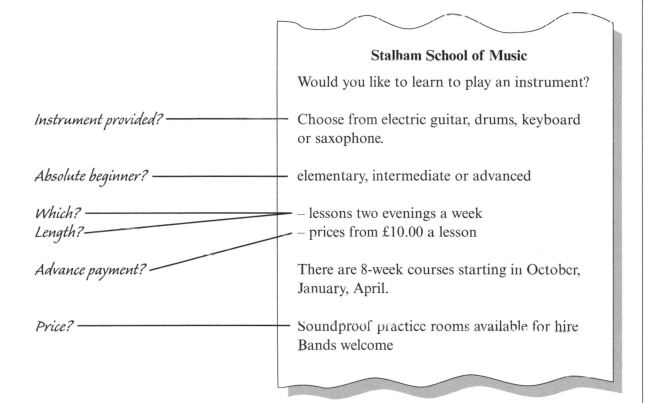

Stalham School of Music

Would you like to learn to play an instrument?

Instrument provided? —— Choose from electric guitar, drums, keyboard or saxophone.

Absolute beginner? —— elementary, intermediate or advanced

Which? ——
Length? —— – lessons two evenings a week
– prices from £10.00 a lesson

Advance payment? ——

There are 8-week courses starting in October, January, April.

Price? —— Soundproof practice rooms available for hire
Bands welcome

Write a **letter** of between **120** and **150** words in an appropriate style. Do not write any addresses.

Exam practice 2: Listening

You will hear five people talking about newspapers. For questions **1–5**, choose from the list **A–F** the reason each person gives for choosing the particular newspaper they buy. Use the letters only once. There is one extra letter which you do not need to use.

A   good articles and photography

Speaker 1 | 1 |

B   useful advertisements

Speaker 2 | 2 |

C   interesting fashion pages

Speaker 3 | 3 |

D   relevant sports coverage

Speaker 4 | 4 |

E   informative reviews

Speaker 5 | 5 |

F   reliable gossip columns

Module 5 Test: How much do you remember?

Part 1 Multiple-choice cloze

Choose which answer A, B, C or D best fits each space.

1 I think it's quite ……… that oil prices will rise soon.

   A probably   B likely   C surely   D definitely

2 You will ……… a lot of opposition if you try to change things quickly.

   A come in for   B come up with   C come out with
   D come up against

3 We gave the job to Gordon because we know he is ……… of doing it.

   A qualified   B able   C capable   D experienced

4 Cook was the first European to ……… Australia.

   A reach   B arrive   C travel   D go

5 Alan hopes to get a good job in the ……… future.

   A close   B near   C soon   D next

Part 2 Open cloze

Think of the word which best fits into each space.

1 Ken fell and hurt ……… when he was mending the fence.

2 Please come with me. I don't want to go on my ……… .

3 When Rachel heard the news, she didn't know ……… to do.

4 I would be grateful ……… you could inform me as soon as possible.

5 Could you tell me ……… the nearest book shop is?

Part 3 Word formation

Use the word given in capitals at the end of each sentence to form a word that fits in the space.

1 Marie always talks about her children with ……… .   PROUD

2 The results are worthless because the experiment was ……… .   SCIENCE

3 You should see Dr Jones as she is a ……… in that area.   SPECIAL

4 Sexual ……… is still a long way off in many companies.   EQUAL

5 *Lord of the Rings* is one of the ……… films I've ever seen.   LENGTH

Part 4 Key word transformations

Complete the second sentence so that it has a similar meaning to the first sentence, using the word given. Do not change the word given. You must use between two and five words, including the word given.

1 Jackie wanted someone to help her cook.

   cooking

   Jackie didn't want to do all ……………………………… own.

2 We did the work without help from anyone so it would be cheaper.

   keep

   We did all the ……………………………… costs down.

3 Will you have a room available next month?

   know

   Could you ……………………………… you will have a room available next month?

4 I am going to move house before the end of the year.

   moved

   I ……………………………… the end of the year.

5 A cure for cancer will be discovered soon.

   someone

   It won't be ……………………………… a cure for cancer.

Module 6 Test: How much do you remember?

Part 1 Multiple-choice cloze

Choose which answer A, B, C or D best fits each space.

1 The courts are very tough on young people who .... crimes.

   A make   B do   C commit   D perform

2 Ted watches the World Cup but generally he's not .... on football.

   A interested   B keen   C enthusiastic   D excited

3 We should use bright colours to make the words ....

   A stand out   B stand up   C stand off   D stand in

4 They were too far away so I couldn't .... what they were talking about.

   A oversee   B overtake   C overlook   D overhear

5 I think you should be honest and .... your mind.

   A say   B speak   C tell   D talk

Part 2 Open cloze

Think of the word which best fits into each space.

1 Sally was very upset and left the room .... tears.

2 Bill couldn't sleep because he isn't .... to so much noise.

3 It was very good .... you to help me last night.

4 I don't understand the relationship .... Chris and Alex.

5 That's the family .... house was damaged in the fire.

Part 3 Word formation

Use the word given in capitals at the end of each sentence to form a word that fits in the space.

1 Ian's very ....; he hates waiting, even for a minute.   PATIENCE

2 The story is slow because of the author's .... style.   DESCRIBE

3 There's a very strong .... between the two girls.   FRIEND

4 We could see the boss's .... with the poor quality of our work.   SATISFY

5 That answer doesn't make sense; it's ....   LOGIC

Part 4 Key word transformations

Complete the second sentence so that it has a similar meaning to the first sentence, using the word given. Do not change the word given. You must use between two and five words, including the word given.

1 Each month Sarah finds it a little easier to live alone.

   used

   Sarah is slowly .... her own.

2 My uncle owned the flat where I stayed.

   belonged

   I stayed in a .... my uncle.

3 This room is in a mess and I am certain it is Luke's fault.

   must

   Luke .... the mess in this room.

4 It seems to me that Pat can't drive.

   get

   I .... can't drive.

5 Brenda doesn't have enough experience for this office.

   too

   Brenda is .... work in this office.

Exam practice 3: Writing

Paper 2 Part 2

Write an answer to **one** of the Questions **1–3** in this part. Write your answer in **120–180** words in an appropriate style.

1 You have decided to enter a short-story writing competition. The rules of the competition say that the story must begin with these words.

   As Danny walked out on to the sports field, he suddenly felt nervous. Would he be able to do as well as everybody expected?

   Write your **story**.

2 A tourist resort in your country would like to attract more young visitors. You have been asked to write an article for an international travel magazine describing the resort briefly and explaining why it is a good place for young people to go on holiday.

   Write your **article**.

3 You have seen this advertisement in an English language newspaper.

   ### HOLIDAY JOB

   We need someone to help us look after our two children (12 and 13 years old) during their summer holidays. They are lively and only speak English. You will spend afternoons with them, organising fun activities and keeping them out of trouble.

   If you think you're the right person for the job, please write telling us why and the dates when you'll be available.

   Write to Mrs Catchpole.

   Write a **letter of application** to Mrs Catchpole. Do not write any addresses.

Exam practice 3: Listening

You will hear an interview with a woman who runs her own company, providing training for businesspeople. For questions **1–10**, complete the sentences.

Fiona's company is called ⬜ **1**

Fiona originally trained as an ⬜ **2**

A friend of Fiona's who was talking at a ⬜ **3** asked for her help.

Fiona got financial help from her ⬜ **4**

Fiona's first client worked for a ⬜ **5**

The courses offered by Fiona's company cost at least £ ⬜ **6**

Businesspeople sometimes need training in how to use ⬜ **7** during talks.

At the end of each course, people give their talks in a ⬜ **8**

Fiona says that talks are most boring when speakers ⬜ **9**

Sometimes when speakers are nervous, they actually appear to be ⬜ **10**

Module 7 Test: How much do you remember?

Part 1 Multiple-choice cloze

Choose which answer A, B, C or D best fits each space.

1 For the Oscar awards ceremony most actors wear a
.... jacket.

   A tuxedo   **B** smoking   **C** dinner   **D** blazer

2 To be .... I have no idea what the
solution is.

   A reliable   **B** honest   **C** trustworthy   **D** fair

3 Helen arrived wearing a beautiful yellow ....
cotton shirt.

   A striped   **B** straight   **C** tight   **D** scruffy

4 If business doesn't improve we are in .... of
losing everything.

   A risk   **B** chance   **C** uncertainty   **D** danger

5 The problem is that, ... from us, Matthew hasn't
got any family.

   A apart   **B** besides   **C** also   **D** as well

Part 2 Open cloze

Think of the word which best fits into each space.

1 If there's one thing Nicola loves it's shopping
.... shoes.

2 We had a couple of bad days but .... the whole
the weather was great.

3 We wanted to know .... there would be time to
go shopping.

4 Your safety is important, so please pay attention at
.... times.

5 I thought I would fail the exam, but to ....
surprise I passed.

Part 3 Word formation

Use the word given in capitals at the end of each sentence
to form a word that fits in the space.

1 The director's first film achieved
.... success.   WORLD

2 I don't care if people think my clothes
are ....   FASHION

3 It's hard to make a fair .... between
different shops.   COMPARE

4 Lisa needs to eat more .... than
she does at the moment.   HEALTH

5 What do you do for a ....?   LIFE

Part 4 Key word transformations

Complete the second sentence so that it has a similar
meaning to the first sentence, using the word given. Do
not change the word given. You must use between two and
five words, including the word given.

1 I'm sure Gill hasn't left yet because her computer is
still on.

   can't

   Gill .... because her computer
   is still on.

2 I partly agree with you, but you have forgotten
one thing.

   extent

   I agree with you .... but you
   have forgotten one thing.

3 The club wouldn't let Jack buy a drink because he
wasn't a member.

   allowed

   Jack .... a drink at the club
   because he wasn't a member.

4 Karen went to work but it wasn't necessary, as there
was nothing to do.

   have

   Karen .... work as there was
   nothing to do.

5 You shouldn't eat in here.

   supposed

   You .... in here.

Module 8 Test: How much do you remember?

Part 1 Multiple-choice cloze

Choose which answer A, B, C or D best fits each space.

1 Peter .... me to go to the party.

   A agreed   **B** persuaded   **C** offered   **D** refused

2 The contract said we couldn't do it but our lawyer found a way .... it.

   A round   **B** across   **C** off   **D** through

3 Many people dream that one day they will .... with someone very attractive.

   A chat up   **B** take out   **C** go out   **D** get married

4 I was very late but I had just enough time to quickly .... to the shops.

   A stroll   **B** dash   **C** creep   **D** wander

5 At first it was hard but in the end I .... to do it.

   A achieved   **B** succeeded   **C** knew   **D** managed

Part 2 Open cloze

Think of the word which best fits into each space.

1 Don't cheat, you'll never get away .... it.

2 In the future you will .... able to watch any film when you want.

3 I'm too busy and I'm too tired. In .... words, I can't go out tonight.

4 Scientists haven't yet succeeded .... finding a cure for HIV.

5 I replied .... I had no idea what he was talking about.

Part 3 Word formation

Use the word given in capitals at the end of each sentence to form a word that fits in the space.

1 Try to make a good .... at the
   first meeting.   IMPRESS

2 I'd like to come but .... I'm busy
   that day.   FORTUNE

3 It is important that all .... look
   after their staff.   EMPLOY

4 This play should be good, it has a
   strong ....   RECOMMEND

5 We are quite different but we get
   on .... well.   INCREDIBLE

Part 4 Key word transformations

Complete the second sentence so that it has a similar meaning to the first sentence, using the word given. Do not change the word given. You must use between two and five words, including the word given.

1 'I didn't break the window,' said the boy.

   breaking

   The boy .... window.

2 It is possible that we can do it for you tomorrow.

   might

   We .... it for you tomorrow.

3 'I must go this afternoon,' she said.

   that

   She said that .... afternoon.

4 I can put petrol in my car but that's about it.

   know

   I .... petrol in my car but that's about it.

5 'Will you lend me some money?' she asked.

   I

   She asked me .... some money.

Exam practice 4: Writing

Paper 2 Part 2

Write an answer to one of the Questions 1–4 in this part. Write your answer in **120–180** words in an appropriate style.

1   Following a class discussion on the subject of clothes and fashion, your teacher has asked you to write a composition with this title:

Some people think you can tell a person's character by the clothes they wear. Do you agree?

Write your **composition**.

2   You have seen this announcement in an international magazine for young people.

> **What's your favourite family TV programme?**
>
> We're offering a prize of £200 for the best article recommending
> a good TV programme to our readers.
> The programme must be suitable for people of all ages.

Write your **article**.

3   You have decided to enter a short-story competition. The competition rules say that the story must **begin** with these words.

It all began with a mysterious text message.

Write your **story**.

4   This is part of a letter from an English-speaking friend.

> *In your last letter you said you were going to do a course in either photography or painting. Which did you choose in the end? What's the course like? Have you made any new friends there?*
>
> *Please write back soon with your news.*
>
> *Chris*

Write your **letter**. Do not write any addresses.

Exam practice 4: Listening

Module 9 Test: How much do you remember?

Part 1 Multiple-choice cloze

Choose which answer A, B, C or D best fits each space.

1 Would you like to be your own ………?

   A boss B manager C employer D chief

2 Val tries not to spend all her wages. She's saving for a ……… day.

   A sunny B wet C rainy D cloudy

3 I am writing to ……… about a report in yesterday's paper.

   A object B complain C express D disapprove

4 Chris has applied for a ……… so he's got an appointment at the bank.

   A cash B deposit C debt D loan

5 The ……… of the people I work with love football.

   A all B both C majority D most

Part 2 Open cloze

Think of the word which best fits into each space.

1 I prefer to spend my money ……… going out.

2 Rose is very careful ……… her money.

3 Everyone ……… been very kind and helpful since my accident.

4 We have a few shops in my village but ……… isn't a post office.

5 If you don't have the cash you can pay ……… cheque.

Part 3 Word formation

Use the word given in capitals at the end of each sentence to form a word that fits in the space.

1 We are looking for people with talent and ……… .   CREATE

2 Sebastian is a ……… advisor in New York.   FINANCE

3 This new phone has a wonderful ……… design.   INNOVATE

4 I think there's too much ……… on TV.   ADVERTISE

5 There was a small cut in Ted's finger but it didn't ……… .   BLOOD

Part 4 Key word transformations

Complete the second sentence so that it has a similar meaning to the first sentence, using the word given. Do not change the word given. You must use between two and five words, including the word given.

1 We must avoid anything that endangers the children at school.

   puts

   We must avoid anything that ……………………………… at school.

2 Keith said he would come at six if he hadn't heard from me before then.

   hear

   'I'll come at six unless ……………………………… before then,' Keith said.

3 Provided you're not a vegetarian, I'll cook for you.

   long

   I'll cook for you ……………………………… not a vegetarian.

4 Judith was late because her car didn't start.

   started

   If Judith's car ……………………………… been on time.

5 Very few people seem to be polite these days.

   hardly

   ……………………………… to be polite these days.

Module 10 Test: How much do you remember?

Part 1 Multiple-choice cloze

Choose which answer A, B, C or D best fits each space.

1 The police went to Turner's house but, not ....,
he had disappeared.

   A amazingly **B** incredibly **C** surprisingly
   D astonishingly

2 You must have insurance in case you ....
an accident.

   A endure **B** receive **C** undertake **D** suffer

3 Sometimes finding the right place to stay can be a lot
of ....

   A hassle **B** nuisance **C** problem **D** difficulty

4 Camping is very cheap after the .... investment in
equipment.

   A starting **B** initial **C** first **D** primary

5 The number of people getting married each year is
on the ....

   A fall **B** reduction **C** decline **D** drop

Part 2 Open cloze

Think of the word which best fits into each space.

1 .... is expected that thousands of people will join
the protest.

2 It's .... time we left; we don't want to be late.

3 Now we're lost! I wish we .... remembered to
bring a map.

4 The aim .... the report is to highlight
recent problems.

5 It's important to prepare everything well ....
advance.

Part 3 Word formation

**Use the word given in capitals at the end of each sentence
to form a word that fits in the space.**

1 A few of us are going .... Do you
want to come?   CLUB

2 I don't know what to say! The prize was
completely ....   EXPECT

3 You're being .... to expect a good
hotel at such a low price.   REAL

4 I have no .... in recommending
this hotel.   HESITATE

5 Dan is .... to the fact that he might
not get the job.   RESIGN

Part 4 Key word transformations

**Complete the second sentence so that it has a similar
meaning to the first sentence, using the word given. Do
not change the word given. You must use between two and
five words, including the word given.**

1 The examiner will show you some pictures.

   be

   You will .... the examiner.

2 Nigel gets nervous when people ask questions.

   make

   People .... nervous.

3 I would have preferred you to tell me earlier.

   rather

   I .... me earlier.

4 We think someone has been rescued.

   thought

   Someone .... rescued.

5 I really want my girlfriend to call me tonight.

   would

   If .... me tonight.

Exam practice 5: Writing

Paper 2 Part 2

Write an answer to **one** of the Questions **1–4** in this part. Write your answer in **120–180** words in an appropriate style.

1   This is part of a letter you have received from a friend in another country.

> As part of my college course, I have to do an assignment about job opportunities for young people in different parts of the world. Please could you write me a short report about your country, saying how easy it is for young people to get a job and what opportunities are open to them. I can then include the information in my project.

Write your **report**.

2   In class, you have been discussing attitudes towards means of transport in your country. Now your teacher has asked you to write a composition on the following subject.

Public transport is only for people who can't afford their own car. Do you agree?

Write your **composition**.

3   This is part of a letter you have received from an English-speaking pen friend.

> Thanks very much for the invitation to stay with you this summer. I'd love to come! Will it be hot? What clothes and sports equipment do I need to bring? Also, I'd like to bring a gift to thank your family — what sort of thing would be appropriate?

Write your **letter**, answering your friend's questions and giving relevant details. Do not write any addresses.

4   You decide to enter a competition which is being organised by an international wildlife magazine. Readers have been invited to send in articles on the following topic:

Should wild animals be kept in city centre zoos?

Write your **article**.

Exam practice 5: Listening

You will hear five people talking about adventurous activities they once took part in. For questions **1–5**, choose from the list **A–F** how each person says they felt about the activity. Use the letters only once. There is one extra letter which you do not need to use.

A   satisfied with a personal achievement

Speaker 1   [ ] 1

B   put off by the attitude of others

Speaker 2   [ ] 2

C   impressed by the way people behaved

Speaker 3   [ ] 3

D   disappointed not to get value for money

Speaker 4   [ ] 4

E   determined to seek financial compensation

Speaker 5   [ ] 5

F   relieved not to feel out of place

Module 11 Test: How much do you remember?

Part 1 Multiple-choice cloze

Choose which answer A, B, C or D best fits each space.

1 As far as I'm .... , the accident should never have happened.

  A worried   B concerned   C disturbed   D distressed

2 Everyone is aware of the .... between pollution and global warming.

  A join   B line   C relation   D link

3 Angela's going home early; she's feeling a bit .... the weather.

  A under   B below   C on top of   D out of

4 Gary's had his car for ten years and it's still going ....

  A long   B far   C strong   D fast

5 The doctor told Jenny to .... red meat completely.

  A cut out   B put on   C take up   D get over

Part 2 Open cloze

Think of the word which best fits into each space.

1 I am writing .... response to an advertisement in yesterday's paper.

2 George is worried about his cat; it's .... its food again.

3 Beckham has been described .... England's greatest footballer.

4 Take your mobile in .... I need to contact you.

5 Fiona has been to a number of European countries, ... as Italy and France.

Part 3 Word formation

Use the word given in capitals at the end of each sentence to form a word that fits in the space.

1 There was great .... in the class before the exam.   ANXIOUS

2 The director's last film was very successful ....   FINANCE

3 The sound of .... filled the room.   LAUGH

4 Next year I want to have a .... lifestyle than this year.   HEALTH

5 He resigned because of worry and ....   FRUSTRATE

Part 4 Key word transformations

Complete the second sentence so that it has a similar meaning to the first sentence, using the word given. Do not change the word given. You must use between two and five words, including the word given.

1 My feet are too big for these shoes.

  not

  These shoes .... for my feet.

2 There were so many people there that Ellen couldn't get in.

  lot

  There were .... people there that Ellen couldn't get in.

3 It looks like a win for England; they're 3–0 up.

  going

  It looks .... to win; they're 3–0 up.

4 Neil did well at university, but he still can't get a job.

  spite

  Neil can't get a job .... that he did well at university.

5 That's a lovely smell; it probably means it's time for lunch.

  if

  It .... ready.

Module 12 Test: How much do you remember?

Part 1 Multiple-choice cloze

Choose which answer A, B, C or D best fits each space.

1 The characters were good but the plot was ....

   A lifelike **B** interesting **C** convincing
   D predictable

2 You can't drive through here; it's .... the law.

   A opposed **B** against **C** outside **D** opposite

3 The events happen in the .... between the two
   World Wars.

   A history **B** period **C** date **D** space

4 When you have read it I'd like some .... on what
   you thought of it.

   A report **B** reaction **C** feedback **D** opinion

5 Science fiction is Maskell's least favourite .... of
   books.

   A group **B** make **C** writer **D** genre

Part 2 Open cloze

Think of the word which best fits into each space.

1 Clive has asked me to help him and I'm unsure
   .... to agree or not.

2 .... written the letter, Maria decided not to post
   it.

3 I'll go instead .... you, if you want me to.

4 I haven't met him .... I can't tell you what he's
   like.

5 We .... our bags searched but they didn't find
   anything.

Part 3 Word formation

**Use the word given in capitals at the end of each sentence
to form a word that fits in the space.**

1 It's a long .... drama set in China.   HISTORY

2 Having been in the same situation I
   can .... with you.   SYMPATHY

3 Alex is hoping to have a career
   in ....   JOURNAL

4 People are worried because of the
   financial .... at present.   SECURE

5 Ben's explanation was highly ....;
   I didn't believe a word of it.   PROBABLE

Part 4 Key word transformations

**Complete the second sentence so that it has a similar
meaning to the first sentence, using the word given. Do
not change the word given. You must use between two and
five words, including the word given.**

1 Someone has to feed the chickens every day.

   be

   The chickens .... every day.

2 These instructions don't have any logic at all, do
   they?

   totally

   These instructions .... they?

3 Someone is making me some new curtains for
   the bedroom.

   made

   I'm .... for the bedroom.

4 I bought the book because I wanted to give it to
   Kathy for her birthday.

   order

   I bought the book .... give it
   to Kathy for her birthday.

5 Don't see the film until you have read the book.

   seeing

   Read .... the film.

Exam practice 6: Writing

Your friend has seen this advertisement for a holiday hotel and is planning to make a booking. You went on holiday at the same place last year. Using the information in the advertisement and the notes you have made on it, tell your friend what the hotel was really like and give him or her any advice necessary.

Food OK, service poor ——————

About 3kms ——————

Nice, but very crowded ——————
Terrible music — comedian worse! ——————

You can hear the planes! ——————

Golden Sands Hotel

* 200 luxury bedrooms
  all with balcony and sea view
* full board in four-star restaurant

* minutes from a long sandy beach
* convenient for shops and nightlife

* free use of heated indoor pool
* entertainment nightly in the bar
* fully-equipped games room for children

* very convenient for the airport

* great value at £220 per person per week

Write a **letter** of between **120** and **150** words in an appropriate style. Do not write any postal addresses.

Exam practice 6: Listening

You will hear an interview with Sally Carson who takes part in long-distance sailing races. For questions **1–10**, complete the sentences.

Sally's latest boat is called | **1**

Sally compares sailing with | **2** | when talking about the role of technology.

Sally says that, in a race, the | **3** | of a boat is as important as its design.

A piece of equipment known as the | **4** | is essential in a single-handed race.

Sally finds the Internet is most useful for finding out about the | **5** | during a race.

Sally regards | **6** | as the most dangerous problem during a race.

Sally's longest race lasted for | **7**

Sally sometimes finds it hard to | **8** | enough in order to get the sleep she needs.

Sally includes visits to the gym, | **9** | and sailing in her training programme.

The title of Sally's book is | **10**

Audio scripts

Module 1

Speaking. Page 17. Exercise 6b.

Both of these celebrations are obviously very proud family occasions, and they both seem to be for one of the younger people in the family; in this one it's this girl's birthday – perhaps it's a special one – it could be her eighteenth – and this one clearly shows the girl's graduation ceremony.

The main difference between the birthday and the graduation is that this one is very informal – everybody's wearing casual clothes and laughing, whereas the graduation ceremony is a much more formal celebration.

I would like to be at the birthday party; it looks a lot of fun, but it might be quite noisy! And although the graduation ceremony looks more formal, I'd like to be there if this was my family, because it's a very important moment in the girl's life.

Of the two, I think I'd prefer the birthday party, though, as it's more relaxed and probably more fun than the graduation ceremony.

Listening. Page 18. Exercise 2.

Speaker 1

I first came out here to stay with friends for a few months after I left university, but ended up not going back. I couldn't believe how laid back it all was here. Everyone is very casual and informal and in the part of the continent where I live, I really loved – and still do love – the fact that you can more or less be outdoors for much of the year. This also means you can get away with living on very little here because you don't have to pay heating bills. Interestingly, though, the thing I miss most about Britain is the seasons – the leaves falling in autumn and the first daffodils in spring. It also feels a long way away from Europe and I feel as if I've lost touch with what's going on there.

Speaker 2

I went there to teach English, and immediately fell in love with the lifestyle so ended up staying for several years. Their priorities are different – for example, people still tend to sit down at lunchtime and eat home-made food together, whereas in the US we just grab something on the move – you know, it's just functional and people are always in a rush. Also, because of the climate, people tend to have a nap or relax after lunch and then work until later, which means shops shut over the lunch period. It took me ages to get used to that, and also to not having dinner until around 9 or 10 in the evening. Unfortunately, I ended up spending too much time with other Americans and so I didn't really become as fluent as I would have liked.

Speaker 3

The people were just as I imagined – polite and law abiding, for example queuing for buses and giving way when they drive and so on. They tend to come over as a bit unfriendly at first, but when they get to know you they're really warm, especially in the north where I am, and would do anything to help you. They're polite in shops, too, unlike in my home town!

I came over here to learn English and then met my wife and got married, so I have been here ever since. But I miss my extended family at home. When I go back they're all there to meet me at the airport, and there'll be a huge meal waiting and people will propose toasts and sing at the table. The problem is that after all these years here I feel strange when I go back to Russia, and yet I don't feel British, either!

Module 2

Speaking. Page 31. Exercise 6b.

A: Well, for me, one of the most important things is how small the classes are.

B: I agree absolutely, it's important for children to have a lot of individual attention.

A: Good exam results are also a big factor, too.

B: Do you think so? Exam results aren't that important to me, not for children that young. Actually, I think it's more important for them to go to a school near their home at this age. It means they have lots of friends who live nearby.

A: That's true. And they can walk there instead of spending ages on a bus, so they have more free time.

B: Yes. And then there's uniform. It's important that they all wear the same clothes.

A: I agree up to a point, although it's not as important as for older children.

B: The least important factor for me is equipment. I just don't think it matters at this age.

A: I couldn't agree more.

Listening. Page 32. Exercise 2.

P = Presenter; L = Leanne; H = Harry

P: It's that time of year again when many school leavers are about to embark upon their college and university courses. Today we've invited into the studio Leanne Wilson and Harry King, – both final year students – for their tips on how to survive the first few weeks. Leanne, we'll start with you. Were you nervous about going to university?

L: Hi. Well, in a way. I'd been looking forward to it but my main sort of panic if you like was that I didn't know anyone.

P: But you met people fairly easily?

L: I met loads. Many of them were on my course but you've got to be careful you don't just stick with these people – you really miss out if you do. And try and be open-minded – just because people don't speak to you doesn't mean they're unfriendly – they could just be shy. The main thing is you know, to get involved with anything and everything. Even if you can't play tennis to save your life, have a go – join the tennis club, Scrabble club, drama society, whatever, just so you meet a wide variety of people.

H: Absolutely. At the art college I'm at there are always so many things going on in that first week. I really wish I'd taken more advantage of all the clubs.

P: Why didn't you?

H: Well, you know I was scared of not doing enough work – when actually it doesn't really matter – it's more important to sort of get to know people, as Leanne says. I was a bit shy, too, and hadn't got too much cash to splash around. But actually, what you have to remember is it won't be that intense for the whole term – you might as well make the most of it while you can – things do settle down and you won't be staying up all night spending money all term.

P: While we're on the subject of money, how did you cope on your student budget?

L: Well, I mean, it's not rocket science, is it? As a student you've got two options. If you want to spend money socialising, you can cut down on what you spend or earn some money. Some people choose to live at home and save on food and accommodation. I felt it was important to stand on my own two feet so I rented a room in a house with some friends and we cut costs by buying books together – second hand or over the net – getting our clothes in charity shops, living on pasta – that kind of thing.

P: So you didn't do what many students do and get an evening job in a bar or supermarket?

L: The thing is, studying architecture, my workload is so high – it would have meant no social life at all. But I obviously got a full-time job in the holidays.

P: Sure. What about going to lectures? I imagine that's very different from lessons at school.

H: That's true. Where I went wrong at first was trying to write down every word the lecturer was saying, which meant I ended up not really listening. In fact, you're normally given the notes so you can just kind of add to them, underline important bits and so on. Quite a few people don't bother going at all actually but I think if you don't, you miss out – I know it's only a basic overview you get in an hour's lecture but it does help you to know which areas you need to focus on and read around.

P: Isn't it difficult to kind of structure your day if you only have a few hours lectures a week?

L: Actually, I didn't find that bit too difficult – I kind of set aside a time when I worked best and stuck to it. My main problem was – and still is – that I have no self-discipline, you know I doodle, email a friend, someone turns up for a coffee – I just waste time really.

H: So do I. It's not that you aren't interested in the subject or anything – it's just that life has a habit of getting in the way. And the work piles up and then you get stressed – all these essays to write.

P: Well, we're very grateful to you both for coming in but I'm afraid we've almost run out of time. Next week we'll be talking to …

Exam practice 1: Teacher's Book

Listening. Page 176. (Paper 4 Part 4).

P = Presenter; A = Anita; D = Darren

P: Today I'm talking to Anita Perry, and her son Darren, who's 14. Now lots of children dream of running away to join the circus, but this is the story of a whole family that did just that. Anita, first of all tell me, do either you or your husband come from a circus family?

A: Not at all. I was a housewife and Terry, my husband, had a good job as an electrical engineer. What happened was, when Darren was three, we took him to see a travelling circus and, for some reason, he just couldn't keep his eyes off the clowns – he was fascinated by them. It's strange because, as a child, I always found them rather frightening. Anyway, after that, Darren became a real circus fan.

P: Right. And so how did this lead to the family actually joining a circus?

A: Well, when Darren was nine, my husband was suddenly made redundant. Although we live in an area of high unemployment, it still came as quite a shock to us. We didn't know what to do, because Darren's two older brothers were just going through university, which was expensive, and there wasn't much work going in the area, so we were pretty desperate.

P: So Darren, what happened next?

D: Well, I said that my dad should try and get work in the circus. We had a car and a caravan, and they always need electricians, so he had the right skills already. At first he thought I was joking, but when I explained that circuses often employ whole families, he began to take me more seriously. I'd read about circuses, and I'd seen some TV documentaries too.

P: So you knew what you were talking about?

D: Not really, but I convinced Dad that he should write away to all the circuses asking if they'd got any work for the three of us. I didn't hold out much hope actually, because I had no idea how easy or difficult it was to get in as a family. But within a week, we'd got an offer from one of the large travelling circuses. Dad was taken on as a spotlight operator, Mum would be selling tickets, and I was accepted as a trainee clown.

P: As easy as that Anita?

A: Well, it wasn't an easy decision to make, and then there was a great deal to organise. I mean, Darren says we had a caravan, but it was only one of those little ones that people take on holiday with them. So it was tough at first, deciding what we needed to take and how it could all be fitted in. We only go away for the summer months,

but that first year it seemed to go on forever. At times I wanted to give it all up, I can tell you. It was a great relief to get home and sort things out.

P: And Darren?

D: Well, I'm not old enough yet to perform in front of an audience, but I've learnt a great deal about clowning just watching the real professionals night after night. People ask about my education, but I only miss the summer term. I follow the same books with a private teacher and I have my laptop computer. It's actually better because on your own it doesn't take long. At school, the teacher wastes a lot of time trying to get everyone to listen and do what they're told, which annoys me. I have to fit in my clowning lessons as well, so I want to get the schoolwork done as quickly as possible.

P: And the future, Anita?

A: Well it was a risk to take, but it's working out, so I guess it was worth it, and we're enjoying it too. We've made lots of friends and, of course, we now have a proper van and a big caravan, so it's quite comfortable. I mean we could've sat at home and got depressed about Terry losing his job, and I'm glad we didn't do that. In a way, I suppose, we had nothing to lose.

Module 3

Speaking. Page 45. (Paper 5 Part 2). Exercise 8a.

E = Examiner; S = Student

E: Here are your two photographs. They show people working with animals. I'd like you to compare and contrast these photographs, and say what you think is difficult about these jobs. Remember, you only have about a minute for this so don't worry if I interrupt you. All right?

Speaking. Page 45. (Paper 5 Part 2). Exercise 8b.

S: They both show people who work with animals. In the one on the left the man – he's the farmer, probably – is in the country with the sheep, whereas in the other one there's a woman in a white coat – she's a, a … kind of doctor who looks after animals. People bring in, er, small animals who live in the home, when they are ill or when they hurt themselves, like this dog.
Personally, I think both jobs must be very hard work. A doctor for sick animals has to study for a long time to learn about all the different animals, and she has to see a lot of, erm, 'patients' in a day. But if I had to choose I would say the farmer's job is more difficult because he has to get up very early in the morning and go out to the fields in summer and winter. He has to work a lot – it must be very tiring.

E: Thank you.

Listening. Page 46. Part 1. Exercise 1b.

P = Presenter; N = Nick

P: When you first went into the rainforest what did you think – what was your reaction?

N: Oh, that was that. I just completely fell in love with it – the heat, the humidity, the snakes, the insects, the animals, the people. I was Rainforest Man.

P: But it can't have been easy to live in that kind of environment.

N: No, it's difficult. It's lonely. You pour sweat, you smell. The insects are like flying motorbikes and you're bitten all the time. And people don't realise how claustrophobic it is – no real daylight gets through the forest canopy.

P: So why did you stay out there so long?

N: Well, the reason I was sent out to the Amazon in the first place was to make a TV documentary about monkeys and birds. But the reason I stayed out there for another ten years was that I decided I had to make one about jaguars.

Listening. Page 46. Part 2. Exercise 2b.

P: Tell us about your first meeting with a jaguar.

N: Well, I'd been out since before four o'clock that morning – trying to photograph a group of black vultures – ugly birds – but it was half past five when she appeared. I'd just looked at my watch because I had to report back to camp at 5:45. Anyway, suddenly there was a change in atmosphere – every hair on my body stood on end. Then I caught sight of her.

P: What did she do?

N: This absolutely magnificent creature – she emerged from the forest greenery about 60 metres away and started walking towards me. The jaguar's coat is really impressive and she had beautiful black markings all over her deep yellow fur. I could even see the whites of her eyes.

P: Then what happened?

N: Time seemed to stand still for a while. I hardly breathed. I don't think she actually saw me – she showed no sign of it if she did – and she had a drink from a river a few metres away, and then disappeared into the forest again

P: Did you take a photograph of her?

N: I couldn't, because I'd used all my film on the vultures. As you can imagine, I was really upset. But after that, I stayed another seven years in the rainforest, and had nine more encounters, all of which I captured on film.

P: Why is the jaguar so hard to find?

N: Because it's a threatened species, it lives only in the very remotest areas. You have to remember that the Amazon forest extends for thousands of kilometres and the territory of a typical male jaguar extends to something like 170 kilometres – in exceptional cases as much as 300 or more.

P: No wonder you don't see them much.

N: Exactly, that's why each sighting is such a thrill. Because what you have to remember is that jaguars are solitary, shy creatures, which have the ability to get through the forest so incredibly quietly that you can be only a few metres away and miss one completely.

P: So how did you eventually track them down, on those other occasions you mentioned?

N: I went thousands of kilometres inland into a less-populated area and made friends with the local forest people. It was while they were helping me look for the jaguar that I had the chance to eat their local speciality – the world's biggest spider. It's 26 centimetres, has eight eyes and tastes revolting. But it would have been very rude to refuse to eat what for them is a very special meal.

P: What do the forest people think about jaguars?

N: Well like me, they don't get to see them very often because jaguars tend to avoid places where humans make their homes. But they certainly wouldn't kill one unless it represented some kind of threat. They have a great respect for these animals actually, regarding them as fellow hunters rather than as potential prey.

P: Studying these animals can't be easy.

N: Oh it's not. One great problem is actually keeping count of how many of them are out there and where they go, because they're so rarely seen. In one project, researchers have been putting what are called 'radio collars' on to any animals they catch, so that they can study their movements afterwards.

P: But you have to catch the animals first?

N: Yes, and they are very frightened of people. You see jaguars don't only live in the forest. In areas where there are cattle and sheep, farmers hunt and kill jaguars because they do attack farm animals, I'm afraid.

P: I see.

N: And when they get too close to civilisation, jaguars can face other problems too, erm, they can pick up illnesses from domestic cats, even dogs, which tend to have a different range of diseases from those found in the forest. But at least, they're not dependent on the one disappearing habitat like so many animals. And there's lots of research going on into jaguars at present, so I'm confident that the animal has a future.

P: Nick Gordon, thank you.

Module 4

Speaking. Page 59. (Paper 5 Part 3). Exercise 5a.

E = Examiner; S1 = Student 1; S2 = Student 2

E: Here are some pictures which show people doing different sports. First, talk to each other about the advantages and disadvantages of doing each of these sports. Then decide which one would be best for someone who doesn't have much spare time. You have only about three minutes for this, so don't worry if I stop you. Please speak so that we can hear you. All right?

Speaking. Page 59. (Paper 5 Part 3). Exercise 5b.

S1: OK, let's begin with swimming, shall we? I think it's a good sport to do because it keeps you fit and you can swim all year, if you have an indoor pool. Most cities and towns have a pool, I think.

S2: It's very boring, though. It's OK in the sea but I don't like public swimming pools. I prefer running because you can go in the open air and run round the parks and …

S1: Yes, and as well as that, you can go with a friend, and it doesn't cost anything. You can go when you want and you can – if you're not fit you can walk or jog. I don't know about golf, though – what would you say?

S2: Well, it's a good sport for meeting people and it's very relaxing.

S1: But it takes a lot of time. I think it's better when you finish work, how do you say – when you're older …

S2: Ah, when you retire. Yes, my father plays it – it's good for people with lots of time, but it's quite expensive if you have to join a club or something.

S1: So, maybe not so good if you have a busy job.

S2: That's true. Well, what about …

S1: Sorry to interrupt, but for me tennis is a good sport.

S2: Yes, tennis is good for meeting people but it's very expensive in my town. You have to join a club and wear, you know, special white clothes.

S1: It's good for fitness though; you have to run around a lot. But what about skiing?

S2: Oh, I don't know – I've never done it. Do you like it?

S1: I like skiing, but it's expensive. You have to travel to the mountains and pay for the lessons and the things you need – you know, you, you have to hire the skis, and the, er, …

S2: Yes, the equipment and clothes. I agree with you. And as well as that it's dangerous. You need to learn. Or you'll spend a lot of time in hospital! With football you can play in the street, with your friends or with …

S1: But you still need to practise and learn the rules, if you …

S2: Well, you can just kick a ball around. It's very popular in my country. What about riding a bike?

S1: I think it depends. If you live in a busy city it's not very good for your health and it's a bit dangerous, I would say.

S2: Anyway, we have to decide which one doesn't take much time. What do you think?

S1: Well, I suppose swimming might be the most suitable, or …

S2: I'm not sure I agree about that. You still have to go to the pool, change your clothes, and then afterwards have a shower, get dry and get …

S1: Or cycling, maybe cycling is better. You can just get on your bike and go.

S2: Well, only if you have a bike. And you should wear a … you know … a hat for safety. Running is even easier and quicker.

S1: So let's decide which one. Running?

S2: Yes, I think so.

Listening. Page 60. (Paper 4 Part 3). Exercise 2a.

Speaker 1

My first parachute jump was the scariest thing I'd ever done. Nothing prepares you for falling out of a plane at 180 kilometres an hour. After all, you can't turn back if you change your mind, can you? When it came to actually jumping, I got very nervous. I had no choice but to do it though, because the whole point was to get people to give donations to a medical research organisation. If I hadn't jumped, I wouldn't have got any money for them. Once back on the ground, I realised I'd loved it and that was the beginning of my big hobby, much to the amazement of my friends and family.

Speaker 2

I grew up surrounded by water – you could see the Atlantic from my bedroom window, and yet I'd never learned to swim. See, I – I just never fancied it, even though my parents and brother swam like fish. I finally signed up for a five-week beginners' course at the age of 35, I mean not because I'd changed my mind about wanting to swim, but just so that I could see the expressions of amazement on my kids' faces. It was worth suffering those awful lessons just for that. But I must admit that, even now, I'd much rather relax at the poolside and watch them splashing about.

Speaker 3

I took up skiing while I was living abroad. I absolutely loved it from the word go – the scenery of course, the sense of speed and complete focus on the task. It's fantastic exercise, too. I hadn't expected to enjoy it though, in fact I had to be talked into doing it by my friends. They'd all skied since they were very small, and kept on at me until I agreed to give it a go. I'm much older now and obviously not as fit as I used to be, but if I could find the money I'd like to take the kids and see if I can still do it.

Speaker 4

I'm not really into risky sports, but I enjoyed snorkelling and quite fancied getting a closer look at exotic fish. My main motive for taking up scuba diving though, to be honest, is because my boyfriend, Tony, said I wouldn't be able to do it. I tend to panic you see, and in scuba diving you have to remain totally calm or things can get very dangerous. It took me ages to gain the confidence to do it, but I was determined to show Tony that he was wrong. So I persevered, and I've now passed all my exams and we're off on a diving holiday together soon.

Speaker 5:

When I was younger and much fitter, I was really into football in a big way. Not just playing it but, you know, going to every Liverpool home match, watching it on TV. And when I wasn't doing this, I was on the computer playing these games, like the one called FIFA and so on. I don't play football competitively any more but I do still enjoy a kick around with my mates or my kids. It's the only way I can really unwind actually, I have a really stressful job and football just helps me to switch off and think of something else.

Exam practice 2: Teacher's Book

Listening. Page 180. (Paper 4 Part 3).

Speaker 1

Because I'm a designer, people immediately assume I'm interested in the fashion pages in the newspaper, but actually we have specialised magazines for keeping up-to-date with developments in the industry – all you get in the newspapers is gossip, and there's enough of that in fashion anyway. No, the only newspaper I get is the local one. It tells me what's on at the cinema, and has really good coverage of my local football team. I'm a real fan, but it's only a local team, so they're hardly mentioned in the national press. The rest of the paper's mostly adverts – I wouldn't buy it just for those, but they're useful sometimes.

Speaker 2

I don't get much time for reading a newspaper, so I buy one of the smaller ones. It's useful for seeing what's on television and I like to know what people are saying about the latest films and plays, even if I rarely get time to go and see any myself. Admittedly, there's more advertisements than news in this paper, and most of the photos are of celebrities at parties, so I skip all that. Even the sports coverage tends to be full of gossip, it seems to be the fashion nowadays. Personally, I'm more interested in the game itself, so I get the results and match reports from the radio.

Speaker 3

My favourite daily newspaper is actually the one that's read by the smallest number of people – perhaps that says something about me! I like it because it only employs top-class journalists and photographers, and they seem to get just the right visual image to go with each story. Even the sports reports are intelligent and well written. I'm not a great one for the arts or fashion, but I find myself reading reviews of plays and concerts which I'd never go and see. And best of all, there's hardly anything about who's dating who and all that rubbish that seems to dominate much of the press these days.

Speaker 4

I work in the advertising industry and so I have a professional interest in newspapers. I'd like to pretend that by choice I'd go for one of the more up-market dailies and read the more serious reviews, but I'm afraid for me the important thing is who's getting coverage, whose photo is appearing on the cover. In my business, you have to know who's saying what about which fashion model or sports personality, otherwise you could easily find yourself using the wrong person to promote a brand. I tend to read one particular paper because the main columnist really does know everybody who's anybody, so you can believe what she says!

Speaker 5

To be honest, we generally manage without a newspaper. I'll look through someone's if I'm not busy at work, but it's usually only glancing at the headlines and pictures. The only time I buy one is when we're booking our holidays – because the Sunday papers are still the best place for those kind of adverts. But I get most of my news from the television these days and if I want up-to-date sports reports, or if I'm looking for a film to go and see, then I can find a much better range of reviews on the Internet. To my mind, newspapers are old-fashioned, they've been overtaken by modern technology.

Module 5

Speaking. Page 73. Exercise 5a.

E = Examiner; C1 = Candidate 1; C2 = Candidate 2

E: Now, I'd like you to talk about something together for about three minutes. I'd like you to look at these examples of modern technology. First I want you to decide on the advantages and disadvantages of each one. Then decide which is the most important and which is the least important. As I said you only have three minutes for this, so don't worry if I stop you. Please speak so we can hear you. All right?

C1: So we have to discuss all the pictures and then say which is the most and the least useful?

E: That's right.

Page 73. Exercise 5b.

C1: OK. Well, straightaway I'm looking at the MP3 player.

C2: Me too.

C1: I think they're fantastic. You've got all your music on one small gadget.

C2: I completely agree with you. And you can listen to them anywhere. But really having a machine to play games on is much more fun.

C1: No, I'm not really that interested in computer games. I find them boring after a while. I don't know what it is … Perhaps because they're always fantasy.

C2: What about some of these other things? You must have a mobile phone.

C1: Oh, yes. You can talk to your friends any time night or day. And if you miss the last bus home you can always get someone to pick you up. But I never have it turned on. I don't like it when people phone me.

C2: Oh, no I love it. Except it's a bit embarrassing on a crowded train …

C1: I hate listening to other people's personal conversations, saying they're on the train and all that.

C2: But you never know when you're going to get a text from one of your mates and they want you to reply immediately.

C1: Let's talk about these household things. I think dishwashers are incredibly useful. Last year we had a holiday in a flat with no dishwasher. It was a real shock having to wash up.

C2: Yes ….

C1: But they do make us lazy, don't you think. They're a bit of a luxury.

C2: Not these days. Anymore than an electric toothbrush is. And the dentists say they're much better for keeping your teeth clean.

C1: Do you think so? I feel they're a bit unnecessary really.

C2: What about microwave ovens? I think they're useful for reheating things but I think food that's cooked in them tastes awful.

C1: You've got to admit they're an incredible time-saver.

C2: That's true. Although we haven't got one at home. There's no more room in our kitchen. Besides, I've never had one so I don't miss it!

C1: That just leaves one thing.

C2: The TV!

C1: Yes. Some people say that they're going out of date now that we can watch programmes on our computers.

C2: But look at that high-definition screen. Isn't the picture fantastic?

C1: It is but you still get the same boring programmes and the same boring advertisements.

C2: Oh, come on. What about all the news? And the films?

C1: To be honest I don't watch TV that much. I'd rather go out and have fun with my friends.

C2: I'm amazed.

C1: OK, it's important but it's not the most important.

C2: So we'd better make our minds up.

C1: I'll go with the mobile phone as the most important and the electric toothbrush as the least important.

C2: No, I'd say that the microwave was the least important.

C1: OK that's fine. So we both think the mobile phone is the most important and the microwave and toothbrush the least. And……..

E: Thank you very much.

Page 73. Exercise 5c.

C2: So we'd better make our minds up.

C1: I'll go with the mobile phone as the most important and the electric toothbrush as the least important.

C2: No, I'd say that the microwave was the least important.

C1: OK that's fine. So we both think the mobile phone is the most important and the microwave and toothbrush the least. And…….

E: Thank you very much.

Page 73, Exercise 3b

E: Can you imagine a world without mobile phones?

C2: Oh it would be impossible. We've got so used to them.

C1: Oh, I don't know. Sometimes I think we use them too much. It's amazing how silly a lot of the conversations are.

C2: But that's always true when people chat to each other. It was the same on ordinary phones.

C1: But you see people holding on to them all the time as though they're frightened to put them down.

E: Which household appliances get used most in your house?

C1: In ours the washing machine, definitely. My brothers and sisters change their clothes every day, even when they're not dirty.

C2: Oh, in ours it's probably the computer or the hairdryer. Someone's always using mine when I want it.

C1: Or the television.. The television's always on in our house even if nobody's watching it.

E: Thank you. That is the end of the test.

Listening. Page 74. Exercise 2a

P = Presenter, N= Nina Cooke

P: Good morning. I'm Anna French and today I'm talking to Nina Cooke as part of our series on Technology and the modern family. Nina, what is really important to you as a working mother?

N: Well, it goes without saying all the things we tend to take so much for granted like dishwashers, washing machines and so on, but I think what I have most appreciated is being able to do my food shopping on-line, because that's something I really can't stand – going to the supermarket. It's so time consuming!

P: But what about other kinds of shopping? Do you still do that?

N: Not if I can help it – well, shopping for clothes for myself is an exception, because I enjoy it and I prefer to try things on, but – you know, there are really good websites for most things, aren't there? You know, CDs, books, toys, household stuff.

P: Do you tend to have your computer on all the time?

N: I do now we've got broadband. It's great to be able to just check on your emails quickly or have the news headlines on the screen. In fact, if it weren't for the crossword I don't think I'd bother getting a newspaper any more. I like doing it on the train on my way to work.

P: And what technology are the kids into?

N: Well, Lizzie is never without her mobile phone. She just sends text messages to her friends the whole time, even when she's been with them all day. I don't know what she finds to say to them.

P: So she prefers this to the computer?

N: So far, yes. As for Tom – well, he spends all his money on computer games, that's his passion – and is very good at pretending he's doing his homework when I think he's probably fighting aliens or something.

P: Do either of them use chat rooms?

N: Tom does when he wants to contact his cousin, who's just gone away to university. At least it's cheaper than using the phone!

P: And I suppose they both do their homework on the computer?

N: Quite a bit of it, yes – they use the Internet to do research for projects and they've also discovered Spell check, which is great because now I don't have to check their work myself.

P: Do any of you use MP3 players?

N: I like listening to podcasts when I'm walking the dog or whatever, and Lizzie always seems to be plugged into her loud music, which I worry about because I'm sure it can't be good for her ears.

P: What's your husband's view on modern technology?

N: Well some of it he thinks is a waste of time – like this satellite navigation system which came with the new car. But he's thrilled with the hands free phone which was also provided, – it means he can catch up with his clients on long car journeys which saves him time because he doesn't have to do it later. And he used to complain about not having time to do things like going to the bank or a travel agency during the week, but that's not a problem any more because you can book holidays and pay bills or whatever on-line 24/7.

Module 6

Speaking. Page 87. (Paper 5 Part 2). Exercise 6a.

E= Examiner; A = Alice; R = Robert

E: Here are your two photographs. They show different types of art. I'd like you to compare and contrast these photographs, and say which type of art you think is more interesting. Remember, you only have about a minute for this, so don't worry if I interrupt you. All right?

Speaking. Page 87. (Paper 5 Part 2). Exercise 6b.

A: Both pictures show art – it's completely different art. In one picture we can see classical art, and the other picture is definitely about modern art. In the first one there are a lot of people looking at the pictures that are on the wall, while in the second picture the people are walking down the street and I get the impression that no one is interested in this, this thing – they are just there. The statue could be a bird or a man – I really don't know what it is. Well, I like some modern art but if you ask me to choose, I think I would choose classical art because I understand it. In the first photo you know what the painters wanted to say. If you want you can learn something about why they were painted. But in the second, if you don't understand it you …

E: Thank you. Robert, are you interested in art?

R: I'm not really very keen on art. I prefer listening to music.

Speaking. Page 87. (Paper 5 Part 2). Exercise 7a.

A: In the first photo you know what the painters wanted to say. If you want you can learn something about why they were painted. But in the second, if you don't understand it you …

E: Thank you. Robert, are you interested in art?

R: I'm not really very keen on art. I prefer listening to music.

Listening. Page 88. (Paper 4 Part 1). Exercise 2a.

One

Hi. Rachel. Thanks for phoning back. Listen, you're going to see the New York City Ballet, aren't you? … Have you still got the brochure there? … . Great. So do they give the exact dates? Oh, really? I didn't realise it was so soon. Thank goodness I phoned you because I'd hate to miss it. I'd better give them a ring. You're going next Friday, you say? Shall I see if they've got any for then because that would be nice, wouldn't it?

Two

To start with, I must admit that I had my doubts. I didn't think Alex Casey would be able to leave the film-script style behind. But even though the characters are a bit predictable, they are so colourful that you can't help but engage with them. And they're portrayed with a good deal of sensitivity, so you really care what happens to them. Then there's the very unusual plot, which keeps you gripped until the very last page. In fact, it would probably transfer very well to either stage or screen and because it's Casey, you immediately think of that. But, actually, it works well enough as it is.

Three

M = Man; W = Woman

M: Can I help?

W: Yes, I'd like to move to the back, so I'm not disturbed so much by the noise of the traffic.

M: Well, it is the holiday period, madam, so we're fully booked and …

W: I appreciate that. But if I'd known how much noise there'd be, I would've gone elsewhere. I might as well put my bed on the motorway.

M: I'll see what can be done. Would you like to take a seat in the bar over there while I have a word with the manager?

W: I'm just on my way to the dining room, actually.

M: Very well, Madam.

Four

S1 = Student 1; S2 = Student 2

S1: So what did you think of it?

S2: It was all right, but you know, it didn't really live up to the hype, did it?

S1: Oh. I thought visually it was really good.

S2: Well, the special effects were OK, I suppose, but I hadn't really expected all that in this sort of film. If you ask me, though, they'd have done a lot better to stick to the plot of the original a bit more closely. Much as I liked Julia Roberts, it just didn't hold my attention, I'm afraid.

S1: Well, I haven't read the book, so I don't know, but I think she was just brilliant.

Five

M = Man; W = Woman

W: I lent him that CD ages ago. I keep dropping hints whenever I see him in the canteen, but either he's forgotten or just doesn't want to give it back to me.

M: Some people are very thoughtless, aren't they?

W: Well, I wouldn't mind, except it was a birthday present and I haven't really listened to it myself yet. My son bought it for me. If I knew him better, I'd ask for it straight out, but I don't want to fall out with someone new like that.

M: It's difficult to know what to do, isn't it?

Six

Don't get me wrong. It's mostly worthwhile stuff they've got there. It's just the way it's been put together that I don't like. I mean, it would be much better if all the works were grouped in some kind of logical way – you know, according to period, theme or whatever. You can't argue with the amount of background information available, which is very thorough, but if all you want to do is see a particularly brilliant painting or watercolour or whatever, you've got to go past all this other stuff to get to it. Some people will be exhausted by the time they're half way round, if you ask me.

Exam practice 3: Teacher's Book

Listening. Page 184. (Paper 4 Part 2).

P = Presenter; F = Fiona

P: My guest today, Fiona Mulligan, runs her own business. Fiona, welcome.

F: Hello.

P: Now your company helps people in a very particular way, doesn't it Fiona? Tell us a little about it.

F: Well, it's all about public speaking. For some of us, standing up and speaking in front of a group of people comes very naturally, but for others it's a rather frightening experience, especially if it's part of their job. That's why I started my company which is called Presentation Skills. It aims to help people get over their fear and speak more confidently in public.

P: So you had experience of public speaking yourself?

F: Yes, because although I was working as an accountant at the time I started the company, I'd trained as an actress and worked in television for many years. But I'd reached the age of 40, it was getting harder to get work in my profession and I was tired of doing temporary work. I decided that I wanted to run my own business, but I wasn't sure exactly what I could do.

P: So where did the idea come from?

F: Well, a friend, a doctor actually, had to give a talk whilst attending a conference. He knew his subject, but was very nervous about actually giving the talk and asked for advice. That's when I realised that many people must suffer in the same way.

P: So how did you get started?

F: Well, the first problem was money – I had none! I applied to the bank for a loan, but they weren't interested. I talked to lots of friends and colleagues, but nobody could really help. In the end I had a lucky break. A rich uncle, who I'd lost touch with years before, heard about my idea through some cousins I'd written to. He was so impressed that he decided to lend me the £10,000 I needed to get started.

P: That was lucky.

F: Yes. Then I needed to find some customers. I telephoned lots of big companies and offered to run a free training session for their staff. I tried supermarkets, financial companies, travel agents, but nobody was interested. In the end, it was the managing director of a department store who asked me to help him with a speech he had to give. He was so impressed that he decided to arrange sessions for all his senior staff. Since then I haven't looked back.

P: So what do your clients get for their money?

F: The basic course involves two days of individual lessons on how to speak in public and costs from £2,500 to £3,500 depending on exactly what's included. For most people the problem is just one of confidence, although some people have to learn things like how to speak loudly enough or how to avoid going too fast – things like that. But some people have special needs, like they have to speak while showing statistics on a screen, which often means using computer equipment, so we train them to use that properly.

P: So you tell people what they're doing wrong?

F: We use a video studio, so that people can see for themselves and, at the end of the course, we take them to a real theatre where they practise giving their talks on stage.

P: And what's the commonest problem people have?

F: They just make the talk boring. They're so worried about how they feel that they forget about how the audience feels. You know, they don't look at the audience, they repeat themselves or, worst of all, just <u>read from notes</u>. That can be really dull.

P: And can you teach people to be more interesting?

F: Well, the important thing actually is for them to be themselves – that's how they'll be most comfortable, and that's how they get over feeling shy on stage. People who are nervous and tense sometimes seem to be <u>angry</u> for example. But when they see themselves on stage, they realise what they look like and that helps them to understand what they need to do.

P: How interesting. Fiona, thank you for … .

Module 7

Speaking. Page 101. (Paper 5 Part 4). Exercise 7a.

E = Examiner; J = Julia; P = Paul

E: Do you think we can decide what a person is like by the clothes they wear?

J: No, I don't think you can judge someone's character from their clothes …

P: To be honest, I haven't thought much about it but I think, er, you can have an idea, for example if they are very casual or very formal. You know if they are similar people to you depending on the clothes they wear. Of course it's wrong to think like that – just because they aren't wearing jeans and T-shirt like me, it doesn't mean they aren't a nice person. Everybody should be allowed to wear what they want, and anyway it depends on what they're doing. If they're going to work they probably can't wear jeans or trainers so you can't really know…

J: Of course. <u>And apart from that</u> it would be very boring if everyone wore the same clothes. It's dangerous if you decide you don't like someone just because they have different clothes.

Listening. Page 102. (Paper 4 Part 3). Exercise 2a.

Speaker 1
During the week, when I'm at work I tend to wear fitted jackets, high heels, straight skirts – <u>you know, quite stylish clothes</u>. The first impression my clients get of me is fairly crucial so I spend time looking for <u>clothes that are businesslike</u>. I can't afford to spend too much on them, though – I don't buy expensive clothes. It's got to the point where <u>I don't feel right in casual clothes</u> so even at the weekends I'll still wear the same kind of thing, but perhaps swap the jacket and heels for a sweater and flat shoes – er, pumps.

Speaker 2
I always wear the same things when I'm not at school – tracksuit bottoms, a fleece or a T-shirt and designer trainers. Nearly all my friends do. I've also got three different football kits – Man United, England and Barcelona. In the summer, I sometimes wear shorts instead of tracksuit bottoms but <u>it's always sports stuff. There's no point in dressing up in smart clothes, anyway – they just get dirty. What matters is feeling relaxed and not having to worry about what you look like.</u>

Speaker 3
Well, I've always had a fairly clear idea of how I want to look – I want to be a designer when I leave school, and <u>I'm always flicking through magazines to pick up ideas. At the moment either very short or very long skirts are cool, worn with trainers or wedges – nothing in between. And low waisted trousers. Strong patterns and crop tops in bright colours – even colours that clash, like lime green and pink – are popular, too.</u> I wouldn't dream of wearing anything sort of frumpy or like my mum wears. I even try to adapt my school uniform a bit to personalise it. So I might wear patterned or striped tights with it.

Speaker 4
I don't think about clothes very much. I suppose I wear what I've always worn – a shirt and tie with trousers and maybe a sweater. I don't spend much money on clothes so most of them are a few years old. I sometimes go into charity shops and my son gives me things he's fed up with. <u>I'll wear anything</u>, as long as it's warm and not too scruffy. I'm certainly not trying to impress anyone!

Speaker 5
I like clothes, but I'm not a fashion victim and I don't dress up. Now I've got kids, my clothes have to be practical, so no high heels and tight skirts these days. Having said that, I don't want to end up living in tracksuits or jeans and baggy jumpers all the time like some mums. I go for casual but well-cut clothes in natural fabrics like silk or cotton. <u>I do tend to spend quite a lot on my clothes but then I can wear them over and over again and they don't drop to pieces.</u> It's an investment.

Module 8

Speaking. Page 115 (Paper 5 Part 1). Exercise 7a.

E = Examiner; G = Giorgio; A = Anna

E: My name is Katie, and this is my colleague Mark. He is just going to listen to us. So you are … Anna … and … Giorgio. Thank you. First of all we'd like to know something about you, so I'm going to ask you some questions about yourselves. Giorgio, where are you from?

G: I'm from Padova, in Italy.

E: What do you like about living there?

G: It's a very nice town, not too big, not too small. The people are very friendly, and they will help you, it doesn't matter if you are a neighbour, or a visitor to the town. The only thing is it can be a little bit boring sometimes – there aren't so many things for young people to do!

E: Anna, where are you from?

A: I'm from Zurich, in Switzerland.

E: Do you like living there?

A: Yes, I do, very much. Although we live in the city we have quite a big house with a lot of space and I love the garden. We always have barbecues, and it's on a hill so we have views over all the city and the mountains.

E: And what do you do in Zurich, do you work or study?

A: I work for an international bank, as a financial adviser.

E: What do you enjoy most about your job?

A: I have a lot of contact with clients and I really enjoy meeting them. And my, er, <u>the other people who work with me</u>, we like each other very much and get on well together.

E: Giorgio, could you tell us something about your family, please?

G: Yes, there are five of us: my mother, my father, and two brothers. One of them is younger than me and one is older. They say in Italy the one in the middle is the best one, but it's just a saying! My brother is a teacher, my father is a teacher and my mother is a teacher, but my other brother hasn't decided yet. I graduated last year and I don't know what I'm going to do. I studied law but I don't want to be a lawyer.

E: Anna, what do you like doing in your free time?

A: It depends on the season. In the winter I like skiing. In Switzerland we have a lot of mountains and it's very pleasant to go there for the weekends. In summer I go walking in the mountains with my husband. After work I like reading books – I like thrillers best.

E: Giorgio, what sort of music do you like?

G: I like rock music most, but I'm really quite, er, <u>how do you say it, I like many different kinds of music</u>. But when I'm quite tired and want to relax it's pop rock because I play the guitar and the best style to play is rock.

E: Thank you. Now, I'd like each of you to talk on your own for about a minute …

Listening. Page 116. (Paper 4 Part 4). Exercise 1a.

P = Presenter; S = Simon

P: Most of us have an interest of one kind or another, whether it's keeping an unusual pet, collecting stamps or gardening. Simon is interested in learning about other people's hobbies – both ordinary people's and those of celebrities. Why is this, Simon?

S: Well, the thing is if you tell me that the bloke sitting opposite me in the train is a teacher, or engineer or whatever, I might be able to guess what sort of things he can do – what he's good at, but really I haven't the faintest idea what he's really like – you know what makes him tick, whereas if you tell me he's a stamp collector or a leading light of the local drama society, you have pretty much drawn a map of his personality for me.

P: You think people reveal their souls through their hobbies?

S: Absolutely. One of the things you can see straightaway, for example, is whether people are happier in company or whether they prefer solitude. So if they enjoy let's say being in a choir, it's often as much the belonging to a group with shared goals as about the singing.

P: And is the same true for people who like curling up with a good book or knitting jumpers? It's not so much the activity itself but the fact they want to…

S: Escape from the world for a bit, yes, – be on their own, usually in the fresh air, actually. Look at Jarvis Cocker from the band Pulp – he likes nothing more than being out bird watching. Or Brian May – he used to be with the band Queen, but he spends hours looking at the night sky through his telescope, being on his own. Other famous people fly kites or model aeroplanes – I suppose it's a release from the tension of being in the public eye all the time.

P: And what about actors? I suppose they need activities to occupy them while they're filming.

S: There's a lot of hanging around, yes. You get to see some very glamorous film stars doing crosswords or Sodoku, or knitting quietly by themselves to pass the time. What seems to be the most popular at the moment though is to bring along board games like Scrabble and Monopoly and play them together. They all seem to take it very seriously and are all determined to win – maybe it takes their minds off the acting and makes them less nervous.

P: What else do people's hobbies tell you?

S: Well, whether you are intellectual or creative, or practical. For example, the Dalai Lama – living God to thousands of Tibetan Buddhists – will spend ages – you know –repairing an old film projector which has no instructions, or with his head under a car bonnet, or taking clocks to bits and putting them back together. He is completely in his element.

P: You wouldn't really expect that of a Nobel peace prize winner, would you?

S: Not really, and rock star Bill Wyman, of the Rolling Stones – is also interesting. He goes around with his metal detector – so far he's found about 300 old coins, and even a couple of Roman necklaces. But it's not the actual treasure itself that motivates him – I don't think he even keeps it – he's just fascinated by the process of archaeology. I've heard that a friend is trying to get him to photograph the things he finds so he can publish a book about his findings one day.

P: Let's hope he does!

S: But perhaps the most interesting thing is the hobbies of leaders and Presidents and so on. The ex Japanese Prime Minister, Koizumi, is fanatical about Elvis Presley. No, really – he has released a CD with his favourite Elvis tunes on and used to do Elvis karaokes, even when he was on official visits, to the discomfort of his advisers, one imagines. North Korea's leader, Kim il Jong collects movies and is so mad about them he even kidnapped an actress once, so that she would make movies for him. These interests completely take over their lives!

P: What does that tell us about our leaders?

S: Probably that they have very addictive personalities. Still it's better than doing nothing, I suppose, although we are difficult to live with. I say we because I'm as bad – I follow a rather indifferent football club around the country and it drives my wife mad. The thing is you'd be surprised how many otherwise normal people have a really weird compulsion – buying rare books on ebay, bungee jumping, you name it somebody will do it!

Exam practice 4: Teacher's Book

Listening. Page 188. (Paper 4 Part 4).

P = Presenter; J = Janice

P: Now it's time for that part of the programme where we talk to people just back from unusual holidays. Today's guest is Janice Dawley, who's been on a singing holiday to Spain. Janice, welcome.

J: Hi.

P: Now, how did you find out about a holiday like this?

J: Well, I've been to Spain a number of times and even had a Spanish boyfriend at one time who was a travel agent, so I know the country quite well. But I found this deal on the Internet where flights and accommodation are included as well as singing classes. I was actually looking for language courses in Spain, because I wanted to brush up my Spanish, and came across this by chance.

P: And you went on your own as well?

J: Yes, although that wasn't my original intention. I was meant to be going with a friend, but she had a fall and broke her ankle, so had to pull out at the last minute. I think if it'd been a simple beach holiday, she'd have come in any case. But in the circumstances, I couldn't blame her. I thought of cancelling myself, because I'd never been away on my own before, and then I thought. 'Well, why not?'

P: And was it lonely?

J: In fact, as it turned out, most people were alone, but we all shared a love of Spain and music, so got on really well. And, you know, at the end we all swapped addresses and promised to keep in touch. So I'm hoping I've made some friends to go away with in future. Although I might consider going away alone again, I think, on balance, it's nicer to have someone to share things with. But I must say it's opened my eyes to what's possible on your own.

P: So how was the trip organised?

J: We stayed in a lonely farmhouse deep in the countryside and, every morning, we'd do four hours of classes. They put us into two groups, with the best singers – some of them had lovely voices – in the higher class and those at elementary level, like me, in another. Although I wasn't that good, I'd once been in a choir, so I already knew the basics of singing which was useful, because the absolute beginners on the course found it very difficult.

P: But you made progress?

J: The classes were tough, but my singing definitely improved. That's because our tutors were professional singers. And they didn't speak any English, so that was fun, and a great way to practise two skills at once. Although we'd been warned about the language problem in advance, some people really didn't have enough Spanish to cope, and that did hold us up at times. It would be my only reservation about the holiday, actually.

P: And when the classes were over?

J: After the lessons, the rest of the day was free. I was happy reading my novel in the sun actually, although trips to different places were available if you wanted. The only one I went on was to Granada – a lovely city which I didn't know. We had a guide – an American student who'd been studying at Granada University for a few years – and she offered to show us around, but I don't think she really knew much about the city, so I didn't bother with that. In the evenings, after dinner, we'd all get together to sing songs and that was wonderfully sociable.

P: So would you recommend this experience?

J: Singing every day really makes you feel good and I felt a long way away from my daily life at home – which is what I wanted. The holiday wasn't cheap, but I thought it was worth every penny. I'd definitely go on another trip like this, but maybe not to the same place next time. There's a two-week tango holiday in Buenos Aires coming up – which I'm sure would be really challenging – but I'm quite tempted.

P: Janice, thanks. And if you'd like …

Module 9

Listening. Page 130. (Paper 4 Part 1). Exercise 2.

One

How's your general knowledge? Reckon you can outwit the competitors on the TV quiz shows? Well, *Quiztime* gives you the chance to show what you can do. Beat the clock to answer questions on a variety of topics, ranging from football to soap operas, natural history to music, fashion to computers. Throw the dice and race round the board, collecting points as you go. Based on the hit TV programme of the same name, *Quiztime* comes in both adult and junior versions and is guaranteed to keep the whole family entertained for hours.

Two

W = Woman; M = Man

W: All I can do is either give you a jacket in another size or issue a credit note. I can't give you a cash refund unless the product is faulty in some way, I'm afraid, because you paid by credit card.

M: But supposing there isn't a blue one in the longer fitting?

W: Well, I expect there will be if you look, or we can order one in for you. A credit note would be valid for up to six months.

M: But that's no good to me, it's a 100-mile round trip from where I live.

W: I apologise, sir, but those are the rules.

Three

The thing is, last month I had a service done and the work alone cost me well over £100. And that's without the parts. What worries me is whether you can trust them or not. I mean, I don't know a thing about what goes on under the bonnet – how do I know they're not just ripping me off and saying they've put new bits in when they haven't? I suppose you'll say I should go to an evening class or something to find out how the engine works, but quite honestly I haven't got either time or interest. I just wondered if you had any ideas on what I could do.

Four

T = Tom; M = Miriam

T: Right. Here we are … I'm not so sure that this is a good idea, Miriam. They did say on the phone that there wasn't one. Why don't we go to a shop and buy a map of the area and then get someone to mark the bus routes on it for us?

M: Oh honestly Tom, why should we spend money needlessly? These places always have maps, it stands to reason. I'm going to go up to that uniformed man over there and ask him to lend me one, then we'll take it next door to the library and photocopy it.

T: OK, but don't say I didn't warn you.

Five

Look, I'm sorry. I accept it was a genuine mistake – these things happen, but surely I'm entitled to some kind of compensation. Had I known there was a midday flight, I'd certainly have chosen it. But when I spoke to your employee on the phone, she said there was only one flight a day and, as you know, with these cheap flights once you've booked, you can't change them. So we ended up having to get up really early in the morning in time to catch the flight she'd booked us on, then had to wait ages at the other end because we were too early – the rooms were still being cleaned.

Six

We're on the train and we'll be arriving around six o'clock, but what I want to know is whether we've got time for a round of golf before dinner, or whether we're down to eat at a specific time. Yes, I know that you didn't make the booking yourself, but I think I read something about the rest of the conference delegates arriving tomorrow morning, so I'm not sure what arrangements have been made for tonight. I seem to have mislaid all the paperwork somewhere, it's probably on my desk somewhere – can you have a look? Or perhaps you could check with the organisers and then get back to me, please? I'm on the mobile number. Thanks.

Seven

It's the latest idea to hit London. A company called Q4U has launched a new service that takes the tedium out of waiting around – be it for prescriptions at the chemist's, picking up dry cleaning or queuing for theatre tickets. Anything that people waste their time standing in a queue for. Customers pay the company £20 an hour and one of their professional queuers does the boring bit on their behalf. The idea has caught on fastest when there's something to be picked up, especially holiday documents. The company says that, given mobile-phone technology, the idea can actually be applied to any time-wasting task. Who knows? Maybe even the dentist's waiting room?

Eight

For both customers and e-commerce businesses, not to mention the mail-order industry in general, the question of delivery has long been an issue. The problem is simply this: that the people most likely to spend serious money having a purchase delivered are the least likely to be in when it arrives. After all they are the ones most liable to possess a job and a busy life. It makes you think that if e-commerce had been around first, then the invention of the walk-in shop would have been welcomed as a brilliant new idea. But, fortunately it looks like a solution is at hand. Tanya Wilde went to investigate …

Module 10

Listening. Page 144. (Paper 4 Part 3). Exercise 2a.

Speaker 1

About four years ago, during a tube strike, I was in a taxi. I was running late for a meeting because as usual at rush hour all the roads were jammed. Suddenly I saw this scooter in the window of a showroom and that's when I had my flash of inspiration. I jumped out of the cab, did all the paperwork in 15 minutes and still got to my meeting on time.

The bike can't go above 50 kilometres an hour but it doesn't seem that slow because you can overtake lines of cars. I must admit it sometimes doesn't start, which is a pain, but when it does go it has shrunk London for me and means I can fit in more business meetings than I used to before.

Speaker 2

I love my bike – it's quite comfortable, with lots of gears. I bought it second hand from a colleague, so it was quite cheap as well.

I started cycling to work around the time of the terrorist attacks on the underground. Like lots of other people I suddenly got very scared and anyway I'd always hated being squashed in with all these other people during the rush hour. It's so much nicer being outside in the fresh air, apart from when it's freezing, of course, and motorists are quite considerate to cyclists these days, although I wear a yellow jacket to be on the safe side. The only problem is all the pollution from the traffic – perhaps I should wear a mask.

Speaker 3

If I drove a car, people would probably try to contact me on my mobile – riding a bike gives me a breathing space to think about things without being interrupted for once, which is great when you have a demanding job like mine. I find I arrive at places in a much better mood.

I've got a Kawasaki motorbike and I'm a passionate enthusiast. It all began 20 years ago when I was a student and I was looking for something cheaper to run than a car. Now I use it every day. When it's windy or pouring down with rain it's not very pleasant but I still go out on it, although my family never thought I would stick with it.

Speaker 4

I'm aware that many colleagues and clients think that lawyers should drive flash cars rather than have a bike. But the great thing about a bike is there's always somewhere to leave it, and you don't have to worry about getting a parking ticket. Mind you, I've had a couple of bikes stolen in the last few years, despite having chained them up. People do often look really astonished when I turn up to important meetings on my scooter, which is great – it's good to challenge people's expectations. Some probably look down on this method of transport but I don't care – the opinions of others don't matter to me in the least.

Speaker 5

I began cycling again because I wanted to get fit, but jogging bores me and I don't like going to the gym. I'm wary of the major roads just from lack of experience, – cars seem to go so fast and you feel very vulnerable on a bike – but I think this will pass eventually and I've not had an accident yet, thank goodness.

I'm really glad I took it up again, because it's so convenient – <u>you always know how long the journey's going to take</u>, whereas you can't depend on public transport, and also hopping on a bus or tube is so expensive these days.

Exam practice 5: Teacher's Book

Listening. Page 192. (Paper 4 Part 3).

Speaker 1

Everyone had warned me that, though it was a wonderful experience, there was always a downside to any trip to Antarctica – long days at sea, rough weather, bitter cold, so I was well-prepared. But when the airline lost my luggage and I found myself standing on the harbour in an open-necked shirt, and lightweight jacket, it nearly put me off going any further. Fortunately, the ship had an impressive on-board shop where I was able to stock up on clothes and equipment. <u>I spent a lot though, and I kept the receipts to send to the airline afterwards – it was their fault, and I wasn't going to let them get away with it.</u>

Speaker 2

I'd come to Winter Park, in Colorado, as a novice skier looking to improve my technique away from the crowds, and it was well worth the extra I'd paid. My previous experience of skiing had been at cheaper resorts in Europe. And though I'd enjoyed it tremendously, I'd also become accustomed to fellow skiers using their poles like elbows to get ahead of you in the queues for the lifts. <u>Here, two queues fed each lift, but there was no pushing, merely a polite 'after you' gesture from the person at the head of the other queue.</u> In Europe, I'd been hopeless at skiing, but I'd become expert at holding my own in a queue!

Speaker 3

Diving is a sport I took up reluctantly 12 years ago whilst holidaying in the Caribbean. My friend decided that the beach was boring and, instead, dragged me out of bed every morning at 7:30 for theory classes, after which I was thrown into the ocean with lots of heavy equipment. It didn't cost much, <u>but the instructors were real bullies and couldn't hide their amusement at how uncomfortable I felt</u>. At the time I said: 'Never again', and meant it. Since then, I have actually tried diving again, and although I don't find it a particularly satisfying activity, it's very much easier than I thought then.

Speaker 4

I'd chosen to go on what's called an 'activity break', and the second day's activity involved climbing with ropes up a large rock, and then abseiling down it. <u>I'd expected the other people to be fitness fanatics who'd make me feel inadequate, but I was pleasantly surprised to find a mixed bunch.</u> Some wanted to overcome a fear of heights – others, like me, had heard it was good for your self-confidence, and didn't cost much. I managed the climb with no trouble, it was easy really and I could have handled something more challenging. Then I stood at the bottom giving shouts of encouragement to those who'd got stuck halfway.

Speaker 5

<u>It's every schoolboy's dream – driving a Formula One racing car round the track.</u> Well, in return for about a month's salary, I made that dream come true, and it was worth every penny. As I was lowered into the car, I was surprised to find no steering wheel. Apparently, they only fix that on once you're strapped into your seat. An instructor leant over and helped me find first gear, and I raced off down the track. But as I entered the first bend, suddenly the world started going round and round … . Moments later, the rescue team arrived, all laughing as they pulled me out. It was such a relief when one said: 'It's OK, the car's not damaged.'

Module 11

Listening. Page 157. (Paper 4 Part 2). Exercise 6.

I = Interviewer, P = Penny

I: In the last few years TV chef Jamie Oliver has been at the forefront of a high profile campaign to make Britain a healthier nation. Not before time, says the chief medical officer, who points out that the level of obesity in this country is increasing faster than anywhere else in Europe. Penny, why is this, do you think?

P: The main issue is not so much adults – although they are certainly not as slim as they used to be – but <u>how many young people growing up today are overweight</u>. The reason is simple, too much junk food – cakes, biscuits, crisps and so on.

I: And in what way is Jamie Oliver hoping to make a difference?

P: Well, crucially by making people aware of the rubbish our kids are eating, <u>focusing particularly on what the school provides for them at midday. Replacing the fatty, processed food commonly used in school dinners with fresh ingredients will make an enormous difference to their well-being as they get older.</u> And therefore how much we have to spend on health-care as a nation.

I: So has the food really been that bad?

P: Well if I tell you that <u>we've been spending around four times more per head on prisoners' food than we do on food for our schoolkids</u>, you will get some idea as to what the quality of the food has been like. It's common knowledge that obesity is linked to a number of diseases such as heart attacks, cancer, diabetes, and strokes. So this situation is really not good enough.

I: I know you've been researching the link between diet and life expectancy in different parts of the world. What have you found?

P: Well, in Japan, for example, where they live longer than anywhere else in the world, deaths from heart disease are almost ten times lower than in Britain. <u>One of the reasons could be that whereas 38% of our calorie intake comes from fat, the Japanese will typically get two thirds of their calories from carbohydrates</u> such as rice.

I: What about other populations you've been investigating, such as the Inuit of Greenland?

P: They have very low rates of heart disease, too, and <u>are very long-living</u>. Which is interesting because they eat very little fruit and vegetables and 60% of their calories come from fat.

I: But doesn't this contradict what you said earlier?

P: Not really, because the kind of fat they eat is the kind you find in oily fish like salmon and mackerel. It's called omega-3, and <u>we've known for a long time that it has huge benefits to the heart and bones. And now scientists are saying that there may also be a connection between omega 3 intake and better mental health, too.</u>

I: I didn't know that.

P: No, it's a very recent discovery. And, moving to a different part of the world, scientists are now also suggesting that turmeric, a key ingredient of curries, may be the reason why <u>older people in India are less likely to lose their memories</u> as early as those in western nations.

I: A good excuse to eat more curry! I'm fascinated by the French, who seem to eat a lot of saturated fat – you know, red meat, butter and so on – and yet manage to remain slim.

P: Now, this is very interesting again because <u>they drink a lot of red wine, as you know, and it now seems likely that it's the chemicals in this which helps protect against heart disease</u>. But it's not just that – it's also their attitude to food.

I: What do you mean? They eat less?

P: It's more that they enjoy their meals, eat slowly and <u>don't have as many snacks as we do</u>. But I believe that the real key to why they don't put on weight is the fact that <u>they have their main meal at lunchtime, as opposed to the British, who tend to have a heavy evening meal instead.</u>

I: It's better for you, you mean?

P: Well, it means that 80% of their calories are consumed before 2 p.m. – at a time when they are more able to convert it into energy.

I: Penny, I'll have to stop you there, but thank you very much for coming into the studio, and …

Module 12

Listening. Page 172. (Paper 4 Part 4). Exercise 2.

P = Presenter, M = Mike

P: My guest today, Mike Morgan has been a leading journalist on a national newspaper for more than 40 years. Mike, what made you decide to take it up in the first place?

M: I kind of drifted into it. I was always good at English and liked writing stories and so on at school, but I was initially quite keen on a career in business and, in fact, I'd accepted a place to study that at college. It was my father who talked me into doing journalism. He just thought I'd be better at it than I would at going into business.

P: What training did you get?

M: In those days, you were taken on by the newspaper straight from school as a kind of message boy. Rather than doing a diploma in journalism as you would now, you had to pick up the skills you needed actually on the job. You had to follow a senior reporter around and if he went to court, you'd go too and then write up the same story. He would look at it afterwards and give you feedback. It was some time before anything of mine actually appeared in the newspaper.

P: What was your first real reporting job?

M: I was a crime reporter, which meant I had to spend a lot of time with the police. In those days, you just hung around them to find out what was going on. They were terribly suspicious of us at first, I remember, but we were given an enormous expense account to buy them drinks, which helped! And after a bit, they felt sure enough of me to let me go out on jobs with them. Unfortunately, I wasn't always allowed to report the things I heard and saw!

P: Are there rules about what you can and can't report, then?

M: There are legal issues, obviously, with privacy and national security and so on. But there are also unwritten rules. I remember when Prince Charles was at university he had four bodyguards looking after him, but he sometimes used to try and lose them so he could meet a girlfriend. So he might go to the toilet in a pub or restaurant and then get out through the window. We always knew what he was up to, but we never printed it – all the journalists sympathised with his situation and didn't want to spoil things for him. It was an unspoken agreement amongst us.

P: So, what makes a good journalist?

M: Well, obviously you need to be confident and articulate and able to get on with all kinds of people. Being able to write well also helps. However good you are though, this is not as important as having bags of energy and commitment. When a big story breaks, you have to drop everything you're doing and work all hours if need be, often under tremendous pressure.

P: And do you still enjoy it?

M: I do, although I won't be sorry to retire. In my day, it was all going out and meeting people to get stories. Now it's much more office based. We have to be computer literate and we do a lot of stuff that printers used to do. In the satellite age, everything has to be instantaneous. It's still just as exciting, but quite honestly it's not what I set out to do.

P: Would you encourage young people to go in for it?

M: Let's face it. Even working on a best-selling tabloid paper you're never going to make your fortune, but you can earn a decent living. No two days are the same and it's great to be one of the first to know what's going on. In some ways it's competitive, like all jobs, but actually that's not such a problem as people might think, because there's also a great team spirit when you're working on a story. So, as long as your family commitments aren't going to be a problem, given the long and unpredictable hours – which is something that has to be borne in mind – then, yes, I'd say, go for it!

P: Mike, thanks for joining us today.

M: My pleasure.

Exam practice 6: Teacher's Book

Listening. Page 196. (Paper 4 Part 2).

P = Presenter, S = Sally

P: With me today is Sally Carson who takes part in round-the-world sailing races, but not, I should explain, as part of a crew, because Sally usually races alone in single-handed yacht races. Sally, welcome.

S: Hi.

P: Now, Sally you've just bought a new boat, haven't you?

S: Yes, it's called *Seabird* and it's much faster than the old one, which was called *Golden Globe*. I'd had it for a few years, and loved it, but it didn't have all the latest equipment, so I decided to change.

P: Yes, because I imagine that if you're out there, in the middle of the ocean, all alone, the technology is pretty important.

S: Absolutely. I usually make the comparison with motor racing, you know, if you put a really good driver into an inferior car, that person's not going to win. But in the same way, a poor driver won't win, even driving the best car in the race.

P: Right. But personal qualities must be important too.

S: Sure. Instinct and skill and technical knowledge are, of course, essential. But the design of the boat can make the difference between winning and finishing further down the field. And in long-distance races, reliability is equally important – if you can't repair your boat, you're not going to finish the race at all.

P: Which one gadget would you never be without in a race?

S: All boats are full of computers for navigation, steering and so forth, but the most important one is the one called the autopilot. If that goes wrong, you simply cannot carry on. That's because if your calculations are wrong by just one degree, and you don't notice, you can end up hundreds of miles off course.

P: Wow. Of the other gadgets, which do you value most personally?

S: Without doubt it's the onboard Internet connection. It means I can keep in touch with the family at home at a time when I'm very much alone, and find out what's happening in the news. But most significantly, it provides weather information, which is vital. If you're going to be sailing into a hurricane, it's best to know beforehand.

P: And what do you do about sleep?

S: When you're alone, tiredness is always the biggest danger because there's nobody else to take over if you've had enough. And there are things like icebergs to avoid, sails to change depending on the wind and so on. I average around five hours sleep over a 24-hour period when I'm racing, and the longest race I've ever done went on for 93 days. I find I sleep best in the afternoons, in bursts of between ten minutes and about an hour.

P: But don't you struggle to keep awake after weeks at sea without a break?

S: No, because you're so excited about the race, the course, the boat and everything that it's difficult to switch off. The problem is more being able to relax sufficiently to get off to sleep, and so sleeplessness can be a problem.

P: And what physical training do you do to prepare for such huge races?

S: Well, sailing is a very physical sport, so you have to be fit and strong with lots of stamina. It's nothing like training for athletics or team sports, though. The best way to train the muscles you need for sailing, is by going sailing. I also go to the gym and go jogging, but there's never enough time to prepare my body as well as I'd like to.

P: And you've written about your experiences too.

S: That's right. My book comes out next week – it's called *Across the Ocean*, and as you can see there's a picture of my old boat, *Golden Globe*, on the cover. Writing that was actually much tougher than sailing, I can tell you, but I was determined to do it all myself.

P: Determination – is that what motivates you to keep sailing and racing?

S: I love the sea. It's as simple as that. I love the sea and I love to race.

P: Sally, best of luck with the new boat and thanks for joining us today.

S: Thank you.